Hara Kei in the Politics of Compromise
1905–1915

HARVARD EAST ASIAN SERIES 31

The East Asian Research Center at Harvard University administers research projects designed to further scholarly understanding of China, Korea, Japan, and adjacent areas.

Hara Kei in 1921

Hara Kei in the Politics of Compromise
1905–1915

Tetsuo NAJITA

HARVARD UNIVERSITY PRESS
CAMBRIDGE, MASSACHUSETTS
1967

Preparation of this volume was aided by a grant from the Ford Foundation
Library of Congress Catalog Card Number 67-27090
Printed in the United States of America

TO ELINOR

Preface

Few countries in modern history have had nonrevolutionary political parties that have grown persistently over an extended period of time. Japan is one of these few. Despite this striking fact, studies of such political groups in Japan have been woefully neglected. Scholarly attention has been directed, for the most part, to the socialist and ultraright groups, almost out of proportion to their actual political influences. Aside from Shinobu Seizaburō's tomes, which are impressive but must be used with care, researches on the parties working within the legal framework have been spotty, especially for the crucial twenty years or so after 1900 when the parties steadily increased their influence in the political order. Recently, valuable studies by Masumi Junnosuke and Mitani Taichirō have helped to rectify the imbalance. But by and large the parties still remain in the relative oblivion of "that sunless ravine between Meiji and Shōwa" (*Meiji to Shōwa no tanima*), as the Taishō period (1912–1925) is sometimes referred to.

Yet, the importance of these parties in Japanese political history is beyond dispute. In their sustained quest for power in the first two decades of the twentieth century they brought into existence powerful political alignments centering around two rival parties. These alignments were fundamentally more complex than those in the 1880's and 1890's, for they involved not only professional party men but also prefectural governors and bureau chiefs, peers, military men, and local political and business leaders. Without question, these party-centered alignments were instrumental in undermining the unity of the ruling cliques — the Genrō, or oligarchs, and their protégés — creating uncertainties regarding the content of leadership that had not been a serious problem when the ruling cliques were firmly in control. Thus, it seems to me, some of the political agonies of the 1920's and 1930's (especially the absence of clearly-defined and consistent leadership and the corresponding unwieldiness of the government) must be assessed in the light of this "intrusion" of the parties into the central arena of political relationships, and not so much a result of the absence of talent.

Moreover, the legacies of party growth in this period are many, particularly in the continuity of patterns of political behavior; the parties are significant for this reason too, quite apart from how one regards the quality of the specific goals they pursued. In striking strategic compromises to gain cabinet positions and in coordinating these offices with party structure and bureaucracy on a national scale for purposes of pork barrel, party men in this period left behind permanent marks on the political personalities of their successors, even on those of party men in the post-World War II period.

It is in the context of far-reaching consequences such as these that I have reconstructed the growth of the parties, focusing in particular on the initial spurt made by the Seiyūkai under its astute leader Hara Kei between 1905 and 1915.

The studies available on this subject, however, tend to be cast in a different framework: they tend, implicitly if not explicitly, to be efforts at explaining the debacle of the Pacific War. There is nothing unique about studies attempting to explain great events in history by examining antecedent developments, and as long as historians generally accept the truism that events seldom occur out of happenstance these attempts will no doubt continue as the pith of history itself. But despite this truism, an analytical disengagement with the "dramatic outcome" is useful and perhaps necessary in some types of inquiry. I think this is true in examining the political parties in Japan in the early teens. In seeing party developments primarily as an antecedent to the disasters of the late 1930's and early 1940's these studies stress the "failures" of the parties, concluding that they handed power to the militarists on a silver platter because, especially after 1900, they sacrificed democratic principles by repeatedly compromising with the forces of "absolutism" (*zettaishugi*). The entire process of party developments, in other words, is seen as a steady decline leading toward disaster.

While this line of argument cannot be discounted entirely, it is not especially illuminating as an organizing theme to explain the *sustained* growth of the parties over some twenty or thirty years. It tends to oversimplify and gloss over important facts, leaving untold the positive and dynamic aspects of party developments. For example, it presents the "compromises" simply as debilitating to the cause of party government, when, in general, they are prerequisites to the functioning of nonrevolutionary parties, and in the specific Japanese case sine qua non to party growth itself. It obscures the motives behind party men in certain concrete situations: there were capricious men, the compromisers, and there were "pures" or "hards," the intransigent noncompromisers; capricious men outnumbered the pures and won, thereby making a tragic denouement inevitable. But if the pures had somehow gained power (as in the Taishō Political Crisis — Taishō *seihen* — of 1912–1913), they would have established party government suddenly and immediately and triggered a sequence of events generically different from that which in fact took place because they would not have stooped to compromises and the like.

By disengaging ourselves from the events leading to the Pacific War, however difficult this might be, I think we can begin to see the fallacies, of which I feel there are basically two, that have given credence to this interpretive slant. The first of these is the fallacy of giving too much weight to one type of documentary evidence, a perennial problem of historians. Many of the documents relied upon by historians of Japanese political history until very recently were written by a small minority of party men — the so-called pures, or hards — and their vigorous supporters in the press. Thus, there has been a decided tendency to judge the broad spectrum of party history through the eyes of these idealists who believed that compromises within the political order indicated submission to "absolutism" and that those in power could be quickly and decisively overthrown (*daha*) if the parties remained firmly united. Yet even Inukai Tsuyoshi, the leading exponent of this point of view, was extremely ambivalent about the viability of this position because he realized, as did the mainstream of the parties, that it plainly defied reality. All party men were sentimentally attached to the idea of "overthrow" because it harked back to the early days of the party movement, but most accepted compromises within the political order and regarded the "overthrow of clique government" (*batsuzoku daha*) as a slogan to incite public demonstrations and not as a realistic political objective. Men of the press and political critics, however, repeatedly condemned party politicians for the discrepancy between avowed ideal and actual behavior. At the same time, they heaped lavish praise on the few who seemingly represented a "pure" position. The myth developed that, aside from a handful, party men were capricious and weak, their thoughts and actions travesties of the principles of constitutional government. This myth, in turn, colored all historiography, Marxist and otherwise, on party history from the 1890's until the dissolution of the parties in 1940.

The second and less precise fallacy is to see the parties as the major cause for the political dislocations underlying Japan's steady drift in the 1930's toward a disastrous war. This view rests, actually, on our present lack of knowledge regarding political discontent in the early decades of the twentieth century. Briefly, we find discontent manifested in two seemingly diverse ways: on one hand we see it in explosive "primitive" demonstrations of the kind suggested by Hobsbawm and Rudé in some European cases; on the other, as Maruyama Masao has pointed out, it is indicated by political passivity, withdrawal, and ennui among critical segments of the educated classes. Although the causes for these political reactions are complex in the extreme, a lion's share of the blame has gone to the parties. It is argued that, because of their relentless pursuit of power, the parties lost sight of their democratic goals and inevitably used their influences in suppressive and corrupt ways, triggering riots in some instances and in others alienating the supporters of party government and demoralizing them into passivity. There is a grain of truth in this reasoning, for the parties indeed failed to excite the imagination of the educated classes, and they did not construct popular bases. Certainly, they cannot be whitewashed of the charge of irresponsibility regarding their lack of commitment to democratic principles. But it should be borne in mind that there is practically no limit to allocating blame for political dislocation and malaise in Japan. And if Maruyama comes close to the mark, as I think he does, in saying that aside from the communists everyone in Japan in the 1930's was a "rightist," then certainly those forces that drove Japanese society toward consensus on the "right" were fundamentally more complex than compromises by party men. Although convenient, it makes as little sense to lay the cause of general political malaise at the doorsteps of parties as it would to attribute general misery in an industrial society solely to the machinations of the industrial bourgeoisie (the "New Power" of the Hammonds), and not to industrialization per se regardless of social and political underpinnings. In short, the ascription of general political discontent to the parties tells us precious little about the roots of that discontent and it tells us even less about the actual process by which the parties enhanced their power, a process that was not by any means natural or inevitable.

For purposes of historical explanation, it seems to me, we must make a distinction that will help us avoid the fallacy of insufficient cause suggested above. By this I mean that an analytical distinction must be made between first, the sustained struggle by the parties (which, while no doubt causing political discontent along the way, changed their status from groups of marginal significance into powerful elites in the government) and second, those driving forces accompanying rapid modernization which generated political dislocations of the sort described by Maruyama. Although the two categories are obviously interrelated and both interact within a broad political environment, they are just as obviously not identical, and the causal lines between the two should be treated with considerable care. The psychological dislocations that drove Japanese society to the "right" had a life of their own, independent of the rise and fall in the fortunes of parties and independent of whether there were parties at all.

In this study, then, I have not posed the question of why the parties caused so much political discontent in society; nor have I asked why they continued to make compromises, thereby failing miserably to live up to ideological precepts — a question that assumes that their growth was natural but that their departure from principles was not. I have asked instead the simple question, why did they grow at all in the sustained way they did? In short, I have isolated for special treatment the politics underlying the steady growth of party power between 1905 and 1915 to see how the parties penetrated the political structure and with what kinds of consequences. It is one of the general conclusions of this study that the growth of the parties in Japan was the result of a crucial transformation among party men from an ideological to a strategical orientation; or, from an attitude of uncompromising opposition to the government based on the ideal of a single, unified, popular party (*mintō gōdō*) to that of realistic compromises within the governmental structure. In particular the successes of one party, the Seiyūkai, under Hara Kei, in pursuing this course of action were decisive in steering party politics in Japan away from multiparties toward two major competing party alignments.

The overall impact by the parties on the content of the political structure was considerable, and for this reason I think it essential to have a firm grasp of this impact on power relationships before trying to assess the political experience of the period on its broad plain. In this respect my study does not pretend to be comprehensive in its coverage. But in this initial inquiry it heeds Namier's good advice to use one searchlight rather than a row of candles in examining historical evidences.

The early chapters cover the years 1905–1912, in which Hara Kei systematically plotted to spread Seiyūkai influence in the bureaucracy and among the local men of power. The later chapters are an account of the impact made by the growth of the Seiyūkai on political relationships during and after the Taishō Political Crisis of 1912–1913. Because I have organized my study around the theme of steady emergence of the parties as powerful elites in the political order, I have not stressed the "failures" of the parties, a story told more than adequately elsewhere. Throughout, however, I have been guided by the assumption of historians that interpretive disagreements do not render history relative, "playing tricks on the dead" as Voltaire once put it, but that they are the bases on which historical appraisals and reappraisals are made and hence, in this sense, not fundamentally divisive to the study of history.

I am deeply grateful to Professor Albert Craig of Harvard University for his kind encouragement and thoughtful guidance from the very beginning of this study. My thanks also go to Professor Edwin O. Reischauer of Harvard for a number of helpful suggestions, and to Professors Peter Duus of Harvard, Irwin Scheiner of the University of California at Berkeley, and Gerald Sorensen of the University of Illinois, Chicago, who read my study in dissertation form and made critical comments on content and style. Above all, I am profoundly indebted to teachers, colleagues, and friends who helped and instructed me during my stay in Japan as a Fulbright fellow between 1961 and 1963. Professors Hayashi Shigeru and Oka Yoshitake of Tokyo University permitted me to participate in their stimulating seminars on modern Japan. Professor Mitani Taichirō and Mr. Itō Takashi, both of Tokyo University, unselfishly shared with me their detailed knowledge of the politics of late Meiji. Mr. Niiyama Shigeki gave me intensive lessons in Japanese, which proved invaluable. And finally, but far from least, Mr. Sakai Yūkichi kept me from languishment with his élan and his untiring assistance throughout my research.

Tetsuo NAJITA

1967
Washington University, St. Louis

Contents

Hara Kei in the
Politics of Compromise
1905–1915

1

Background

The remarkable isolation of Tokugawa Japan, which gave the Japanese people two hundred years of domestic peace, was brought to a dramatic end by the steamships and guns of the West. By mid-nineteenth century the seas surrounding Japan could no longer keep the Black Ships away as they had other ships in the past, and for the first time in centuries Japan faced the grim prospects of bombardment and marching armies. This prospect set in motion a revolutionary effort, beginning with the Meiji Restoration of 1868, to modernize — to achieve wealth, national integrity, and empire. In embarking on this totally uncharted course, the leaders of Japan looked to the West for models. They saw China as the "sleeping lion," incapable of defending itself against the West, and did not look to it for inspiration: they went to observe the West, learning there the art of making steamships and guns and studying diverse political, economic, and social structures.

By the time our story begins in 1905, Japan had proven to the world the success of its modernization. It had undertaken far-reaching legal, political, and educational reforms to alter radically the rigid society of Tokugawa Japan. It was also well along in its industrial revolution; it had outstripped all other Asian countries in wealth. Above all, Japan had become a world power, defeating China in 1895 and signing a treaty on an equal basis with Great Britain in 1902, then climaxing the great effort to become a world power with a stunning victory over Russia in 1905. Japan had become an empire. Most important, the threat of foreign invasion to the nation was gone, and an unprecedented feeling of relief swept through the country.

Yet there remained a basic unease in society. Some, like the poet Ishikawa Takuboku, hoped the uneasiness was the reaction of "old Nippon" against the growing influences of Western thought. Others, like the critics Tokutomi Sohō and Miyake Setsurei, saw, with apprehension, the victory itself over Russia as the cause of the decline in national unity and purpose. But the most deep-seated problem continued to be discontent over the distribution of political leadership, as in the previous thirty-five years. There was widespread distrust in society against the handful of men, the so-called ruling cliques or *hambatsu*, who controlled the government. Opposition to these leaders was spearheaded by the political parties which dedicated themselves to the formidable task of breaking the monopoly of this narrow elite in power.

By 1905, when war with Russia ended, the parties had already had fifteen years of experience outside the legal political structure and another fifteen within it; but the government, for the most part, was still beyond their control. Indeed, it seemed to observers that the few leaders who had directed Japan's rise as a world power were now in a position to consolidate and freeze their monopoly over the government. But once the Russian threat to the nation was removed the parties, led by new men and armed with new techniques and attitudes, refocused their attention on the struggle for power, and in the next decade — the decade known as "late Meiji-early Taishō" — challenged and irrevocably undermined the hegemony of the ruling cliques.

THE PARTIES IN THE CONSTITUTIONAL ORDER

Party men in late Meiji were engrossed in a relentless struggle to gain access to key centers of government. Faced with certain hard political realities (a limited electorate, the inertia of rural political behavior, an unfriendly bureaucracy, and a legislative process they did not fully control), they did not concern themselves primarily with propagating the ideas of political democracy and organizing rice-roots support, but on competing for influential positions at the cabinet level. Yoshino Sakuzō, critic and exponent of democracy after 1915, described this commitment to power in a nutshell when he observed: "It was by seizing control of the cabinet that the political party was able, for the first time, to expand its influence throughout Japan." [1] Two factors were especially instrumental in defining the stratagem for gaining power. One was the institutional arrangement of the Meiji political order within which party men operated; the other was a tightly knit factional resistance to party growth.

The parties became part of the formal political structure in 1889 with the establishment of the Lower House by the Meiji Constitution. This was an advance, because the parties had not previously enjoyed legal status; as in the case of the German Empire, however, the institutional arrangement established by the constitution was unfavorable to them. Among the institutions created by the constitution was the House of Peers, a body not popularly elected, and therefore immune from dissolution. There was also the Privy Council, which held extraordinary powers to advise the throne. Cabinet ministers could hold seats in that council, but its members were mainly imperial appointees from outside the cabinet. The bureaucracy and the military services also lay beyond the extended reach of the parties. Above all, the Lower House did not control the cabinet. The selection of a prime minister was an imperial prerogative; but since the Emperor did not make substantive political decisions the task of advance selection of a prime minister fell on the Genrō Council. This council was not technically created by the constitution, but it was given extraordinary advisory powers by the Emperor. The Genrō (oligarchs, elder statesmen, leaders of the ruling cliques) were a handful of men who had received special commendation from the Emperor for meritorious service (*genkun yūgū no i*)[2] and who, for the most part, shunned party leadership in the Lower House. In short, the constitutional order established in 1889 was a restrictive one for the parties, with the legislative and administrative processes clearly beyond their control.

Despite these structural disadvantages of the political framework, party men believed that party government was attainable within that frame. The constitution did not specifically deny the establishment of party cabinets, nor did it spell out the method and process by which prime ministers were to be selected except to leave the matter to imperial prerogative. The selection of prime ministers by the Genrō, in other words, was not an explicit constitutional privilege. Therefore, party men believed it was within the limits of the law for the prime minister to come from the majority party in the Lower House. Their main task, then, was to gain control over the major legislative and administrative centers in the political structure and establish the practice of having the Emperor approve for the prime ministership a candidate selected by the majority party.

Moreover, party men, and many political critics as well, believed that party government best fulfilled the "spirit" of the Meiji Constitution. In this view, party government was a legacy of the Emperor Meiji, who had decreed in the Charter Oath of 1868 that all state affairs should be decided by public discussion (*banki kōron*). A tradition developed that government should be run jointly by the Emperor and people (*kummin kyōji*) because there existed between them an inviolable bond of unity (*ikkun bammin*) in which the imperial will and the general will were one. To party men, this bond between Emperor and people symbolized the change from the feudal, class-oriented Tokugawa society to the modern, egalitarian order of Meiji: it guaranteed equality and unlimited mobility to all; it was the bedrock on which "Japanese democracy" and the claim for party government rested.[3]

Believing, then, that party government was possible and right, party men set out to expand their influence in the political structure. At the outset they harassed the government by using their legal weapons of submitting votes of no confidence and rejecting the government's budget. These tactics were not without effect since they caused disorder in the Diet, disturbing to the men in government. Party men, however, were inadequately prepared for the task of expanding party power within the political order: having been shunned by the leaders of government for fifteen years, they had developed a strong attachment to the idea of total opposition (*daha*) to the government. And having accepted the legal status given them by the Meiji Constitution, they faced the extremely difficult and baffling task of trying to discard this attitude and to work instead with the government within the political order while maintaining a posture of defiance against it. This ambiguity in their political stance intensified petty factional disputes existing among them and impeded their plans for a durable united front against the leaders in the government. By the end of the 1890's party men were being driven by political reality to agree that the task of overcoming the structural disadvantages of the constitutional order called for less harassment of the government and more hard-headed, realistic, negotiations by new men skilled in the art of giving and taking power.

In 1892, one of the parties, the Jiyūtō, had struck out in this new direction by establishing a compromise relationship with Genrō and Prime Minister Itō Hirobumi. In September 1900 this same party, now called the Kenseitō, forced its president, Itagaki Taisuke, into retirement and again joined with Itō to form a new party — the Seiyūkai. This was an important advance: it reflected adjustment by a party to the constitutional order; it meant a rejection of the tactic of total opposition, if not of the sentimental attachment to it; it meant the acceptance of gradual expansion within the system. Moreover, the formation of the Seiyūkai also showed that there were prestigious men in government who were not completely opposed to the parties. This was a source of great encouragement to party men foundering in their search for political recognition. Finally, the union between party men and Itō meant the introduction of new blood to the party movement. The Seiyūkai was opened to men with administrative experience, previously excluded from the parties, who agreed with the new realistic approach of party men and believed in the ultimate goal of party government.

There was another dimension, however, to the problem of party expansion that offset the developments leading to the formation of the Seiyūkai. This was the emergence of the Yamagata faction as the dominant group in the Meiji political structure. Unlike Itō, who was flexible and open-minded in his views on the parties, Yamagata and men in his faction were bitterly opposed to the parties and consciously blocked their growth.

YAMAGATA AND ITŌ IN PARTY HISTORY

The factions in power were called the "ruling cliques" and their political monopoly "clique government." Of these,

Satsuma and Chōshū (named after the great feudal domains in southwest Japan) were of major historical importance because their leaders had directed the Meiji Restoration of 1868. By 1880, however, Satsuma had lost its ablest leaders — Saigō Takamori in 1877 to the Satsuma Rebellion and Ōkubo Toshimichi by assassination in 1878 — so that Chōshū became dominant. In this Chōshū faction two Genrō stood out among the others: one was Itō Hirobumi, the other Yamagata Aritomo.

Itō was a civil administrator, the principal architect of the Meiji political order, a skilled diplomat supremely confident of his powers of persuasion; he was also the most prestigious Genrō, commanding the respect of friend and foe alike. As a political architect, Itō — as one recent study suggests — tended to see the Meiji state as a "work of art." [4] Hence he moved with great intimacy from one part of the political structure to another, seeing to it that all the parts functioned smoothly. At one time or another he was president of the Privy Council, leader in the Genrō Council, speaker of the House of Peers, prime minister, and then president of a party in the Lower House. At none of these places, however, did Itō create a power base; he left behind only "admirers" [5] and he was proud not to require an extensive faction behind him.

Yamagata was a field general. In the eyes of the public especially, he was stern, reticent, and definitely overshadowed by the brilliant Itō. [6] But Yamagata's role in creating the Meiji order was considerable, second only to Itō's; and, quite unlike his more confident colleague, he was intensely oriented to power. With much candor he once told Saionji Kimmochi: "Power is indispensable so I do my best to maintain mine." [7] Yamagata cultivated a factional empire. He had the following of army generals like Katsura Tarō, Kodama Gentarō, Terauchi Masataka, and Tanaka Giichi, and of such influential civilians as Shinagawa Yajirō,

Kiyoura Keigo, Aoki Shūzō, Shirane Sen'ichi, Nomura Yasushi, Ōura Kanetake, Hirata Tōsuke, Yoshikawa Akimasa,
and Komatsubara Eitarō.[8] While these men, with the exception of one or two, have fallen into obscurity, they were
extremely powerful as a group, dominating the upper ranks
of the bureaucracy, the House of Peers and the Privy Council.

Yamagata held his faction together by ties of loyalty. His
own loyalty to the Emperor was absolute. Those who knew
him have said: "To begin with, his loyalty was different
from that of others. The other Genrō and ministers were
loyal too, but his loyalty alone was on a different plane.
How shall I describe it — should I say pure, immaculate?
It was a plane where personal interests meant nothing."[9]
In turn, Yamagata expected absolute loyalty of his following. Cold and noncommunicative to those he disliked, he
reciprocated the loyalties shown him with warmth, affection, and tangible rewards. He arranged that his supporters
receive titles and important posts in the cabinet, the House
of Peers and the Privy Council.[10] He also looked after their
personal lives, as he did in finding a mistress for Katsura.[11]

The emergence of the Yamagata faction as the most influential one in the political structure coincided with Itō's
attempts to find a working compromise relationship between
the main bodies of the political order and the parties in the
Lower House. A tense relationship between Itō and Yamagata was unavoidable, and it became increasingly evident
in the course of the 1890's. In 1892, Itō strongly protested
widespread government intervention at the polls: directing
the election were Yamagata and his faction, whose policy
was "charge the enemy" (tokkan), involving extensive intervention at the polls to split the parties and then manipulate them.[12]

Viewing this approach as obstructionist and bankrupt, Itō
began searching for ways to hammer harmonious links be-

tween the parties and the ruling cliques. He tried to dissuade the parties from their harassing tactics and to integrate them into the mainstream of the political order. He
gave their leaders a cabinet — the Okuma-Itagaki Cabinet,
1898. And finally, in 1900, he became president of a party:
the Seiyūkai.

Yamagata and his faction bitterly opposed Itō's policies
and intrigued to undermine them. They caused the collapse
of the Ōkuma-Itagaki Cabinet inside of four months, and
when Itō assumed the presidency of the Seiyūkai Yamagata
accused him of violating the "national political essence,"
hoping to disrupt Itō's leadership of that party.[13]

Itō's chances of making his moderate views prevail over
Yamagata's hinged on whether he could unify the Seiyūkai
into a power base for himself. But, unfortunately, Itō was
not interested in such an undertaking. Orderly government
was more important to him because, aside from his deep
concern over mounting difficulties with Russia, he himself
had designed the principal bodies in the political structure
and, accordingly, his loyalties were distributed evenly
among them; it was emotionally impossible for him to ally
himself with one segment of that structure at the seeming
expense of the others. Thus, his commitment to the Seiyūkai
and the Lower House was not firm. In fact, he was dis-
interested in the internal affairs of the Seiyūkai and with
that party's main concern of expanding its political influence
— its reason for accepting his leadership.[14] After his fourth
cabinet of 1900–1901, which collapsed within seven months,
Itō's interest in the Seiyūkai cooled. He gave Seiyūkai support to Prime Minister Katsura Tarō for his navy expansion
program (late 1902, during Katsura's first cabinet, 1901–
1905) without consulting party leaders and without bargaining for power. Ranking party leaders defected in protest while uneasiness and dissatisfaction prevailed among
those remaining. While the Seiyūkai faltered over this in-

cident, Itō resigned as president of the party (March 1903) and took refuge in the Privy Council. Although he resigned in part because of pressure from Yamagata, he left the party believing its internal affairs irrelevant to his political position. He could neither understand nor cope with the constant bickering for more power that he had encountered in the party, and for this reason he was more than ready to end his leadership of it.

Because Itō failed to convert the Seiyūkai into a political base for himself, his position vis-à-vis Yamagata steadily deteriorated, and chances for support of the parties by moderates in the ruling cliques also waned. Itō remarked in 1906 that men around Yamagata "do not know the broader political issues and are nothing more than policemen." [15] But it was these "policemen" who blocked off and controlled most of the structure designed by Itō himself. In 1906, Itō left the political scene at the capital (Tokyo) to become governor general of Korea, completing his isolation from the leaders in government. Shortly before Itō's assassination by a Korean nationalist, Hara Kei approached Prime Minister Katsura (Katsura's second cabinet, 1908–1911), asking that Itō be returned to Tokyo: "I asked this of Katsura because I know that he and Yamagata are secretly pleased that Itō has been in Korea for so long. The other day Saionji told me that he had explained to Itō that even though he was beneficial to Korea, he, Itō, should return home to further the cause of constitutional government. Itō was said to have been exuberant upon hearing this. . . . Yamagata and others want to keep Itō in Korea as long as possible." [16]

With Itō gone from the center of government and the Yamagata faction firmly entrenched in the major bodies of the Meiji constitutional order — the House of Peers, the Privy Council, the Imperial Household, the bureaucracy, the army — the stage was now set for the politics of the post-1905 period. The parties, particularly the new Seiyūkai, had given up the tactic of total opposition and assumed as their most pressing task, the spreading of influence within the political structure. But this turn toward political realism resulted in a modus vivendi between the Seiyūkai and Itō that proved abortive, leaving that party torn by internal dissension and uncertain as to its leadership. Thus, the brief conciliation with Itō was more than offset by the emergence of the Yamagata faction as the single most powerful group in the political order. The objectives of the parties, therefore, were defined vis-à-vis that faction, to press against it and undermine it thereby enhancing their position. It was in this context that Hara Kei emerged to gain control over the Seiyūkai.

Hara joined the Seiyūkai in 1900 on the coattails of Itō, but he was not in the small coterie of Itō's trusted advisers. The latter severed their ties with the Seiyūkai when Itō did. Hara remained in the party and thrived in the absence of Itō, championing the task of party expansion. He was suited to this task, for, like Itō, he believed in orderly government and was free from the psychology of total opposition that plagued party men. But unlike Itō, he was not a Genrō-politician because he was not of the ruling cliques — he shared with party men an "outsider mentality." Above all, he coupled his personal ambitions for power with a clear understanding of what party men needed most: an increased voice in the councils of government. Perhaps it was because his strategic goals were defined in realistic terms such as this that he proved instrumental in the successful growth of the parties in late Meiji-early Taishō (1905–1915).

2

The Basis of Political Compromise
(1900–1905)

As a political realist, Hara Kei practiced the art of
the possible, defining his goals and limiting them to what
could be achieved.[1] While some goals, he felt, were desirable but unattainable, others were at once desirable and
possible to achieve. He believed that party government in
Japan was desirable; that conditions made its establishment
possible; that with dedicated leadership (which, he became
convinced, he could supply) it would even become inevitable. At the same time, he did not feel that the Yamagata faction would suddenly surrender or wither away out of some
principle of necessity, creating a vacuum for the parties to
fill. On the contrary, the political monopoly of that faction
would persist unless the parties, and the Seiyūkai in particular, unified themselves into solid, congruent bodies to challenge the faction in a sustained way. The overriding political
issue as Hara saw it was the strategic use of party power,
not argument over principle.

Between 1905 and 1915 one party, the Seiyūkai, dominated the Lower House. With its leadership securely in the
hands of Hara, it did not divide and regroup as parties constantly tended to do throughout much of party history before World War II. By maintaining a majority control of
the Lower House, the Seiyūkai prevented the manipulation

of that house by the Yamagata faction and forced Katsura
Tarō, chief protégé of Yamagata, to work continuously with
it and its astute Hara.

THE BACKGROUND OF HARA KEI

Hara Kei was born in 1856 as Hara Kenjirō, the second
son of a high retainer to the feudal lord at Morioka in the
northeast. The northeast was the last stronghold against
the forces of the Meiji Restoration led by men from Satsuma
and Chōshū of the southwest. At the age of sixteen, Hara,
like many others, went to Tokyo in search of success. Because of his place of birth he found himself an outsider, and
this early experience left a deep and lasting impression on
his political character.[2]

Hara came to harbor an intense hostility toward the
ruling cliques of Satsuma and Chōshū who monopolized
power. In time, as these cliques increasingly took on the
appearance of a Yamagata faction, Hara's animosity shifted
to this group, which he frequently called the "bureaucratic
faction." To Hara, these few who deigned to consider themselves the guardians of power and sole possessors of loyalty
to the Emperor had failed, out of blind prejudice, to realize
that loyalty and talent in Japan were not sectional.

Hara argued that his predecessors from the northeast had
struggled against Satsuma and Chōshū during the Meiji
Restoration as loyalists acting in the belief that they were
benefiting the entire nation. Throughout his career he continued to defend the samurai of the northeast. Thus, for
example, when an imperial rescript of 1914 commemorating
the campaign against the northeast suggested that these
samurai were traitors, he used his political influence to have
it revised.[3]

From the northeast himself, Hara feared that he would
be unable to rise in society. A burning ambition was kindled
in him to overcome that stigma and surpass the leadership

of the ruling cliques. In time, he concluded that a nationally based political party could take him to this unchallenged position.

The above explains Hara's patient drive between 1900 and 1918 to become prime minister; it helps explain his almost exclusive concern with acquiring power; and it also explains why, as prime minister (1918–1921), he did not initiate reforms worthy of his epithet "commoner."

Another point which adds insight into Hara's political character can be drawn from his early background. Although painfully aware of the monopoly of power that excluded him, he also realized that inroads into that monopoly could best be made through the careful cultivation of personal contacts.[4]

Hara's early career was marked by repeated failures to find avenues that would lead him to success. The route of the scholar was blocked since he had failed the middle-school examinations. Likewise, he failed the examinations to enter the naval and foreign service schools (1875). Four years as a servant of God (baptized "David" into the Catholic Church in 1872) could not satisfy his ambitions. After three years of study in the school of law attached to the Ministry of Justice Hara was expelled (1876) when he objected to the invasion of privacy of thought by school authorities. And after two years as editorial writer for the *Yūbin hōchi* he was forced to resign by a rival faction (1882).[5]

It was not until Hara had established ties with men in high government positions that he began to make rapid advances. Under the auspices of such influential men in the bureaucracy as Inoue Kaoru and Mutsu Munemitsu, Hara launched a temporary career in the government. Through Inoue, Hara entered the foreign ministry in November 1882, became Inoue's private secretary in 1888, and joined the Seiyūkai in September 1900. Through Mutsu, he rose steadily through several posts to the rank of vice-foreign minister in 1895. Hara admired this talented leader, whose political views were broad and liberal for his day, and his friendship with Mutsu verged on adoration. Hara never forgot the patronage of Mutsu and Inoue: as a party politician he, too, would become a patron, granting personal favor to those who showed promise by promoting them to high posts in party and bureaucracy. In offering these favors to others he was fulfilling in a real sense his obligation to Mutsu. This fond remembrance of the goodness shown him, an outsider, by men like Mutsu was the heart of his benevolent paternalism toward the rank and file — the *"oyabun"* image that Oka Yoshitake has so vividly described.[6]

Because of these favorable relationships with Mutsu and Inoue, Hara's attitude toward the ruling cliques necessarily underwent revision. While his hostility toward Yamagata and the adherents of transcendental government remained unchanged, he could no longer see these cliques as an undifferentiated target of attack. He saw a positive side in some of them which he felt the parties should recognize. He believed, therefore, that the attitudes of party leaders should undergo fundamental revision — from opposition to a willingness to deal at close range with select men from the ruling cliques. He persuaded party men to work on the assumption that an alliance with Itō was a positive act.[7] In Hara's eyes it was not degrading to join with Itō and Inoue to establish a political party; on the contrary, he felt this to be necessary for party growth.

HARA'S RISE IN THE SEIYŪKAI

Hara was a bureaucrat for fifteen years. On the intimate advice of his mentor, Mutsu, he left the bureaucracy in 1897. He spent the next three years fruitfully as editor for the *Ōsaka mainichi*. Then, in September 1900, under the auspices of Inoue, Hara began his career as party politician.

Hara joined the Seiyūkai convinced of the rise and eventual domination of the government by the political parties.
But he was not as yet certain that the road to power for
him, personally, would be that of a party leader, for (unlike
Itō and Inoue, whose careers were underwritten by the fact
that they were Genrō) Hara, already forty-five, had no solid
basis of political power. Disappointed with the weak and
ambivalent leadership of Itō,[8] Hara's commitment to the
Seiyūkai developed rapidly as positions of leadership opened
to him. By 1909 Hara admitted: "I have no possible choice
but to devote myself entirely to the Seiyūkai. . . . Itō
agreed and gave me strong encouragement."[9]

At first, Hara held the post of chief secretary (kanjichō).
In this capacity he managed the party's finances, establishing a foothold in the party; his continued control in this
area, moreover, was an important factor in his rise in the
party to virtually undisuted leadership.[10] Of Hara's role in
party finances Saionji Kimmochi, president of the Seiyūkai
1903–1913, commented: "Hara loved money. He was not a
miser, since he certainly knew how to use it. . . . He liked
to handle money, in much the same way that we enjoy art
objects. I entrusted the matter of party finances entirely to
him."[11]

Hara's position in the Seiyūkai, however, was not secure
at the outset. He was not a Diet member; he had been a
bureaucrat — not an asset at this time. He did not belong
to the small circle of close advisers to Itō[12] nor did he have
a faction of his own. Itō, however, saw great potential in
Hara and told a young politician: "He will someday become
a pillar of the state. Young men such as you [Ishikawa
Hanzan] should cast your lot with him."[13] In December
1901, Itō promoted Hara to minister of communication to
replace Hoshi Tōru, who had resigned for alleged involvement in bribery. Still, the party as a whole was under the

control of leaders such as Hoshi, Hayashi Yūzō, and Kino-shita Kenkichi, of the old Jiyūtō.

Jiyūtō men had joined the Seiyūkai under the assumption that because they managed the party rank and file they would be able, in turn, to control Itō. Itō, who had formed the party to establish a workable system between all branches of the government, could not unify the party. Hara was at first a witness to this tension between Itō and Jiyūtō leaders, but he benefited directly in the end. Late in 1902, high-rank-ing members of the Jiyūtō group bolted from the Seiyūkai when Itō summarily gave Seiyūkai support to Katsura Tarō (Katsura's first cabinet, 1901–1905).[14]

Leadership in the party was also being vacated in other ways which gave Hara opportunity to advance. Hoshi, the powerful leader of the Jiyūtō faction, was assassinated on April 21, 1901. Furthermore, in early 1903 Itō left the party to assume the presidency of the Privy Council. The net re-sult was that only a handful of leaders remained, making the situation ripe for Hara to take steps to assume leader-ship of the party. He made a series of moves that were the first illustrations of his skill as a politician.

First, Hara gained a Diet seat in August 1902. Although he assumed that all party leaders should belong to the Lower House, his candidacy for a seat was realistically aimed at countering the criticism that he was a bureaucrat. Furthermore, by becoming a Diet man Hara could scheme for control over key factions whose leaders had left the party. Seiyūkai Diet men were divided informally into eight regional groups or factions (*chihō dantai*) which selected representatives to the party council (*kyōgiin*) and, above all, maintained close communications with the various re-gions. Of these eight regional groups the two most powerful were the Kantō (east-central) and the Kyūshū (southwest) groups. After becoming a Diet member, Hara quickly used his influence as chief secretary — manager of party finances — to acquire the factional support in the rank and file that he had lacked in the beginning. He gained control over the Tōhoku (northeast) and the Kantō groups which had lost their leader Hoshi (see above) and thus responded favorably to overtures from Hara.[15]

The Kyūshū group owed most of its allegiance to Matsuda Masahisa, who had been a symbol of the party movement during the 1870's and 1880's.[16] Hara formed an alliance with him — an alliance maintained until Matsuda's death in March 1913. Matsuda's popularity in the party was far greater than Hara's, and because of his popularity he was a latent challenge to Hara. Had Matsuda sought to surpass Hara he probably could have done so, but he was not aggressive by nature. Tending to be something of a dandy and a spendthrift he was no match for Hara, whose eyes were fixed on matters of political power. One political critic, Uzaki Kumakichi, a prolific writer of this period, described the shift of power into Hara's hands in this way: "The inner chamber of the Seiyūkai is occupied by the right and left ministers to the president, Hara and Matsuda. . . . Matsuda does not attend to party details and so power has shifted to Hara. Hara's position is like that of a vice-president and he has in his hands all the keys — be it in the matters of party finances or distribution of personnel . . . inevitably, the executive staff will be dominated by Hara." [17]

Hara's other major alliance was with Saionji Kimmochi, Itō's choice as successor to the Seiyūkai presidency. Tokutomi Sohō, the brilliant, if conservative, critic once described Saionji with three English "in's" — "intelligence, indolence, and indifference." Later, he said that Saionji only seemed "indifferent"; but "indolence" remained unrevised.[18] Saionji himself admitted as much in the late 1920's when Japan was about to plunge into a period of militarism: "I have never possessed the ambition, or should I say desire, or should I say courage, to break open new ground out of dissatisfaction with existing conditions, or to stem the tide of a violent trend. I am still the same today." [19]

For all his cultivation of a limpid style and his love of *ars poetica* — he seems to have been more than a dilettante in these matters — Saionji was a weak political leader who, given his relative lack of interest in politics, probably should not have become involved in it at all. An aristocrat by birth, he never gave up the notion of transcendental government, while all along he seemed to champion the cause of the liberals. Although Saionji occupied such positions as journalist, party president, and Genrō, from which he could have wielded considerable influence, he did not advance any of the liberal ideals he was presumed to have upheld. For example, he recalled that his experience as a journalist in the early 1880's (for a liberal newspaper, *Tōyō jiyū*) "did not mean that I was strongly advocating popular rights nor that I was firmly committed to the newspaper business. It was nothing more than half play, of indulging for a while in some pleasure." [20] While he might not have described his presidency in the same way, his basic attitude was the same: the powers of the Seiyūkai president were great, but he did not use them; his role as party leader was passive.

Hara agreed with Tokutomi that Saionji could neither execute policies nor carry out reforms and was, moreover, "irresponsible" because as president of the party, he remained "indifferent to political power." [21] Saionji, however, added prestige and, because of this, unity to the Seiyūkai — hence the importance to Hara of maintaining a close alliance with Saionji.

Once the alliances with Matsuda and Saionji were intact, Hara turned his attention to two major factions in the party. One group had belonged to a government party and had ties with the ruling cliques; the other was the remainder of the Jiyūtō faction. These two factions were involved in a bitter feud between 1900 and 1904, constantly throwing the party directorate (*sōmuin*) into disorder. By working closely with Matsuda and Saionji, Hara managed to postpone indefinitely the formation of a new directorate on the ground that the factional dispute had rendered that body inoperative. In this way, control over party affairs, properly the function of the directorate, fell into the hands of the party secretariat (*kanji*), which was empowered — aside from its financial responsibilities — to handle emergency situations. The chief secretary was none other than Hara. Shortly afterward the party directorate was reinstated, but with only two members — Hara and Matsuda.[22]

Thus, while Hara ostensibly shared party leadership with both Saionji and Matsuda, he in fact held it in his own hands. By the last months of 1904 Hara had become the party's chief negotiator: he was now ready to begin his career as party leader. As chief negotiator he directed the Seiyūkai over a course of party expansion during the next ten years, using a variety of complicated tactics in this pursuit of power. Many subscribed to his ways; many others were highly critical of them. But few in his day, and fewer subsequently, understood the purpose of Hara's strategies. Most often he struck observers as a cold and mechanical tactician and little else. What then were the attitudes and beliefs of Hara's political character that underlay his quest for power?

HARA KEI: PARTY POLITICIAN

Hara towers above other party politicians in pre-World War II Japan. In September 1918, he became the first prime minister who held a seat in the Lower House and who was at the same time president of the majority party. He refused highly coveted aristocratic titles — even rejecting a posthumous title in his will — to create for himself the "commoner" image.[23] A handsome and neat person, he lived frugally, as few politicians in his day did. Hara skillfully tempered his stubborn and argumentative nature with courtesy even toward his political foes. He was not an eloquent speaker but he excelled as a leader of men. To the party rank and file he showed genuine warmth and affection, especially after his assumption of the presidency in 1914. He took part in regional party rallies to raise the prestige of low-ranking Diet men. Although personally frugal, he gave to all party men at election time half again the funds requested. Throughout his career he combined calm words of encouragement with firm warnings to preserve party unity: "Even though our party controls an absolute majority, should we, even in the slightest, lack unity of action and feeling, this majority will be useless. When we reflect on our party's history, we find that at every Diet session there was the fear that fragmentation would result. . . . Should the majority of the Diet members act with great care and firm unity, we will advance toward constitutional government." [24]

Judged by standards of democracy as conceived in some Western countries, Hara's marks might be low. It can be argued correctly, for example, that he did not crusade for democracy. He did not plan basic structural reforms and, still less, social legislation. From this point of view, Hara seems to have failed to grapple with the fundamental issues for the survival of a constitutional system. He appears nothing more than a skilled tactician. There can be no doubt as to Hara's superior skill as a political strategist. A cursory reading of his faithfully-kept nine-volume diary shows that his interest was almost exclusively politics. A closer reading reveals a master in the art of politics who pressed his opponents in moments of weakness, parried their thrusts, and retreated when necessary.

Underlying this involvement in political maneuver, however, was a much more complex figure. Hara was a politician whose actions were grounded in a consistent view of reality, whose dedication to his party was truly rare in his day, and who, because of this devotion to party, was committed to the principle that the majority party in the Lower House should control the government and the military services.

In Hara's eyes each political situation was important because society was dynamic, ever-changing. Reminiscent of other samurai educated in the last years of the Tokugawa period, he saw the political leader as one who grasped the "trends of the time" (*jisei*)[25] and gave positive direction to the "progress taking place everywhere in society."[26] By the same token, Hara believed that change was gradual and required proper historical conditions: it could not be forced nor was it ever complete. Early in his political career (November 1880), he wrote: "Can there be a basic principle that dictates changes in the political structure? Then again, can there be a basic force which says there will not be changes in the political structure? A principle or force such as this does not exist. Thus, by submitting to the time and taking advantage of the trends, changes may be found to be unnecessary, and then again, they may be unavoidable. To alter or not to alter the political structure is simply a question of what the conditions of the time are."[27]

Hara argued that if the forces of an age dictated certain reforms, then the only course open was to utilize those forces and carry out reforms: "If changes are not carried out when conditions require them, high and low will be torn asunder and it will be impossible to maintain the political structure. . . . If changes are carried out when conditions are not yet ready for them, then chaos will result in all quarters of the land. . . . Therefore . . . to know what trends should be seized to carry out reforms is a truly complex matter."[28] From the foregoing we can understand the confident Hara: "No matter how the bureaucrats seek to control the parties, in the end, the parties will triumph."[29] We can also understand the cautious and realistic Hara:

"Constitutional government cannot be realized in a day, but by a step-by-step process." [30]

Hara's consistent attitude toward change in history made him the opportunist his critics were quick to point out because he could select and cite conditions to support his policies. Thus, he argued in 1919 that manhood suffrage would be established in the end when conditions made it "natural" and that this was "not that dangerous." [31] But that same year he passed a moderate suffrage bill which lowered the required direct tax from ten to three yen, and defeated the manhood suffrage bill on the grounds that the nation was not prepared for it. Hara argued in favor of a gradual increase in suffrage: "I do not have any objections to a gradual increase of voters and, moreover, it will not be harmful that the so-called manhood suffrage be established in the future when conditions in the nation are ready for it." [32]

During his editorship of the *Ōsaka mainichi* (1897–1900), Hara concluded that conditions indicated the possibility of ultimate party domination over the political structure. Believing that under proper leadership the divisive tendencies of political parties and their "irresponsible" concern with opposition could be corrected,[33] he wrote in July 1898 that the march toward party government could begin: "To discuss whether or not political parties are necessary for constitutional government is a thing of the past. The task today is to work toward the advancement of political parties . . . as political parties should advance, toward the establishment of pure party cabinets." [34]

To Hara, the ambitious outsider without a firm political base, a majority in the Lower House was the instrument of party power against the ruling cliques. Hence he stressed one-party domination of the Diet. In principle he did not reject a two-party system, but he saw no virtue in struggling within the Diet with other parties. His reason was clear:

a perpetual majority in the Lower House would force the ruling cliques to work continuously with that majority, while a two-party system would permit the government to play off one party against the other. Strengthened by his success in building a powerful Seiyūkai, Hara raised to the level of dogma his belief that the majority in the Lower House would control power: "Constitutional government is government by majority." [35] Whatever else he compromised, this he did not, even after the Seiyūkai had been reduced to a minority in 1915.

It was on this issue that Hara and the Genrō Inoue and Yamagata never agreed. Thus Inoue, once Hara's benefactor, told Hara: "I want you to cease being party-centered and be nation-centered instead." [36] Likewise, Yamagata told Hara: "There is one thing I cannot agree with you on, and that is your idea of acquiring a majority." [37] And on another occasion Yamagata said of Hara: "Hara is party-centered, but I want him to be more Emperor-centered in his views." [38]

To Hara, accusations such as these were unfortunate because in his idealized view devotion to party meant devotion to country. Behind this idealization, however, were the stark facts that it was only through the party that he could satisfy his political ambitions; only through it could he overcome the profound psychological frustrations inherited from his youthful days as an outsider. Therefore he could not rise above the party to assume a transcendental position, purveying the interests of the entire nation, as Inoue and Yamagata wished. By necessity, his patriotism was partisan politics: he could not help but see party control over the government in a rational manner as a positive good for the nation — as national progress itself. This view grew stronger with each of his successes, and he never tired of expressing it again and again, as in this passage from a speech to his party in the spring of 1914: "Those who do not understand

existing conditions often slander us at the slightest provocation for promoting party unity for selfish gain only. Obviously, expansion and unity benefit the party. But if we
should consider the matter from the question of promoting
constitutional government, then the actions of our party are
natural. In any country, there must be an organization with
a sense of responsibility that will direct the affairs of state.
This is especially true of a constitutional state. If we want
to continue to shoulder the burdens of the state and contribute our services to the nation, we must constantly strive
to expand the power of our party." [39]

In emphasizing government by a majority party, furthermore, Hara rejected the practice by other men of using the
Emperor in cabinet changes. Hara did not question the
constitutional position of the Emperor nor the rights of men
to advise him; he made a clear distinction, however, between the activities of the throne and those of everyday
politics. Hara would deny the advisers of the throne a right
to make independent decisions regarding the exchange of
power — a view clearly contrary to Yamagata's view of his
own role as adviser to the throne: "The Imperial Household
will be able to stay outside the sphere of political struggle
only when the Genrō select, as a matter of custom, [a prime
minister from] one or the other of the parties that controls
the majority." [40]

Hara's notion of government by Diet majority had important implications in another area: he felt that the majority party should control the military services. In July
1898, on the eve of becoming a party politician, he wrote:
"There are those who believe that the military is something
separate, but this is an extremely erroneous assumption.
Ministers of the army and navy are pure administrative
officials. On the basis of the present administrative organization, military ministers need not necessarily be appointed
from the military. Hence, if a military man is not available,

it is permissible that a civilian be selected." [41] And in October 1921, at the twilight of his career, he appointed himself temporary naval minister. This was to last only for the period that the naval minister was at the Washington Conference, but the act was unprecedented and it was made against stiff opposition from the military. In a curtly-phrased memorandum to Yamagata and the army, Hara asserted his right as prime minister to interpret the rules governing the administrative system. While Hara doubted that the army would change in the near future, he noted that "this precedent . . . is definitely a progressive step in the present system." [42]

Hara, then, was more than a tactician. Underlying his fondness for political maneuver was his commitment to party and party government and a view that history was dynamic. However, he was convinced that changes could not be forced. He believed in political compromise as beneficial, and he became a master at it.

In early 1905, without prior consultation with other Seiyūkai leaders, Hara worked out an agreement with Prime Minister Katsura Tarō to establish the First Saionji Cabinet. For the first time, a party became directly involved in a power exchange. This agreement marked the beginning of Hara's plans to direct his party to new heights of power.

COMPROMISES WITH KATSURA

The Meiji Constitution did not define the procedure for exchanging power. Leaders of the ruling cliques, the Genrō, customarily decided who should be prime minister and when. With the advent of victory over Russia, however, the Genrō retired into the background, leaving the reins of government in the hands of their protégés and reserving for themselves the right to advise and interfere, but not shouldering the responsibilities of decision-making. Now, the principal figure of the ruling cliques on the active po-

litical scene was Katsura Tarō. Under Yamagata's surveil-
lance, Katsura served as prime minister from 1901 to 1905
— the longest single term of any prime minister. Katsura
was Hara's partner in compromise and his adversary as well.

Born in Chōshū in 1846, Katsura was ten years Hara's
senior. In October 1901 Itō resigned for the fourth time as
prime minister, and Katsura gained that office for the first
time. Because of his late start as a politician rather than to
the difference in their ages — he was only five years younger
than Itō — Katsura was never considered on a par with Itō
or Yamagata or Inoue. This (as his close confidant, Tokutomi
Sohō, took pains to show) kindled in him a burning desire
to be recognized as their equal.[43]

During his prime ministerships the Anglo-Japanese Treaty
was signed (1902), victory over Russia was gained (1905),
and Korea was annexed (1910). No other politician could
be credited with as many historic achievements and still fall
short in the estimation of the public. Katsura was widely
disliked for his seemingly insatiable ambitions, and he was
also ridiculed for his "smile-and-tap-on-the-back" conduct
or "niko-pon-shugi," a term that originated and became
known throughout Japan at that time as a description of
Katsura.[44]

Actually, Katsura was a talented politician, undoubtedly
the most talented among Yamagata's men. He brought with
him to the prime ministership a backlog of experience as an
administrator — for example, as governor general of Taiwan
1896–1897, and as army minister 1898–1900. Like Hara,
furthermore, Katsura was attached to political reality and
had a genuine fondness for politics. "If he had been on our
liberal side," Saionji once remarked, "he would have been a
match for Hara in politics." [45]

Katsura shared with Yamagata a bitter animosity toward
the parties and party government. If Hara's first purpose as
party leader was to undermine the Yamagata faction, Kat-

sura's was to manipulate the parties: he stood for transcendental government. Unlike other men in Yamagata's faction, however, he had a penchant for independent action. As a young man of twenty-four (1870) he feigned illness to have himself exempted from further military service so that he could study in Germany. He studied advanced military organization and tactics there for four years; it was on the basis of this training that he rose steadily in the army and then in politics. As army minister in the 1890's, furthermore, he showed that he was adept at drawing support from factions in the parties for Prime Minister Yamagata without prompting from the latter.[46]

As prime minister, Katsura increasingly asserted his independence as a political leader and virtually acted as the chief representative of the Yamagata faction. Because he chose this role as liaison between the Seiyūkai and the Yamagata faction, he simplified problems of communication for Hara. By not having to wage constant battle against the Yamagata faction Hara could concentrate on using Katsura as a shield behind which he could establish a foothold in such important centers as the bureaucracy. For Katsura, electing to deal single-handedly with Hara led him into decisions he did not foresee when ties between the two men were first established.

In spring 1905, Katsura and other government leaders wanted a peace treaty with Russia signed as quickly as possible. At the same time, because the weakened military and economic position of Japan was not widely known, they anticipated strong opposition from the parties and the public to a treaty. Katsura, therefore, needed Seiyūkai support and began holding private conferences with Hara.

Aware of Katsura's predicament, Hara pressed his advantage and demanded control over the "management of postwar affairs." If power were not granted, Hara warned, he would allow the Seiyūkai to lead mass demonstrations

against Katsura.[47] Katsura agreed to a Saionji cabinet in exchange for Seiyūkai support of the treaty with Russia. Katsura was not defenseless, however; he had the confidence of
the Genrō, and his influence in the House of Peers far exceeded Hara's. The price Katsura asked in exchange, therefore, was that the Saionji cabinet not be a party cabinet and,
furthermore, that it not deviate sharply from his policies. In
return for these concessions Hara demanded that Katsura
prevent interference in cabinet affairs by the Genrō, the
Privy Council, and the House of Peers.[48]

On April 17, 1905, Hara related the details of the compromise first to Saionji and then to the entire party.[49] When
Katsura got in contact with Yamagata (not directly, but
through Hirata Tōsuke), Itō had already been consulted and
had expressed approval. By then the compromise was an accomplished fact, with the timing of Katsura's resignation
the only question left.

The first round of compromise with Katsura was settled.
Hara now brushed aside proposals from the minority party
and the Seiyūkai rank and file to demonstrate against the
government.[50] When the riots exploded on September 5,
1905, against the "unfavorable terms" of the Portsmouth
Treaty, the Seiyūkai was passive. Hara was conveniently
vacationing in Morioka, his home town in the northeast.[51]

In late December 1905 Katsura officially resigned, and in
January 1906 the First Saionji Cabinet was established. As
agreed, it was a compromise cabinet. The minister of communication was the adopted son of Yamagata; the minister
of agriculture and commerce was "convenient" because of
his ties with the House of Peers; the minister of education
was selected on the basis that it was "necessary to include
someone from Satsuma"; and the minister of finance was
"inadequate" but had Inoue's backing. Furthermore, the
cabinet agreed not to deviate from Katsura's policies. Finally,
at the insistence of Yamagata, Saionji assumed the prime

ministership as "Marquis Saionji" and not as "Saionji, president of the Seiyūkai." [52]

If the discussion ended here, it would be difficult indeed to uphold the argument that the politics of compromise undermined the ruling cliques; it would seem, on the contrary, that the compromise had ended in a sacrifice of Seiyūkai power. The First Saionji Cabinet was undeniably weak — it certainly did not mark the emergence of party government. Power, however, did not come into the hands of the parties suddenly or totally; it shifted gradually toward the parties and always in relation to other groups, particularly the Yamagata faction. In this process, the First Saionji Cabinet marked an important turning point: the establishment of a compromise relationship that allowed Seiyūkai party expansion to take place.

While Katsura quite confidently described the compromise relationship in this succinct fashion, "The House of Peers is mine; the Lower House is Saionji's," [53] this relationship could not be permanent. Hara could not agree to Katsura's division of power, and he used the compromise relationship to enhance the growth of his party. He did not surrender the House of Peers to Katsura, but constantly sought to establish connections in that house to divide and overcome it. Neither could Hara keep to the promise that the cabinet would not deviate from Katsura's policies: his plans to expand party influence in the bureaucracy and among local men of influence involved policies that were contrary to those of Katsura. Under these circumstances, Katsura could not always keep his promise to mediate with the Peers and the Genrō on behalf of the Seiyūkai. Moreover, he could not keep the bargain "the Lower House is Saionji's." Katsura retained control over a small government party in the Lower House and was receptive to overtures from the minority party in that house to join with it against the Seiyūkai.

Thus, although the compromise arrangement outwardly

preserved political peace, it was, from the outset, the well-spring of much of the political dynamism of the period. Through it Hara gained the office of home minister, which he would now use to challenge Katsura and the Yamagata faction in unprecedented manner and degree.

3

The Pragmatic Uses of Power
(1906–1908)

The creative political leader, James MacGregor Burns
has suggested, is one who maximizes his impact on politics
by integrating his perception of the political environment
with tactical priorities which he arranges according to their
bearing on "long-term strategic ends." [1] Although "creative"
might not be appropriate for Hara, he had the keen political
sense of perceiving elements in his environment which were
directly related to strategy. While many of his contempo-
raries, like Tokutomi Sohō, saw in their political environment (late Meiji) "spiritual unrest" and the loss of "national
purity" caused by the excessive proliferation of democratic
ideas,[2] Hara saw "progressive trends" everywhere in his environment.[3] He singled out in particular those trends which
meshed with the political priorities agreed upon by party
men: he pointed to the dramatic transformation of the
bureaucracy in size and content, and he pointed to some
crucial structural changes taking place at the town, village,
and district (gun) levels of the regional bureaucracy. To
Hara, these "trends" were "progressive" because they buttressed his belief that the parties could break the power
of the Yamagata faction and establish, in the long run, the
hegemony of the Lower House over the entire political system.

THE CHANGING NATURE OF THE BUREAUCRACY

Hara was aware of "natural" changes taking place in the bureaucracy and was prepared to use them. What had been a bureaucracy dominated by a narrow elite largely from Chōshū and Satsuma was being transformed into a massive bureaucracy (from twenty-nine thousand in 1890 to seventy-two thousand in 1908) made up of university graduates and, at the upper levels especially, of graduates from the Tokyo Imperial University. These men from Tokyo University advanced rapidly to the upper echelon of the bureaucracy in the post-1905 period, the more successful of them controlling the top posts of vice-ministers, bureau chiefs, governors, and so on. To illustrate, below are two charts:

		Vice-ministers		Bureau chiefs	
Year	Cabinet	Total	Tokyo University graduates	Total	Tokyo University graduates[4]
1902	Katsura I	7	2	27	9
1907	Saionji I	7	3	31	20
1912	Saionji II	7	7	36	28
1916	Okuma II	7	7	29	26

	1867–1905		1905–1925	
Prefecture	Governors	Tokyo University graduates	Governors	Tokyo University graduates[5]
Tokyo	17	0	6	4
Osaka	13	0	9	8
Nagasaki	13	0	9	8
Niigata	18	0	10	6
Chiba	11	1	8	6
Aomori	15	1	12	11
Yamaguchi	9	0	8	8
Kōchi	15	0	9	7

These Tokyo Imperial University graduates were a whole new breed of bureaucrats whom Hara called the "up-and-coming." They shared a common educational background. They were of a different generation from the leaders of the ruling cliques — most were in their mid-thirties or early forties; their geographical origins were national in scope; their social background was heterogeneous — many were commoners.[6] For these reasons, they owed little allegiance to the Meiji ruling cliques and, partly because of this, found the problem of advancement to higher and more important positions especially frustrating.

The mobility structure in the bureaucracy was complex. The prefectures were ranked according to importance: that is, according to the amount of funds allotted by the central government. Above the prefectural governors were bureau chiefs, of which each ministry had about half a dozen, not all of equal prestige. Above these were vice-ministers and ministers, and finally there were the members of the House of Peers, envied by high-ranking bureaucrats because they were not subject to the vicissitudes of frequent cabinet changes and popular elections and, therefore, had optimum political security.

Conscious of the problems facing "up-and-coming" bureaucrats in this complex mobility structure, Hara aimed to use his appointive power as home minister to persuade them to rely on his party for movement upward rather than on the traditional ruling cliques. To Hara, success in this was crucial because control of the bureaucracy was essential to party growth.

The bureaucracy was the most efficient channel through which national influence could be gained. Its structure was rational and pervasive, stretching from the central bureaucracy in Tokyo to the forty-seven prefectures and municipalities headed by the governors and their staffs, on down to the districts (*gun*) and towns and villages. Backed by a police force and supported by government funds, the bureaucracy could act with a degree of effectiveness and speed against which the party, with its more informal and less powerful hierarchy, stood little chance of competing.

The bitter experience of being at the receiving end, of being kept at arm's length by an unfriendly bureaucracy, made party men agree that the obvious solution lay in establishing control over the bureaucratic apparatus. Rather than reduce its function, however, as one nursed in the school of nineteenth-century liberalism might urge, party men intended to redirect the bureaucracy for party ends. The logic behind the assertion of Hara that politics was power (echoed by men such as Ōishi Masami of the minority party) lay precisely in the realization that without controlling the bureaucracy a party could not survive as an effective political group. It was not, therefore, the desire of personal glory alone that underlay the quest for power by party men. In the case of Hara and the Seiyūkai, the expansion of party power and the maintenance of that strength were involved. In the case of Ōishi and the minority party — Kenseihontō, then Kokumintō in 1910 and Dōshikai in 1913 — survival was at stake.

Next to the prime ministership, the position that offered the greatest opportunity to expand party power in the bureaucracy was that of home minister. The home minister appointed the governors, was head of the police, and had a controlling voice over civil engineering projects throughout the country: he had under him, in other words, the entire regional bureaucratic structure. It was hardly by chance that Hara was home minister in the three cabinets in which he served between 1905 and 1915.

HARA AND SOME EARLY APPOINTMENTS AS HOME MINISTER

Immediately after having been sworn in as home minister for the First Saionji Cabinet (January 1906), Hara turned to gain control of his ministry. He began with the police, and his approach was meticulous: "I called on Yoshikawa Akimasa [the previous home minister] and took down the names of the leading figures and their followers in the central and regional offices. . . . He, too, suffered from the high-handedness of the metropolitan police and was troubled by the expanding influence to the regional level of Ōura [Kanetake] and his faction." [7]

Hara intended to make the police system responsive to his directives as home minister. The police had been used repeatedly against the parties in the past; principally through Ōura, metropolitan police chief 1898–1900, its members had intimate ties with the Yamagata faction. Hara first purged the metropolitan police of Ōura's men in what he described as a "pervasive change-over in personnel." [8] Next, he revised the rules governing the chain of command so that the metropolitan police chief became directly responsible to the home minister. Under the previous rule the police chief and, in turn, the entire police apparatus below him could act on orders from the prime minister as well as the home minister; because of this ambiguity in control over the police the Yamagata faction had maintained a paramount influence by placing men loyal to the faction in charge of it.

More important than changing the rules, Hara named a police chief who would, in fact, subordinate himself to Home Minister Hara. He selected Anraku Kendō (a Satsuma man who had once served under Yamagata and Itō), offering him the post on the condition that he would cooperate with Hara and with the understanding that the job would become his again in future cabinets in which Hara was home minister. By cooperating with Hara, Anraku's continuance in office when Hara was out of power was doubtful; but if Hara should return to power, so would Anraku. Anraku accepted Hara's terms, and between 1906 and 1915 his movements in and out of the bureaucracy coincided with those of Hara. [9]

What Hara had done was to place the post of metropolitan police chief under patronage: a police chief under him could not serve under Katsura and Ōura and, of course, vice versa. In short, the era in which the police had been consistently hostile to the parties had come to an end; the police was no longer the monopoly of the ruling cliques.

Having established control over the police Hara turned to other areas of the home ministry, making two appointments of lasting importance for him. One appointee was Mizuno Rentarō, the other Tokonami Takejirō; both had been graduated from Tokyo Imperial University in the early 1890's. Hara saw great promise in these two, saying of them: "Both recognized that the activities of the bureaucratic faction were inadequate" and "both supported progressive policies." [10] He named Mizuno to the important post of bureau chief of civil engineering (*doboku kyoku chō*) and Tokonami to the equally important and perhaps more prominent post of bureau chief of regional affairs (*chihō kyoku chō*). Later, during Hara's second tour as home minister (1911–1912), Tokonami served as vice-home minister and Mizuno as bureau chief of home affairs. Mizuno yielded the higher post to Tokonami; Tokonami, in turn, conceded an appointment to the House of Peers to Mizuno in 1912. When Katsura organized his third cabinet (December 1912), both men resigned with Hara. When Hara became home minister again in February 1913, Tokonami was appointed to the influential post of chief of the railroad bureau, while Mizuno advanced to the post of vice-home minister. In the spring of 1913 they formally joined the Seiyūkai. Both resigned with Hara in 1914, and during the post-World War I period they rose to ministerial level once again, under Hara's auspices.[11]

Tokonami and Mizuno were outstanding examples of bureaucrats out of the Tokyo Imperial University who cast their lot with a political party. (For further examples, see

Appendix A.) They were part of a late Meiji development aptly described by one scholar as "the party-ization of the bureaucracy" (the common description being "the bureaucratization of the party").[12] The most important group of bureaucrats among whom this "party-ization" took place was the governor class. Governors and their staffs were crucial liaisons in the disbursement of government funds on the local scene, close to the party's power bases throughout the country. Hence, the success of party expansion depended on Hara's ability first to gain control over the bureaus of civil engineering and of regional affairs by appointing men like Tokonami and Mizuno, and then over the governors who implemented the general directives from these bureaus throughout the country.

HARA AND THE GOVERNORS

Hara defined his attitude toward the governors in a questionnaire he sent them in January 1906: "If there are projects that you consider urgent in your metropolitan or prefectural areas, submit a detailed statement of your views. Furthermore, if you have any requests concerning national policy, include these in your statement." [13] Sending a questionnaire was unprecedented, and it brought on confusion and uncertainty among the governors. Although Hara did not admit it, the questionnaire was a test to see which governors were "efficient" — in Hara's terms — and acceptable, thus providing him with a working file for future appointments. Without openly stating his views, he made it plain to the governors that their success in the bureaucracy would depend on their ability to adapt themselves to his policies. In a speech to the governors in May 1906, he told them "the establishment of political parties is a natural trend," adding casually, "but there is no need for you to distinguish between one political party and another." [14]

His appointment policy, however, left no doubt in the minds of the governors that Home Minister Hara acted as party politician. He expelled the "inefficient" and promoted the "efficient"; he shifted strong "Seiyūkai governors" to weak Seiyūkai areas and weak or noncommitted governors to strong Seiyūkai areas. The first such shuffling of governors came in July 1906: six governors were suspended; thirty-six officials below the rank of governor were expelled from office; six were promoted to governorships from minor positions in the prefectural secretariat (*jimukan*); four others were promoted from lesser to more important prefectures.[15]

The second series of reshuffling came in December 1906 and January 1907; six governors "resigned of their own volition" and sixteen others were transferred or promoted. Then, in March and April 1908, just before the general election of May, five more were suspended, three others "resigned of their own volition," and fourteen governors were shifted about or promoted.[16] During 1906–1915 Hara was home minister roughly half the time (1906–1908, 1911–1912, 1913–1914) and made at least forty-one suspensions (there were forty-seven gubernatorial posts), and numerous and extremely intricate reshufflings and promotions. Although precise knowledge of the conditions surrounding each of his moves may be unavailable today, there can be no doubt as to the general motive that lay behind them.

Hara described his appointment policy as the "selection of the up-and-coming" and the "dismissal of the aged."[17] In principle, the Genrō did not object to Hara's reasoning because they had always asserted the same rationale; but his selections were unmistakably connected with plans for the growth of his party. He wrote in his diary: "Governors with divided loyalties or who are incompetent will be moved about without reservation."[18] He would suspend from office those who were "ill" or "inefficient" and *"who opposed the policies of this cabinet"* (emphasis mine).[19] Furthermore, he noted that a governor (Kawakami Chikaharu of Tōyama) was suspended because he "worked against this cabinet by allying himself with Ōura Kanetake's faction." Another (Ishihara Kenzō of Chiba) was also suspended because he "opposed my policies and gave support to the Katsura faction." [20]

Of those who "resigned of their own volition" he would say they were "underlings of Ōura and arms of the bureaucratic faction," [21] or, "they are products of the police and definitely inappropriate for the times." [22] On the other hand, he wrote of those he promoted: "I promoted Vice-Governor Yoshihara to governor of Kōchi prefecture because he was one of those who always defended us." [23] In much the same way, he wrote in 1911 that he had appointed a bureaucrat (Inuzuka Katsutarō) to the governorship of Osaka because he was a "progressive person." [24]

Fully aware of Hara's appointment policy, Seiyūkai Diet men were known to say on their tours, "if you want a change of governors, come and see me." [25] Men on the local scene often took up the offer, and sometimes appealed directly to Hara himself to have prefectural bureaucrats transferred. Whatever the route, unpopular local bureaucrats were brought to Hara's attention and removed. We see this in operation, for example, in the following account by a reporter in one of the prefectures: "Another case in point is the building of a normal school in the city of Hamamatsu which came up last year (1912). It was decided by Governor Matsui and Chief of Home Affairs Kojima . . . to build it in the Ōe district of Hamamatsu. The Seiyūkai group, however, actively campaigned to have it shifted to the Nagori district instead. Chief of Home Affairs Kojima did not listen to their demands . . . but the Katsura cabinet [third, December 1912–February 1913] collapsed . . . and once again Hara became home minister. . . . Matsui and Kojima were removed and Kasai and Wada were brought in as replacements by Hara. The normal school . . . was duly transferred to the [Seiyūkai] district of Nagori." [26]

Clearly, then, Hara was biased in his "selection of the up-and-coming" and his "dismissal of the aged." As it usually turned out, those who supported Hara were indeed "up-and-coming" and those who did not were usually old and heavily committed to the Yamagata faction; hence, he could claim a semblance of objectivity in making his appointments. "Up-and-coming" governors, however, were not unanimously behind Hara. For a while he could suspend them as "inefficient," but it was clear to observers that they were being suspended because of their support of opposition groups. The latter came to be known as "anti-Seiyū governors" while those who worked for the Seiyūkai were called "Seiyū governors." [27] (For examples, see Appendix B.)

Steadfast Seiyū governors were not numerous, but their impact far exceeded their number. They represented a group from the governor class, which was firmly allied to a party for the first time. As committed Seiyū governors they became persona non grata to the Yamagata faction, and their future as administrators or political leaders hinged on Hara's proximity to power.

Although Hara kept in touch with these jobless (*rōnin*, or masterless) governors and occasionally invited them to dinner, it is not certain what they did when out of office. When in power, however, their activities were unmistakable: they coordinated the policies of the central government with those of the prefectural governments; they distributed, according to their Seiyūkai bias, contracts involving government funds for building schools, parks, railroads, and dams; they used their appointive powers to purge the local bureaucracy of opposing elements; they cultivated the electoral base for the Seiyūkai, especially in areas where the party was weak; and finally, they gave official backing to the party at election time.[28]

Perhaps the best known, and certainly one of the most extreme and fiery, examples of the Seiyū governors was Mori Masataka. Mori exemplified that group of Tokyo Imperial University graduates (class of 1893) who, because of differences in education, generation, and geographical origin, owed little allegiance to the Meiji ruling cliques. As a minor bureaucrat in the home ministry, Mori found that his upward mobility was greatly hampered by those already entrenched in positions above him. In 1897 he complained to his friend Mizuno Rentarō regarding the matter of rising in the bureaucracy: "The alternatives end with these: we either come to Tokyo frequently to lade flattery on our superiors, or else, establish ties with the ruling cliques. . . . No matter how we work — especially those of us from the northeastern area who have no clique of our own — we are always deprived by them of our accomplishments. . . . This is particularly true for those of us who are university graduates. . . . I feel I should stop serving any further in this benighted home ministry." [29]

By the turn of the century Mori was ready for an alternate route. In 1907, Hara promoted him from a minor prefectural post to governor of Ibaraki, launching his career as a Seiyū governor. At Niigata prefecture (1911–1912), Mori used the following tactic: on the pretext of retrenchment he announced a cutback in new schools from a projected twelve to five; areas denied the new schools, of course, were opposition areas. As a result of negotiations and bloody riots in the prefectural diet of Niigata, nine new schools were built instead of the revised plan for five. In other words, four of the seven opposition areas swore support to the Seiyūkai and got their new schools; the three that continued to oppose the Seiyūkai went without new schools. [30]

Mori's blatantly partisan policies led to his expulsion by Katsura in 1912; he was reinstated by Hara to Miyagi in 1913. There Governor Mori continued his strong-arm tactics,

dismissing one hundred twenty men from the local bureaucracy within a few short months. In 1914 he was expelled
by Ōkuma (anti-Seiyūkai cabinet). In 1916 and again in
1918, Hara brought Mori out of forced retirement to serve
as a Seiyū governor. Finally, in 1921, while he was serving
as prime minister, Hara appointed Mori to the House of
Peers.[31]

The emergence of a group of vigorous Seiyū governors
like Mori could not go unnoticed by the Yamagata faction.
For example, Takazaki Shinshō (governor of Osaka), who
owed unswerving loyalty to Yamagata, complained to the
latter in January 1913: "Of late, if one is not a member of a
political party, neither as official nor private citizen can he
accomplish anything. Thus, bureaucrats in general, and especially prefectural governors, have tried to take advantage
of the majority party and now they reek like party politicians."[32] Thus, Home Minister Ōura, working for Katsura,
had to expel Seiyū governors and make counteractive appointments. Hara noted in his diary in 1912 that Seiyū governors Abe Hiroshi, Andō Kensuke, Yoda Keijirō, Inuzuka
Katsutarō, Kawashima Junkan, and others were expelled
from office.[33] To replace them, however, Ōura had to select
men who were also "up-and-coming" university graduates.
Governors such as Izawa Takio (Tokyo Imperial University,
1895) were not committed to any party at the outset but,
because they opposed the excesses of the Seiyū governors,
came to be recognized and used by men such as Ōura,
whether they wished it or not, as anti-Seiyū governors. Ultimately they did not cast their lot with Yamagata and the
exponents of transcendental cabinets, but with the rival
party to the Seiyūkai.

A case in point is Shimooka Chūji (Tokyo Imperial University, 1895), a Kenseikai party leader in the late teens
and early twenties. Promoted by Katsura from governor of
Akita prefecture to bureau chief of agricultural affairs in

1913, he was optimistic of his future as a bureaucrat for the Yamagata faction. Therefore, in spite of the fact that the Third Katsura Cabinet was on the verge of collapse (the Taishō Political Crisis, 1912–1913), he wrote to a friend in this carefree manner: "Seen as a whole, the general commotion in society is nothing extraordinary. The future of those of us of the so-called bureaucratic faction is extremely bright — like a spring sea." [34] But this same Shimooka left the bureaucracy and joined the anti-Seiyū party, the Kenseikai, in 1915. At this time he wrote to Yamagata, who thought highly of him: "I cannot at all acknowledge the emergence of a transcendental cabinet [Terauchi cabinet, 1916–1918] in this day and age as a regular development of constitutional government." [35]

By forcing his rivals to take countermeasures, Hara unwittingly set in motion an opposition which, while at first inchoate, became an important force behind the formation of a strong second party: highly talented young bureaucrats eventually joined the opposition party and became leaders in it. Thus, Hara's appointment policies had implications that went beyond just strengthening his party's position. By the mid-twenties, when these policies might be said to have reached the saturation point, the entire governor class and the bureau and section chiefs below them were informally categorized according to party affiliation. [36] In the period under consideration this was not the case, for the process had just begun.

Although many bureaucrats had party connections, some managed to remain unaffiliated. Between Mori Masataka and Izawa Takio — outstanding Seiyū and anti-Seiyū governors respectively — was a group of noncommitted or weakly committed governors. Some, because of family background and ties with high government officials, proceeded directly from governor status into the House of Peers. [37] Others claimed to be Seiyū governors but managed to remain in office without interruption.[38] These uncommitted governors enjoyed political immunity: they could work for whomever was in power and evade the almost certain expulsion meted out to strongly committed governors when their party was not in office.[39]

What should be stressed, however, is that whether or not a governor was strongly committed to the Seiyūkai, he had to carry out the policies of that party to a certain extent. He could refrain from the excessive measures taken by some, but he had to cooperate or else face expulsion. He would be ranked as an anti-Seiyū governor or considered "inefficient," which probably amounted to the same thing to Hara. Hence, a commitment notwithstanding, Hara manipulated the governors, using them as arms of his party; and, as a result of two other terms as home minister, he retained and expanded his control over them. The net result was the growth of Seiyūkai power and the undermining of a key base of power of the Yamagata faction.

The abuses that this system brought were many, constituting a persuasive body of negative evidence against the parties in the 1930's. The coalition of party and bureaucracy, when backed by the force of authority, became a suppressive weapon free of any adequate institutional checks. Party men, however, were bound by the logic that the most effective way to compete against the unfriendly and powerful bureaucracy was to gain control of it and use it for party ends. Opposition groups counteracted by repeating the process of acquiring power at the top and re-directing the powerful bureaucratic apparatus. The result was a constant jockeying for power at the top that was always extremely intense.

THE PLAN TO ABOLISH THE "GUN" (DISTRICT)

Hara's drive into the ranks of the governors was an integral part of a broader scheme to extend party influence down to the level of towns and villages, a scheme involving the destruction of the *gun* (district).[40] This plan illustrates the pervasiveness of his plan to expand party influences in the bureaucracy; at the same time, it shows the precarious quality of the compromise that had brought Hara to power in the first place.

The regional administrative structure of Japan was completed between 1887 and 1890. At its base were the towns and villages, next were the *gun* or districts, and above them were the prefectures. Both the prefectures and the towns and villages had a traditional base, coinciding roughly with the feudal territorial units (*han*) and the natural agricultural units, respectively. The *gun*, however, lacked this base.

Standing midway between the towns and villages below and the prefecture above, the *gun* were thought of as the vital link between officialdom (*kan*) and the people (*min*). The *gun* chiefs were bureaucratic appointees nominally under the governors, and the *gun* councils represented the people in towns and villages. To Yamagata, the principal architect of the regional structure, the *gun* were the crux of his idea of "self-government." [41] Instead of providing "self-government," however, the function of the *gun* was to assure domestic stability. Men of "wealth and reputation" who shared Yamagata's view of the Meiji state were appointed *gun* chiefs; although they were technically under the prefectural governors, they held broad administrative and emergency police powers which they used (as in the 1890's) to assure orderly local government by interfering at the polls.

Sixteen years after the *gun* were established Hara proposed their abolition. He made his views clear in an address to the governors one month after assuming office (February 1906): "In devising the policies for the management of postwar affairs, we must administratively accompany the *progress taking place everywhere in society* and, moreover, we must stimulate that progress. I intend to *respond to the trends of the time*. . . . I believe it our natural duty to complete the task of the postwar management on this basis. . . . I will submit to the Diet a bill revising the city-town-village system. . . . I will submit for consideration, at the same time, the abolition of the *gun* system. Briefly, the reason for abolishing the *gun* is this: the city-town-village system has an ancient tradition of self-government and so, with good legislation, unlimited development can be expected of these. Such is not the case with the *gun*." (Emphasis mine.)[42]

What were his reasons for wanting to abolish the *gun*? Stripped to the minimum they were clearly these: one, there were sound structural reasons that called for abolition; two, abolition would be a devastating blow to the Yamagata faction; and three, the end result would be the expansion of party power.

The *gun*, to Hara, were becoming unnecessary in the Meiji structure. Because of a reduction in financial aid for local projects by the government during the war with Russia, the five-hundred-odd *gun*, lacking the power to levy taxes, were becoming ineffective. Furthermore, many functions of the *gun* were being pre-empted by towns and villages. Industries and public works, for example, were flourishing and being controlled locally, quite apart from *gun* supervision. In Hara's view, therefore, the towns and villages should be permitted to grow; their taxing powers should be expanded; they should be encouraged to consolidate for the sake of greater efficiency, rendering the *gun* invalid. The *gun*, in short, restricted natural progress and should be destroyed. From Hara's own defense of his bill: "The towns and villages of today, generally, have not developed fully. Hence, they are being spurred on by the developments in the nation, and are in the process of consolidation. The consolidation and growth of the towns and villages is a natural trend. Unless the towns and villages combine and grow, it will be extremely difficult to carry out local projects. . . . Because I feel that this development is a result of stimulation from a pervasive and inevitable progress, I hope that the towns and villages will be permitted, as much as possible, to grow and consolidate. As the towns and villages are permitted to grow gradually . . . it will become increasingly difficult to recognize the need for the *gun*, standing at a midway point." [43]

Although Hara defended his bill in the Diet on grounds of natural changes in the regional structure, he had in mind other reasons of greater importance — breaking the strength of the Yamagata faction, and extending the influence of his party. The Yamagata faction's regional basis of power was tightly knit and extensive. Its core consisted of that class with "wealth" and "reputation" on which Yamagata relied for the maintenance of stability and the preservation of the "national purity" in the countryside. Although lacking the proud heritage and the power of the Prussian Junker, men from this class nonetheless staffed the major positions in the local bureaucracy (the governors, and especially the *gun* chiefs and town and village chiefs and their councils). Moreover, they dominated influential semi-bureaucratic organizations such as agricultural associations (*nōkai*) and industrial cooperatives (*sangyō kumiai*). These organizations, which were established at the turn of the century, received government subsidies to promote agriculture and industry in the countryside; hence they grew and expanded with nourishment from the bureaucracy. Sponsoring and directing the movement to expand these associations were men like Hirata Tōsuke and Komatsubara Eitarō, peers with long experience in the home ministry and dedicated followers of Yamagata. [44]

The influences of this faction throughout the regions were what Hara set out to destroy under the guise of responding to the trends of the day. He manipulated the governors from above, as we have seen, and then hoped to destroy the *gun* chiefs below them. Then, as we shall see later, he planned to undercut the economic significance of the semibureaucratic cooperatives which Yamagata's men sponsored by making his party the sole arbiter in the distribution of government largesse. There can be no doubt that in this integrated plan of attack the abolition of the *gun* loomed large in Hara's mind: "The major issue behind the abolition of the *gun* system is the complete destruction of the Yamagata faction. I intend to abolish the *gun* system and ruin that faction with one stroke." [45] His strategy was to push through the bill abolishing the *gun* and then diminish the initiative powers of town and village councils staffed by conservative men of "wealth and reputation" and expand the appointive and emergency powers of the town and village chiefs. These chiefs (retired bureaucrats of the governor class) would be appointed by the home minister and placed directly under the governors, whom he would control from above. Since the lines between these chiefs and himself would become much tighter than before, he could compel them — just as he could the governors — to be responsive to the demands of the local party branch offices and not to the town and village councils. In other words, by abolishing the *gun* Hara aimed at squeezing the bureaucracy from above, right down to the level that was closest to the party's power bases.

The implications of his plans were clear. If he succeeded, he would drastically undermine the regional power base of the Yamagata faction. And with the added control over the regional bureaucratic structure that the abolition of the *gun* would bring, he would win sweeping victories at the polls: "I plan to abolish the *gun* and decisively defeat the Yamagata faction. On the basis of that strength, I will face the prefectural elections this year [August 1907] and, after that, the elections for the Lower House next year [May 1908]." [46]

The preliminary skirmishes came in February and March 1906. On March 17 Hara submitted his bill to abolish the *gun* to the Lower House, where it passed without dissent. But it was pigeonholed in the House of Peers,[47] and Hara girded himself for the main struggle that was yet to come. First he convinced a somewhat hesitant Saionji in this fashion: "If, with good fortune, it should pass, Yamagata's faction will have lost considerable prestige, and the public will praise the cabinet. If, with ill fortune, it should not pass, it will not matter as we will be representing public opinion." [48] Then, overriding stiff opposition from others within the cabinet who believed, quite rightly, that the bill would antagonize Yamagata, he submitted his bill again in 1907.[49]

Convinced that public opinion was on his side and that a victory would break the Yamagata faction's regional base, Hara was determined to have his bill passed. Passage of the bill meant opening the bureaucracy for party penetration down to the local level. By using his power as home minister to appoint town and village chiefs he would be able to win sweeping victories in the forthcoming elections. Passage of the bill, furthermore, would show that he was capable of directing the entire decision-making machinery, including the Lower House, the House of Peers, and the Genrō. The stakes were big, the psychological implications even bigger; and he could not go unchallenged. This was the first overt confrontation between Hara and the Seiyūkai on one hand and the Yamagata faction on the other, and the infighting was fierce and complex.

HARA CONFRONTS THE YAMAGATA FACTION

While most critics in the presses missed the political content of Hara's bill, hailing it in some cases as a significant step toward the reduction of administrative expenses, or denouncing it as disruptive to the entire agricultural sector of the economy (as was argued by commentators supporting the views of the agricultural associations), Yamagata's men had not been deceived. They saw with pristine clarity the power implications behind Hara's move. They took the offensive against Hara with a drive to defeat him in his own bastion, the Lower House. This caught the astute Hara temporarily off guard, for he had anticipated that the stumbling block to his bill would be the House of Peers. He had not expected that the bill, which had passed the Lower House without opposition in March 1906, would meet with stiff opposition in that house. But Yamagata's men in the Daidō Club established an alliance with the minority party, the Kenseihontō, and particularly with the reform faction (*kaikakuha*) in that party, to vote against the *gun* bill.[50]

This Daidō Club-Kenseihontō coalition is of considerable importance in understanding the emergence of a countervailing force against the Seiyūkai. Of the Daidō Club little need be said: it was directly under Katsura and Ōura, and was one in the line of many small government parties whose objective was to gain the balancing votes between the two major parties — Yamagata's idea of a multiparty or "triangular party system" through which the government could manipulate the Lower House. Something more must be said, however, of the reform faction of the Kenseihontō, whose responses to Seiyūkai expansion grew steadily in the course of the decade.

The beginnings of the reform faction, which can be traced to the turn of the nineteenth century, were rooted in a growing displeasure among a few Kenseihontō men with their party's position vis-à-vis the ruling cliques. As had Hara, these men had concluded that the tactics of opposition were inadequate, and in late 1906 they banded together into what came to be known as the reform faction.[51] The platform of this faction was seemingly based on the naive belief that members of the ruling cliques could be persuaded to join the party movement. But underlying this bit of naiveté was the realization among men of the faction that the minority party could not compete against the Seiyūkai.

Opponents of the reform faction within the minority party, notably Inukai Tsuyoshi, urged a "union of the people's parties," which meant, in effect, a search for alliance with the rapidly growing Seiyūkai. Men of the reform faction contended that such a policy would only contribute to the plans of the Seiyūkai to penetrate further into the local electoral bases of the minority group. Instead of seeking a union with the Seiyūkai, synonymous with committing political suicide, they argued that the only real alternative was to persuade a powerful member of the ruling cliques (the favorite choice being Katsura) to join with them to resist the Seiyūkai.[52]

Initial action came in December 1906. The reform faction let it be known in no uncertain terms that party president Ōkuma Shigenobu because of his lack of vigor, and Inukai because of his unrealistic obstinacy, were persona non grata to the party. It then announced its objective of reforming party structure (hence, "reform faction") in order to facilitate party growth. This meant revising key party organs to shift the balance in favor of the reform faction, thereby minimizing the influence of Ōkuma and Inukai. With a control over the majority, the reform faction carried out a series of structural changes in line with this aim[53] and took the drastic step of forcing Ōkuma, the founder of the party, to resign his presidency by rejecting his platform (January 19, 1907). Having gained the upper hand over Ōkuma and Inukai, it then reached the agreement with the Daidō Club to oppose the *gun* bill, hoping that this would result in an alliance with Katsura.

In light of this threat to his bill, Hara turned to split the coalition by drawing men from the Daidō Club into the Seiyūkai. But its leader, Ōura Kanetake, countered Hara by secretly persuading Saionji to reject all Daidō men from the Seiyūkai. Hara could not disguise his anger when he discovered what Saionji had done. He reminded Saionji that the aim of the Seiyūkai was not to exclude bureaucrats of the Daidō Club from the party but "to expand absolutely the power of the party," and he told Saionji that before making decisions of this kind he should consult with Matsuda Masahisa or himself about actual conditions in the party. Utterly exasperated, he entered in his diary: "If he . . . is absent-minded about such matters there is no hope for the future." [54]

Hara's displeasure with Saionji's leadership is a constant theme in his diary. It was particularly intense in this case because of the speed and unity of action with which the Yamagata faction threatened Hara with defeat. In the end, Hara lured five members of the Daidō Club to join the Seiyūkai. This maneuver plus support from a few independents (for example, Ozaki Yukio and Hanai Takuzō) enabled Hara to overcome the Yamagata faction's challenge in the Lower House. In committee action, the bill was reported to the floor by a thirteen to eleven vote and the final passage on March 22 was by a close one hundred eighty-eight to one hundred sixty-four tally.[55]

Hara now turned to the House of Peers. There he started his long and difficult drive to divide and overcome that house, which he despised: in his eyes it was a bastion for conservatives who viewed the parties with lofty contempt. Throughout his career as party leader he seized every opportunity to promote party men into the House of Peers; in 1912, he finally managed to have a party man (Sugita Teiichi) named to the house. His aim, he wrote at that time, was "to destroy the tradition in the House of Peers to treat party men with disdain — as if they were lowly outcasts." [56] His contempt for the peers, then, was equal to theirs for the parties. And he would break their power by splitting their ranks.

He gained allies with influential peers like Hotta Masayasu (Kenkyūkai) and Senge Takatomi (Mokuyōkai),[57] and he drew the support of a few groups disaffected from the Yamagata faction — for example, a group of barons (Dōshikai) and a group of viscounts (Danwakai).[58] By splitting the House of Peers he would deliver still another blow against the Yamagata faction which controlled that house, thus greatly advancing the cause of the parties: "If both the Mokuyōkai and the Kenkyūkai [leading groups in the House of Peers] should support the cabinet, the situation in the House of Peers will change drastically and great strides will have been made toward the realization of constitutional government." [59]

It was obvious that Hara had no intention of conceding to Katsura's formula "the House of Peers is mine. . . ." Thus, while Hara would reassure Katsura in later talks (April 1909) that he had no close connections in the House of Peers, he would also tell Katsura that as long as the Yamagata faction remained "oppressive" in that house those on the receiving end would "naturally lean towards the Seiyūkai." [60] Moreover, he told Katsura: "Gradually the idea of political parties will be accepted in the House of Peers, too." [61]

But the Yamagata faction — Kiyoura Keigo, Hirata Tōsuke, Komatsubara Eitarō, Mishima Yatarō, Ōura Kanetake, etc. — moved swiftly to preserve the unity of the peers against Hara. With telling effect, these men persuaded the majority of the peers to preserve the sanctity of their house — a house that must remain transcendent to the petty interests of parties. Thus, for most of them, Hara's argument that the *gun* were becoming obsolete fell on deaf ears. Clearly, it was the ability of these men to maintain a high level of esprit de corps among the peers that prevented the passage of the bill. By the same token, it was not weakness or ambiguity of purpose on Hara's part that turned near victory into sudden defeat. Hara gained one hundred eight votes, which reflected the effectiveness of his maneuvers; but his enemies gathered one hundred forty-nine votes. Then, having beaten Hara in this test of strength over the *gun*, they proceeded to ostracize those peers who insisted on maintaining ties with the Seiyūkai, rendering them powerless and finally, in the election among the peers for seats in July 1911, preventing their re-election almost to the man.[62]

The defeat over the abolition of the *gun* was a bitter one for Hara, greater than he would admit. At least, he never again was to confront the Yamagata faction in the same way he did over the *gun*. The defeat, however, reconfirmed his belief that the realization of party government involved an arduous and complicated struggle. With characteristic optimism, he continued to believe that time would bring ultimate victory — that history was on his side. He took solace in the fact that his defeat had not been crushing: "The Yamagata faction was extremely active — hence, the result. But even so, its power is not so fearful. The fact that the House of Peers, with which we have no ties, moved the way it did for us . . . indicates that Yamagata's influence in the House of Peers is not overly great." [63]

The passage of the bill to abolish the *gun* finally came in 1921, during Hara's first cabinet. Coming at a time when its psychological importance was gone and when greater reforms were being demanded from progressive quarters, the passage of the bill came as an anticlimax. In early 1907, however, the *gun* issue was not at all insignificant: in its passage or defeat were involved the issues of whether Hara could, in fact, make major inroads into the House of Peers and whether he would be able to extend his appointive powers to the local level and in so doing win massively at the polls; and, above all, it involved a deeply personal matter of testing his own strength with that of the Yamagata faction.

THE BREAKDOWN OF COMPROMISE

The struggle over the abolition of the *gun* led to a breakdown of the compromise relationship between Hara and Katsura. Katsura had agreed to support the Saionji cabinet vis-à-vis the Genrō and the House of Peers and Hara, on his part, had agreed that the cabinet would not depart radically in matters of policy. Hara's plan to abolish the *gun* strained this agreement because it was clearly a scheme to enhance the growth of his party at the expense of the Yamagata faction. For this reason, Katsura did not act on behalf of the cabinet in the House of Peers and he did not abide by his formula "the Lower House is Saionji's." To Hara, Katsura's promises were "completely empty words." [64]

Chances for a rapprochement between Hara and the Yamagata faction had been temporarily sealed off, permitting opposition to mount against the Saionji cabinet in its last year. Yamagata appealed to the throne, protesting Hara's mild handling of socialists, forcing Hara to counter Yamagata's "wicked scheme" with a successful appeal of his own. Suppression, Hara argued, should be preceded by "education and reform of social conditions." [65] In early 1908, the Daidō Club and the reform faction of the Kenseihontō submitted a no-confidence vote against the Saionji cabinet that came within nine votes of passing. There was also growing opposition from the Genrō Inoue Kaoru and Matsukata Masayoshi, who, reflecting the views of business leaders, opposed the cabinet's economic policy.

By the end of 1907 Saionji wanted to resign. [66] At the insistence of Hara, this was delayed until after the general elections of May 1908. In August, in spite of the Seiyūkai victory at the polls, the First Saionji Cabinet resigned and made way for the Second Katsura Cabinet.

Compromise, however, was re-established as easily as it had broken down. Katsura needed support from the majority

Seiyūkai, especially to have his budget passed. Hara seized this opportunity and maintained close ties with Katsura to influence policy-making. In spite of a tendency for the politics of compromise to break down, it had to persist as long as the Seiyūkai retained control of the Lower House, and Hara continually pressed this advantage to preserve party power. Thus, the foothold he had gained in the bureaucracy did not divide and disappear. His activities vis-à-vis the peers did not cease. And even though he had failed to abolish the *gun,* he had served notice to Katsura and men of the ruling cliques of the emerging power of the Seiyūkai. Moreover, by forcing Katsura into compromises with him he could work out still another plan he had in mind, besides abolishing the *gun,* to reach down to the men of influence at the local power bases: this was his economic policy, which, in retrospect, accomplished what he had aimed at in trying to abolish the *gun.* Hara's impact on the processes of government, then, was far from finished; his strategic goals remained fixed in his mind, his long term objective unimpaired.

4

The Cultivation of a Local Power Base
(1909–1911)

Sometime in early 1911 Hara was alleged to have said to Inukai: "It is absurd that a segment of the public should call me a tool of the ruling cliques. Reaching a mutual understanding with them is not surrender. Rather, it is a case of using the ruling cliques. Political parties cannot advance unless they take power. . . . What can we accomplish without power?"[1] Although these may not be Hara's exact words, they undoubtedly represent his views: use the ruling cliques to maintain party strength and, through negotiation, seize the reins of government to weaken these cliques. This is clearly evident in the Seiyūkai's consistent support of an economic policy that would maintain party strength. At the top level Hara negotiated with Katsura to shape economic policy, while below, party cadres throughout the country maneuvered to influence the disbursement of government funds. Keeping close contact with Prime Minister Katsura was a stratagem to preserve and extend party strength by making certain that the interests of local powerholders (*chihō yūryoku sha*) were satisfied. Then, assured of a continuing majority, Hara would again press for an exchange of power and try to weaken the Yamagata faction by isolating Yamagata from his principal protégé, Katsura.

PARTY EXPANSION THROUGH A POSITIVE
ECONOMIC POLICY

In the election of March 1904, the electorate in Japan numbered some seven hundred sixty thousand voters; in the following election of May 1908, the figure had soared to one million five hundred ninety thousand voters.[2] The war boom had ushered in "the age of the nouveau riche" (*narikin tenka*),[3] and with it more people than ever before, enough to double the electorate, were now paying the minimum ten-yen direct tax that entitled male citizens to vote. Along with this sudden spurt in the size of the electorate came an increase in corruption: person-to-person contact at election time was much more difficult than before, raising substantially the cost of elections; "election-brokers," often local businessmen, emerged on the scene to buy out votes for ten and fifteen yen apiece from those who had gained the right to vote but who had little experience or interest in voting.[4]

The impact of the above was that the electoral bases (*jiban*) were made extremely unstable. It became difficult to predict which way local power holders, the fulcra of the electoral bases, would swing the blocs of votes they controlled. These local political leaders were no longer simply the "men of wealth and reputation" on whom Yamagata based his system of "self-government"; by late Meiji they had become much more diversified and vocal in their interests. Aside from a few like Ozaki Yukio and Inukai Tsuyoshi who held "iron *jiban*," therefore, Diet men for the most part were constantly plagued with political insecurity and greatly feared Diet dissolutions and new elections.

In each of the elections held in the decade under study (1908, 1912, 1915) there was a substantial number of newly elected Diet men. Returns show that fifty percent and more were not being re-elected, indicating the extremely fluid and unstable condition of the local political bases. For example, in 1912, one hundred seventy-eight out of the total of three hundred eighty-one seats were newly elected.[5] In 1915 the Seiyūkai was reduced from one hundred eighty-nine strong in the Lower House to one hundred five, while the minority party grew from ninety-seven to one hundred fifty. There were one hundred ninety-five newly elected men that year.[6]

In seeking to establish small electoral districts, Hara expressed his concern over the unstable electoral bases: "In looking over the results of the recent general elections, we find that not even one-half of the Diet members are being re-elected for the second time and rising, as a result, to important positions. In the election of 1908, for example, little over one-third of the Diet members were re-elected, and just shy of two-thirds were elected for the first time." [7] To solve this problem of insecurity facing Diet men Hara took a twofold approach. For one thing, he attempted to revise the electoral system. In the large district system in existence, Seiyūkai Diet men found themselves competing against each other and dividing votes among themselves, thereby enhancing the chances of a weaker third candidate. Furthermore, expenses were high in the large district systems. Hara, therefore, submitted a bill (March 1912) to establish a small electoral district system, but it was turned down by the House of Peers as a selfish scheme.[8]

The other and more important approach to ease the insecurity of Diet men was the pursuit of a "positive policy," that is, a vigorous spending policy. Taxes would be raised and loans floated at home and abroad to boost the economy; more schools, parks, roads, dams, and railroads would be built than ever before.[9] A positive policy did not mean the satisfaction of local interest for its own sake, or the promotion of the agrarian sector of the economy; it meant party expansion by pork barrel, and it involved coordinating the activities of governors and their staffs with those of party headquarters, the regional groups, and the local branch offices.

Sympathetic to the Seiyūkai, Hara's biographer Maeda Renzan wrote: "For many years the Seiyūkai consistently emphasized the need to develop roads, rivers, harbors, and railroads. It grew by joining these to the hopes of the farmers and the small city people of the regions. The opposition belittled this as the Seiyūkai's party expansion program. The Seiyūkai, however, believed that the program beautified the entire nation and therefore argued that the growth of the party was a result of good government." [10] Opponents of the Seiyūkai, however, saw things somewhat differently: "How has the Seiyūkai, which controls the majority in the Lower House, been able to become the powerful party that it is today? It certainly did not achieve this because its policies were welcomed by the people. It enticed the simple folk of the regions by carrying out needless civil engineering projects under the fancy title: the management of postwar affairs. Consequently, government expenses rose to extreme proportions and the entire financial structure was endangered. During the ten years following the war, the nation has not been able to recover and there are signs of disaster ahead." [11] Whether seen in sympathetic terms or not, the phenomenon being described was the same: a positive economic policy to expand party power.

In launching this spending program, Hara warned the governors that "the rise in administrative expenses is entirely unavoidable." [12] True to his warning, the peacetime budgets of 1907 and 1908 went far beyond the wartime budget of 1905:

Year	Cabinet	Budget[13]
1905	first Katsura	421 million yen
1907	first Saionji	602 million yen
1908	first Saionji	636 million yen

Over and above the rise in the regular portion of administrative expenses, an increase in armaments was agreed upon (eight new army divisions and fifty thousand additional tons of warships) and the railroads were nationalized at a cost of four hundred eighty million yen. For a large segment of the population, therefore, peace did not bring a reduction of fiscal burdens. On the contrary, to help defray growing expenses "emergency" wartime taxes which had been levied on general consumption goods such as textiles and kerosene were renewed in 1906 and increased in 1908.[14] From late 1906 on, as Japan's economy sank into a period of unabating slump, complaints against the spending policy grew louder, as in the vociferous but unsuccessful antitax movement (1907–1914) which demanded retrenchment.

The basic Seiyūkai spending policy, however, remained unchanged. The Seiyūkai contended that a positive spending policy — a crude form of pump-priming — and not a passive retrenchment policy was needed to boost the slumping economy. This argument, however, was not based on economic analysis but on the indisputable fact that government funds were essential for the maintenance of party strength. The satisfaction of local economic demands through bureaucratic channels was not a new phenomenon; but what had once been an almost purely local affair was now, in late Meiji, being coordinated by party men into a national scheme for party expansion.

In the fall months of every year before the Diet convened in December, and preceding and following elections, branch and regional rallies were arranged by Diet men in Tokyo and party officials in the branch offices.[15] In 1909, to take an example, the following series of major rallies were held:

Date	Rally[16]
October 2	Kyūshū regional rally at Ōita prefecture
October 27	Joint Chūgoku-Shikoku regional rally at Shimonoseki
November 14	Hokushin regional rally at Niigata prefecture
November 14	Miyagi prefecture branch rally at Sendai
November 15	Hokkaidō branch rally at Sapporo
November 16	Tōkai regional rally at Nagoya
November 31	Tokyo rally to climax all the rallies

Regions like Kyūshū, Chūgoku, Hokushin, and Shikoku were made up of about a half dozen prefectures and had at party headquarters (*hombu*) in Tokyo groups of Diet men named after the regions they represented. There were eight of these "regional groups" (*chihō dantai*),[17] each acting as liaison between the executive staff (*kambu*)[18] at party headquarters and the branch offices, usually one to a prefecture or a municipality, throughout the country. They elected representatives to the party's board of councillors (*kyōgiin*),[19] which had close contact with the executive staff. More important, they organized regional rallies. At these rallies the interests of an area were expressed, and the policies of party headquarters were in turn transmitted. In this way the rallies served as meeting points for the two main segments of the party — headquarters and the branch offices — and, aside from Saionji, party leaders from headquarters made a point of attending them.

At predetermined train stops in nearby and distant prefectures, welcoming committees (*kangeikai*) composed of local political leaders[20] came out to meet party men from headquarters in Tokyo. These party leaders then went on tours to examine sites for new schools, railroad lines, and roads, or, as one party leader put it, "to investigate the actual conditions of transportation and industry . . . and, furthermore, to assess party strength there." [21] In other words, they reminded local leaders during these tours of the continuing interest of party headquarters in the economic development of the particular area and, at the same time, of the continuing need for increaesd local support for the party. In areas where the party was weak the men from headquarters made exaggerated promissory speeches. One critic of the time described Seiyūkai strategy this way: "Their [Seiyūkai leaders] one most effective weapon was to tour their rivals' electoral bases and make promises as though right away railroads would be laid and roads built. In this way, local leaders were persuaded to join the party." [22]

After the sightseeing and speechmaking were over, the guests from party headquarters retired to a large city in the area where branch (in the case of one prefecture) or regional (several prefectures) rallies had been scheduled. The presence of party leaders from central headquarters lent an aura of prestige to these rallies and to an area as a whole. It also imparted a feeling that rewards would be quick in coming: prior to the banquet that invariably brought the rallies to a festive end, the leaders reiterated the promises they had made all along the tour. From Hara's entry in his diary, for example: "Returned from Fushiki by special train to Takaoka and from there left for Kanazawa at 4 p.m. . . . A branch-sponsored reception was held . . . and I delivered a speech affirming our positive policy." [23]

Sometimes there would be an election of local party officials; always, there were resolutions. The latter voiced some of the major requests of an area and usually began on a general note: "We pledge to promote the development of our national welfare and to support a positive policy." [24] Resolutions with specific requests followed: "We resolve the rapid completion of the Ukoshi and the Kaigan railroad lines. . . . We are agreed that the Tōhoku Technical High School should be built in this prefecture [Yamagata]," [25] and, "we resolve that the Iwakoshi railroad be completed immediately and also that transportation facilities of all kinds be developed extensively in this prefecture," [26] and again, "we resolve that the Tōhoku University be completed rapidly, that the Sapporo Agricultural College be raised to the status of a university; and that high schools for dyeing and weaving be established. . . . We resolve that plans be laid for the development of railroads and harbors in Tōhoku and Hokkaidō so that transportation facilities can be developed without delay in these areas." [27]

The enthusiasm radiating from the tours and rallies served to reaffirm the specific promises made to local politicians. Such assurances were inviting, and the Seiyūkai rapidly increased its membership. One observer noted: "For a while, at least, popular feeling has risen almost in unison to support the Seiyūkai. If one is not a member of the Seiyūkai, he has no influence at all." [28]

This meant that the six or seven hundred thousand new voters on the scene were being induced to vote for the Seiyūkai. Note the successes of the Seiyūkai in the 1908 and 1912 elections for the Lower House in the table below.

The situation in the prefectural assemblies reveals the same pattern. In the election of September 1907, the Seiyūkai captured eight hundred forty-seven seats of a total of one thousand five hundred sixty-three seats compared with the minority party's two hundred ninety-two. In the election of September 1911 the distribution remained much the same and the Seiyūkai controlled relatively, or absolutely, thirty of the forty-seven prefectural assemblies while

Year and (election)	Seiyūkai[a]	Minor- ity party[b]	Splinter groups	Total	Electorate[29] (second election 435,000)
1898 (fifth)	105	103	92	300	450,000
1898 (sixth)	120	124	56	300	502,000
1902 (seventh)	191	95	90	376	983,000
1903 (eighth)	175	85	116	376	958,000
1904 (ninth)	133	90	156	379	760,000
1908 (tenth)	188	70	121	379	1,590,000
1912 (eleventh)	209	95	77	381	1,506,000

[a] Until 1900, Kenseitō.
[b] Until 1910, Kenseihontō; then Kokumintō until 1913, Dōshikai through 1915.

the Kokumintō, its closest competitor, held only seven; the rest were in the hands of minor factions.[30]

With this growing power, Seiyūkai men in the prefectural assemblies gained control over key committees that handled subsidies, investigation of new projects, and loans through the powerful agricultural and industrial banks (nōkō ginkō, semibureaucratic banks). Through these committees they pressured governors and their staffs to disburse funds according to Seiyūkai plans.[31] The implications can be gathered from the following account: "The township of Kakekawa was an isolated [anti-Seiyūkai] stronghold, but each year subsidies from the prefectural government for the building of the town's arts and crafts school for girls were reduced, while the gun agricultural school was shifted into the marshes. . . . The townsfolk have been truly oppressed and thus, after the main anti-Seiyū figure, Yamazaki Junichirō, passed away, 200 leaders of the town joined the Seiyūkai and that stronghold collapsed. Under these cir-

cumstances, leaders in the city of Shizuoka are also arguing
that they will not be able to retain their life investments if
they continue to antagonize the Seiyūkai. . . . Many others
are saying that they should join that party soon so that the
Yasube dam will be repaired and strengthened. . . . In the
end, the city of Shizuoka will share the same fate as the
town of Kakekawa." [32]

Party pressures of the sort just described could be applied only with close cooperation from the bureaucracy.
They reflected the manipulation of the prefectural bureaucracy by the home minister from above and the party from
below. The outcome was a complex interest structure (see
accompanying scheme) in which local party leaders, governors and their staffs, and Diet men were deeply immersed,
binding party and bureaucracy intricately together at almost
all points. Even below the prefectural level the fastening of
ties went on, as the majority Seiyūkai continually persuaded
governors to oust opponents of the Seiyūkai from the local
bureaucracy and to appoint in their places men affiliated
with the Seiyūkai.

The intertwining of the Seiyūkai and the bureaucracy
enabled that party to manipulate funds to suppress the opposition and, at the same time, to satisfy its interests. It
was with a real sense of pride and accomplishment that
Hara observed concrete results of his spending policy. Par-
ticipating in tours and rallies in the north, he wrote in October 1910: "This port was started during my tenure in office
. . . and it is now in its second stage. In a year or two, it
will have a depth of twenty-one feet two inches. . . . It is
a fine port and can be expanded as needed." [33]

In short, promises by party men had to be fulfilled to a
certain degree if the support of local political leaders was
to be retained. As negotiator for the party, then, Hara had
to influence policy-making at the top level, assuring the

INTEREST STRUCTURE: PARTY AND BUREAUCRACY UNDER HARA[a]

PARTY LEADER

EXECUTIVE STAFF
(transmits policy)

BOARD OF COUNCILLORS
(partly appointed by president, partly elected by 8 regional groups)

(transmits requests from below; reports on party strength)

EIGHT REGIONAL GROUPS
(voice local requests, transmit policies from above)

REGIONAL RALLIES
(transmit requests for new projects and for dismissal of local bureaucrats)

HOME MINISTER

BUREAU OF REGIONAL AFFAIRS

BUREAU OF CIVIL ENGINEERING

BUREAU OF RAILROADS
(aggressive appointments and directives for allocating government funds)

GOVERNORS
(allocate funds and contracts to consolidate party base)

PREFECTURAL ASSEMBLIES
(pressure governors to spend according to Seiyūkai)

GUN CHIEFS[b]

BRANCH OFFICES
(demands by local men for schools, dams, railroads, and general "regional industrial development")

LOCAL ELECTORAL BASE
(electorate — 1.5 million in 1908 — votes in blocs controlled by "men of influence." The latter include prefectural assemblymen; local administrators — e.g., heads of post offices, principals of schools, etc.; presidents and managers of banks, business associations, and various manufacturing and construction industries; and leaders of town and village councils.)

[a] The more important relationships are drawn with heavy lines.
[b] *Gun* chiefs declined in significance because this system of allocating government funds bypassed them.

continued flow of funds from above through his positive policy. It was this problem that gave meaning to the politics of compromise between 1909 and 1911; and the main issue was railroad development.

THE BROAD-GAUGE ISSUE

Railroads became a major political issue with their nationalization in 1906.[34] In late Meiji, railroads were the main form of mechanized transportation and were crucial for economic development throughout the country. Competition to gain railroads was fierce, because prefectural towns depended on them for survival and growth; with the nationalization of railroads every prefecture petitioned the government for the improvement and proliferation of railroad facilities.

To Hara, the demand for railroads was another "natural trend," and he intended to have his party act as the channel through which this demand would be met. Railroad expansion was the core of the positive policy, as Hara indicated in a speech at a regional rally in June 1910: "We felt at that time [following the Russo-Japanese War] that, to respond to the impending emergency, we had to carry out financial readjustments and, at the same time, plan for future developments. *We felt our most urgent task to be the development of transportation facilities:* that is, the *improvement and building of railroads and harbors.* Consequently, we first nationalized the railroads and then established a policy of gauging transportation facilities throughout the country and gradually connecting these with the various harbors. . . . I feel that our majority control in the Lower House and the conspicuous growth of our party throughout the nation are due to *popular approval* of the policies that our party has taken up to now. . . ." (Emphasis mine.)[35]

Despite strong opposition from Foreign Minister Katō Kōmei, Genrō Inoue Kaoru, and business leaders, the First Saionji Cabinet had nationalized the railroads in March 1906.[36] Seventeen firms had been bought out at a price of some four hundred eighty million yen to be covered by loans, half domestic, the other half foreign.[37] Katsura had planned nationalization of the railroads in 1904, and Hara's tacit promise not to deviate from Katsura's policies implied support of this plan. There was no basic disagreement here, and the execution of the plan provided seemingly conclusive evidence that Saionji's cabinet was dominated by Katsura.

After having established government control of the railroads, the Saionji cabinet started what seemed like an ambitious twelve-year (1906–1918), one hundred and seventy-five million-yen expansion program. But only six years later (1912), thanks to the Seiyūkai's positive policy, the program had grown into a massive project with committed funds totaling seven hundred five million yen.[38]

Fully aware that the positive policy would draw strong opposition, Hara removed railroad expenditures from the regular budget and placed them in a special category (spring 1907). This meant, in the first place, that a general retrenchment policy would not effect railroad development; secondly, it allowed profits from the railroads to be automatically earmarked for new railroad lines. Hara next laid plans to establish a railroad bureau with a separate budget and special powers to float loans. Here again there was no disagreement between Hara and Katsura, and the latter carried out the plan in 1909 during his second cabinet, naming Gotō Shimpei, his principal backer in railroad as well as other matters, to head the new bureau.[39]

Both Hara and Katsura, then, were agreed on the nationalization of the railways; both were agreed, furthermore, on the creation of a separate railroad bureau. Underlying these

superficial similarities, however, was a fundamenal discrepancy between their reasons for supporting these policies.
Katsura, the military man, sought to transform Japan's trunk
lines from the existing narrow gauge (ca. three feet seven
inches) to the broad gauge (ca. four feet ten inches) — his
reason was logistic. But underlying this strategic reason was
his desire (as well as that of Gotō, who was largely responsible for working out the details of the plan) to use this
project to pre-empt further Seiyūkai influence on railroad
developments.[40] Hara, the party politician, wanted to preserve Seiyūkai influence over railroad-building by using
government funds for the continued spread of narrow-gauge
lines throughout the countryside — his reason was party expansion, and he sensed that it was for the same reason that
Katsura insisted adamantly on the military need for broad-
gauge lines.

By late 1909, it was widely publicized that the Second
Katsura Cabinet was planning to convert Japan's trunk lines
to the broad gauge. According to this plan, which army leaders had been urging since the 1890's, one line would extend
from Tokyo in the east to Shimonoseki, on the western tip
of Japan. Another would stretch from Aomori at the northern tip down along the Japan Sea coast, again to Shimonoseki. Cars with strategic military goods would be brought
to Shimonoseki, loaded onto barges, transported across the
Japan Sea, and fitted directly onto the broad-gauge lines
already there in Manchuria. In the reverse process, cars
would bring raw materials from the mainland and be chan-
neled to key industrial centers.

Katsura, Gotō, and military planners had urged nationalization of the railroads precisely to lay these broad-gauge
lines. Accordingly, in their plan, local railroad expansion
would be returned by the government to private capital.
This was neither a rejection of government management of
railroads nor ardent support of control by private capital,

but recognition that government spending on local railroad lines would reduce funds for the broad-gauge plan. By late 1910, plans for the broad gauge were completed. The program would cover a twelve-year period and the cost was estimated (or, rather, underestimated) at two hundred thirty-eight million yen.[41]

Faced with a policy that could undermine Seiyūkai power, Hara had to defeat it. In early 1909, after a six-month trip to Europe and America, he began to maneuver for advantage: "The year before last, Katsura and I reached an agreement that the cabinet would be turned over to us. Because of this, I felt it wise to take this opportunity to use this same method again." [42]

In his initial round of talks with Katsura in the spring of 1909, Hara probed him regarding his relations with "anti-Seiyū" groups, especially the reform faction of the minority party, and reassured him that he had no close ties in the House of Peers. Then, he agreed to give Seiyūkai support to Katsura on condition "that power should be exchanged smoothly." [43] Having reached an understanding on these points, he turned to give that compromise concrete meaning.

In coming to power in August 1908, Katsura had promised a program of financial retrenchment. The Seiyūkai immediately protested this. For example, from a Kyūshū regional rally of September 1908: "Although financial retrenchment is urgent, we are strongly opposed to a passive policy which will place a brake on the growth of vital national industries." [44] And this position was reaffirmed in the party's platform of January 1909, part of which reads: "The Asian sphere has become increasingly peaceful. In this situation, it is imperative that the nation's resources be fully developed. . . . Efforts should be made, therefore, to adjust finances, promote industrial development, install transportation facilities, expand educational facilities, and carry out domestic improvements in all areas." [45] Despite Katsura's retrenchment policy, then, the party's support of a continued spending policy had remained unchanged; in October 1909, Hara called on Katsura to tell him this: "My views are frankly these: If there is a surplus in the budget then this should not be used in a passive but in a positive fashion. . . . There is a great deal to be done in the area of *transportation and harbor development.* . . . Consequently, as we have agreed in private that the exchange of power should be restricted to you and Saionji, *you must not attempt, in spite of this, to undermine our positive policy.*" (Emphasis mine.) [46]

Hara's warning was directed to Katsura with full knowledge of the latter's broad-gauge plan. To Hara, this plan was clearly harmful to the Seiyūkai because private capital could not cover the funds withdrawn by the government from local railroad projects, and these projects would be left uncompleted throughout the country: in other words, party promises made annually at rallies throughout the regions would go unfulfilled, and economic ties holding together local men of influence and party men would be weakened.

Hara urged, therefore, that the government should not switch to a costly broad-gauge program, however important it might be for national military strategy. Rather than concern itself with gauge connections between Japan and Manchuria, the government should concentrate on extending already existing narrow-gauge lines to all sections of the country. He urged that the government borrow from abroad to extend these lines and use the profits from them to pay off interest on foreign loans so that still another several hundred millions of yen could be borrowed to maintain the flow of funds for railroads. Obviously it was not military strategy that concerned Hara, nor was it really the cost of broad-gauge lines; rather it was the tactical allocation of funds in all the regions, which the broad-gauge plan would deny him, that deeply disturbed him. Thus, reminiscent of his later stand against universal suffrage, he told Katsura that even though the broad gauge might be necessary in the long run for logistic reasons it was not now a pressing need. For Hara, the civilian party politician, there were more important and less expensive projects to be carried out: "The broad gauge may be necessary in the distant future, but unlike Europe and America, Japan does not need, at present, to transport goods over long distances. Consequently, if harbors were developed in suitable places to connect the railroads, then the goods can be collected in these areas. There is no need to change over to the broad gauge now. Furthermore, the *broad gauge will consume an inordinate portion of the funds set aside for the extension of railroads and will therefore cause postponements in many areas.*" (Emphasis mine.)[47]

Throughout the summer and fall of 1910, Hara toured the regions — Kinki and Tōkai in June, Hokushin in September — to reaffirm the party's policy of improving transportation facilities. By November, Hara's position against Katsura had stiffened: support for Katsura would be contingent on, first, the postponement of the broad-gauge plan, and second, assurances of an exchange of power. Otherwise, he would reserve for his party the right to "freedom of action." [48]

THE BROAD GAUGE POSTPONED: THE MUTUAL
UNDERSTANDING OF JANUARY 1911

By "freedom of action" Hara was hinting that the Seiyū-kai might form an alliance with Inukai Tsuyoshi and the Kokumintō to submit a vote of no confidence against Katsura. A no confidence vote was a weapon of party men that could cause considerable embarrassment and turmoil for the government. The politics of compromise, seen from the point of view of the ruling cliques, was, in part, to guard against such occurrences.

Opposition against Katsura had swelled. His handling of socialists in the Great Treason Case (*Taigyaku jiken*), in which twelve anarchists were convicted on highly controversial evidence and executed (January 25, 1911), drew considerable protest. Hara himself noted with displeasure the "reckless suppression" of the socialists by the "bureaucrats," and he urged Katsura to give clemency to the convicted anarchists.[49] He also objected to Katsura's plan to grant the governor general of Korea the power to decree without reserving the right of review for the Diet in Tokyo.[50] Finally, a petty issue involving a textbook rendition of dynastic legitimacy in the fourteenth century was used to stir up antagonism against Katsura.[51] Even men close to Yamagata viewed the incident as "truly serious government mismanagement,"[52] and it proved to be extremely embarrassing to Katsura.

The ingredients necessary for a successful vote of no confidence were there; Inukai therefore appealed to Hara for a "union" — that is, dissolution of the parties and establishment of a new, unified party against Katsura. With good reason Hara suspected Inukai of wanting to take over the Seiyūkai and knew, moreover, that many in the Kokumintō were not behind Inukai but behind the reform faction which sought an alliance with Katsura. From the outset of his career as party politician Hara had discounted the notion of a "union of people's parties," and he could not agree to Inukai's plan: "The old Shimpotō men [Inukai's faction] are always coming to us with offers for a union . . . but their real motives are vague. Public opinion will not sympathize with a simple banner like 'Down with clique government,' and, by causing disturbances throughout the land, we will have inadvertently brought about many years of adverse conditions. The political world around us is not the simple one they picture." [53]

Although a union was not possible, joint action against Katsura in a vote of no confidence could be taken. The broad-gauge issue still remained unsettled, and rumors were rife that Katsura would turn the cabinet over to Terauchi Masataka, a general in Yamagata's coterie, and not to Saionji. Hara therefore pressed Katsura for an early settlement to prevent this. Katsura, however, bided his time, feeling that although he had to reach an agreement with the Seiyūkai to avoid a no confidence vote his position was not desperate. He was aware that Seiyūkai leaders were ready to negotiate, so that he believed he could save most of his program and still retain Seiyūkai support.[54] Katsura was not wrong, but he was being much more optimistic than the situation warranted.

On December 14, 1910, Hara and Katsura finally sat down for some frank talks. Playing on Hara's ambitions for power, Katsura announced his plan to retire from politics after the Diet session was over and perhaps — and this he left enticingly vague — have Hara himself form the next cabinet. He curried Hara's favor by agreeing with him ("in a way reminiscent of Itō," Hara noted hopefully[55]) that political parties were permanent institutions in Japan. But Hara was not thrown off guard by Katsura; his demands remained rigid and explicit. Under no circumstances would he support a cabinet under one of Yamagata's men: it must be Seiyūkai-controlled. And Katsura must postpone the broad-gauge plan because it was inconsistent with his party's platform.[56] Although Katsura conceded the next cabinet to the Seiyūkai, he insisted on Seiyūkai support for the broad gauge. Katsura's position, however, was weak, because Hara made it clear that the Seiyūkai was determined to vote the plan down in the budget committee, and that he personally would not allow outright submission by his party to Katsura on this critical issue. Katsura's alternatives were clear: he could insist on having the broad-gauge bill passed and face public denouncement by the Lower House, or he could concede and resign from office peacefully.

On January 26, 1911, a "mutual understanding" was formally reached. The Seiyūkai would support Katsura's budget and, reluctantly, his plans for administering Korea. In return, Katsura would hand over the cabinet to the Seiyū-kai and postpone the broad-gauge plan "for a year." The funds set aside for the first year of the broad-gauge plan, some five million yen, would be returned to the regular railroad development program. To the very end Katsura was unwilling to give up the broad-gauge plan, but Hara prevailed: "Katsura still insisted that he wanted the broad-gauge plan passed since it was basically his plan and not Gotō's. I argued, however, and Katsura agreed, that a plan like this one that undermined the footing of party men could not contribute toward the advancement of the parties, and that, without this advancement, progress toward constitutional government was unthinkable." [57]

By postponing the broad-gauge plan Hara killed it. In the spring of 1911, Katsura urged that Hara retain Gotō Shimpei as chief of the railroad bureau to continue investigation on the broad gauge, but Hara repudiated the suggestion. When Saionji's second cabinet was formed in August 1911, Hara himself headed that bureau. Thereafter, the broad-gauge plan failed to become a serious issue and finally, between 1919 and 1921, it was permanently blocked when Hara launched a massive narrow-gauge railroad expansion program.[58]

In view of Seiyūkai tactics for party expansion, Hara had won an important victory. The security of the party's power bases depended on the flow of funds through a positive policy. In shaping economic policy at the top level to conform with this positive policy, Hara had played a crucial role in the growth of party strength.

First, he had strengthened his position in the decision-making process, giving to the policy of nationalizing the railroads a content and direction that clearly diverged from those of Katsura, Gotō, and the military leaders who had initially planned the nationalization policy. He had preserved his party's program of laying narrow-gauge lines throughout the countryside, which both he and the rank and file knew must continue as the heart of the party's positive policy. In short, in defeating the broad-gauge plan Hara had maintained the vital link that bound party and bureaucracy into a single structure in which governors and their staffs, as well as Diet men and local powerholders, disbursed funds in terms of local partisan politics. Thus the regional political structure was being transformed, through party growth, from the system of "self-government" planned by Yamagata into a pervasive, party-oriented interest structure.

Although a master at compromise, Hara had not surrendered on an issue that threatened to undermine the economic basis of party strength: in his eyes, therefore, he had advanced the cause of party government. He had proven in this crucial test, as he told Gotō later on: "Party power will be the decisive factor. . . . Arguments will not be enough."[59] Understandably, Hara was elated with the compromise.

"Elated" would hardly describe Katsura's emotions, although he had his rewards too. His budget had been passed and the minority party's no confidence vote (February 23) resoundingly voted down two hundred one to ninety-three.[60] In Katsura's view, however, the compromise was not a real "understanding." As a protégé of the Meiji Genrō, he could not help but see the structural changes taking place in the central and regional bureaucracies as disturbing signs. As a military man, the postponement of the broad-gauge lines was a bitter defeat. Moreover, he still faced Hara, whose schemes to increase his party's power did not stop at shaping economic policy. Hara would insist that, as part of the mutual understanding, Katsura commit himself to the cause of Seiyūkai expansion. There was an undertone of uneasiness in the understanding between these two men that inevitably developed into open conflict between them.

5

Prelude to Conflict
(1911–1912)

Through Hara the Seiyūkai had gained, by 1911, a firm foothold in the bureaucracy. It had launched an extensive program to increase its strength throughout the regions and, moreover, it had begun to influence policy-making at the highest level. As its chief negotiator, Hara now grew bolder in his dealings with Katsura. He seized the initiative, pressing Katsura for more concessions. The Yamagata faction was still firmly entrenched and confident of its strength; but, in the key relationship between Katsura and Hara, the balance had begun to shift in Hara's favor. As Hara's influence grew, Katsura was forced to adjust his tactics, causing uneasiness in the ranks of the Yamagata faction and ending in an unprecedented struggle with the Seiyūkai in the Taishō Political Crisis (Taishō *seihen*)[1] of the winter of 1912–1913.

This crisis was touched off by a conflict between two contradictory positions, both having separate historical roots. The Saionji cabinet, representing the principle of civilian government, adopted the policy of financial retrenchment being urged by business leaders — a policy to solve the problem of economic recessions that were endemic in the decade after 1905. Contrary to this, the army demanded the immediate establishment of two new army divisions, a policy aimed at allaying the fears of military strategists of Japan's position as a power in Asia.

While this disagreement is important as a precipitant of the political crisis and as a specific illustration of the tensions existing in the Japanese government between the civilian and military branches of the state, it should be distinguished clearly from the main predisposing issue to conflict, which was the imbalance in the compromise relationship between Hara and Katsura. This imbalance precluded the chances for a settlement between the Saionji cabinet and the army and produced instead the explosive events at that particular juncture in Japanese political history. The Taishō Political Crisis, then, must be woven into the logical fabric of the politics of compromise and the growth of Seiyūkai power.

KATSURA'S ANNOUNCEMENT OF THE MUTUAL UNDERSTANDING

Party expansion through personal diplomacy went hand in glove with Hara's more systematic structural approaches. Through direct personal persuasion Hara intended to split the Yamagata faction: he would draw Katsura to the side of the parties and isolate Yamagata. Katsura was Yamagata's principal protégé. Some could compete with Katsura for Yamagata's favors; none could rival his political skills and attachment to politics. The loss of Katsura to the Yamagata faction would be a serious blow to that group and a major gain for the parties.

With these considerations in mind, Hara told Katsura: "There is the fear that the words 'compromise,' 'compromise' might have already made the people weary"; and he insisted that Katsura publicly announce that the mutual understanding was more than just "compromise." [2] Hara knew that many in the Seiyūkai rank and file strongly opposed compromise with Katsura and demanded a pure Seiyūkai cabinet. Katsura had written off these demands as "irresponsible speeches," [3] but Hara and other Seiyūkai leaders felt an explanation was necessary to satisfy the party. To appease Hara, Katsura had repeatedly agreed with him on "progress in society" and the "spectacular development of ideas." [4] As a further term of compromise, Hara now asked Katsura to personally add to the "progressive trends" by publicly stating his commitment to constitutional government.

On January 28 Katsura handed the draft of his speech to Hara, which the latter found "too simple" and "an inadequate piece of work." [5] Furthermore, Hara learned that he could not make major changes in the draft since Katsura had shrewdly read it to the Emperor in advance. Katsura, in any case, delivered his speech at a Seiyūkai luncheon on the following day. He referred to the "spectacular transforma- tion of ideas" and then said: "For a long while, we have recognized that your party seeks to contribute its services to the state on the basis of sound political views. . . . It is our earnest desire to come to a mutual understanding with you, and, together, bring about the realization of constitu- tional government." [6] Katsura said nothing to give the plati- tudes concrete meaning, but an unprecedented event had taken place: the most powerful member of Yamagata's fac- tion had publicly announced that he would work continu- ously with the Seiyūkai to realize constitutional government. Hara believed he had gained a major victory: "I do not know how the public will evaluate the agreement reached, but I took this course of action because I believed it would serve to quicken the pace toward constitutional government. . . . Regardless of what he [Katsura] believes or what the con- ditions around him are like, he decided there was no alter- native but to open up a brand-new phase for himself. Those who suffer from nearsightedness will say I have been bureauc- ratized but I acted without regard to them. . . . Someday the remainder of the ruling cliques and the bureaucrats will resist us from their isolated fortresses, but, on account of Katsura's decisive precedent, members of the ruling cliques and the bureaucrats can now sever their ties, at least out-wardly, with the past." [7]

Hara continued his divisive tactics against the Yamagata faction by flattering Katsura and playing on his ambitions for power: "We have had many Genrō, but, up to now, they have all been of the pre-constitution era. Those of the post-constitution era begin with you. (Upon hearing this, Kat-sura's face lit up with pride.) You must, therefore, try to be different from these other Genrō." [8] Moreover, he reminded Katsura that the mutual understanding was a binding com-mitment to assist the Seiyūkai: "A while back, we agreed over and over again that the mutual understanding was not a temporary affair. Consequently, will you support our cabinet fully, and, at the same time, refrain from interfering in our debates? Katsura replied, 'Of course.' . . . After hav-ing specifically said that you will work for the advancement of constitutional government, I will consider our mutual understanding void if you simply support what it [House of Peers] supports and reject what it rejects.[9]

Katsura, however, had ambitions of his own; the mutual understanding did not, therefore, resolve the problem of power interchange. It was nothing more than a short-term agreement based on mutual advantage. Still, because Kat-sura had publicly announced his support of the Seiyūkai he had weakened his position, making it extremely difficult for him to bargain with Hara for support. Hara's price would be too high.

RESPONSES BY KATSURA

Compromise had proven more to Hara's advantage than to Katsura's; the latter had to restore his political position and then work out a permanent solution in his relationship with Hara. Katsura was flanked by the Genrō and the House of Peers on one side, and the Seiyūkai and the Lower House on the other. This midway situation offered great potential to him because he had influential contacts on both sides; nevertheless, his position was unstable.

On one hand he had to pacify the Genrō, especially Yamagata, because it was his duty and because his prestige was enhanced when they did not interfere in his activities. Thus, a day after the compromise was reached, he wrote Inoue as though nothing of importance had happened: "As the situation in the Lower House is now under control, I beg you please not to worry. The future of the nation, too, is moving in an increasingly favorable direction." [10] To Yamagata, Katsura wrote that opposition from the Seiyūkai rank and file was only "slander and gossip" by "people in positions of no responsibility," and that there was no need to worry since the Seiyūkai could be exploited at will. [11]

On the other hand, Katsura had to make concessions to the Seiyūkai that displeased him and disturbed Yamagata. To save his legislative program, he made an embarrassing public statement announcing his support of the Seiyūkai. He handed the cabinet exclusively to that party although he knew that Yamagata wanted a coalition cabinet. [12] The Second Saionji Cabinet, unlike the first, included no one from the Yamagata faction. Furthermore, he was not consulted regarding the composition of that cabinet, and his principal nominee for chief of the railroad bureau, Gotō Shimpei, was turned down. The rest of the cabinet was selected entirely by Saionji and Hara. [13] Katsura complained to Yamagata on August 30: "As I related earlier, the cabinet has finally been formed, but I wonder what will come of it? I am especially concerned over the minister of finance, whose abilities are entirely dubious." [14]

The question lurking in the minds of Yamagata and others in his faction was that if Katsura were displeased with Saionji's second cabinet why had he agreed to its formation in the first place? Unwittingly, Katsura had been used by the Seiyūkai to promote the spread of party influence in the bureaucracy, clearly contrary to the wishes of the Yamagata faction. Katsura, however, could not afford to lose the backing of the Yamagata faction because it controlled the House of Peers. His boast "the House of Peers is mine" was empty unless he had support from this faction. Yamagata's men in the House of Peers had found the mutual understanding degrading, and publicly dissociated themselves from it: "Historically, everyone in the Kenkyūkai . . . belongs to the Yamagata faction. And so we do not have a special relationship with this present cabinet [second Katsura]. The activities of the Kenkyūkai, needless to say, will remain transcendental to the Katsura-Saionji cooperation." [15] But because he had to deal with Hara, Katsura could not enjoy the luxury of remaining "transcendental" as could the peers, and he inevitably faced growing distrust from them.

Katsura's first tactical move following the mutual understanding was to regain the confidence of the Yamagata faction by reaffirming his commitment to the "transcendental" sanctity of the House of Peers against the parties. Elections among counts, viscounts, and barons for seats in the House of Peers were held every seven years, and these elections were scheduled for July. Katsura knew that Hara was eager to gain office before then so that he could interfere in the elections by such means as offering ministerial seats to influential peers. Katsura refused to resign until the elections were over.

On July 10 the elections among the peers were held. Groups supporting the Seiyūkai were erased: of the Dōshikai (counts), only one pro-Seiyūkai member was re-elected; of the Danwakai (viscounts), every pro-Seiyūkai member was defeated. Katsura had seen to it that connections Hara had carefully built up against the Yamagata faction were destroyed.[16] Furthermore, Katsura refused to name Seiyūkai supporters to fill any of the vacant appointive seats.

In Hara's view Katsura had "broken his promise," for

mutual understanding had implied that Katsura would help the Seiyūkai cause in the House of Peers. In Katsura's view, however, Hara had agreed in the mutual understanding to give up his designs in the House of Peers. Hara had indeed conceded this to Katsura; but he added, "should they [peers] struggle against us . . . we will have to take suitable action for self defense." [17]

Having ostensibly regained the confidence of the Genrō and the House of Peers, Katsura handed the cabinet over to Saionji on August 30, 1911. He did not, however, fully erase the doubts about himself in Yamagata's mind even though he had purged the peers of Seiyūkai influence, because he began almost immediately to consider forming a political party of his own. Because of Yamagata's distrust of his political ambitions, Katsura was unable to strike out in his new course of action in neat and orderly fashion; there were unexpected pitfalls along the way. But an opportunity to form a party against Hara and the Seiyūkai began to take shape in the emerging conflict between the Saionji cabinet and the army.

HARA AGREES TO A RETRENCHMENT POLICY: WINTER 1911–1912

The demand for administrative retrenchment began as soon as Japan had ended its war with Russia. The war had placed a severe burden on the populace, and with peace reestablished there was widespread hope that expenses would be cut and taxes reduced. The military, accused of spending more for armaments than the national resources could handle, came under especially severe criticism. Some critics even contended that the sacrosanct Meiji goal, "a wealthy and a militarily strong state" (*fukoku kyōhei*), was no longer applicable since, thanks to the military, it had led to an "impoverished state" (*hinkoku kyōhei*).

The Genrō Inoue and Matsukata took up the demands of

business leaders and pressed the government to carry out retrenchment. By 1911 Saionji was completely under their sway. All along, however, the Seiyūkai had contradicted demands for retrenchment with a vigorous spending policy: now Hara had to be persuaded to accept retrenchment.

Upon assuming office in August as both home minister and chief of the railroad bureau, Hara began immediately to lay plans for his positive economic policy.[18] He would float a foreign loan of three hundred to four hundred million yen for railroad expansion. For the fiscal year 1912 he would request sixty million yen for railroads; and, in line with his plans, he selected strategically located harbors, four in particular, to be developed into terminal points for his railroads.[19]

Resistance to the positive policy, however, had grown sharply. Hara's main opponent in the cabinet was Yamamoto Tatsuo, the minister of finance, whom he saw as an enemy of the Seiyūkai. Only gradually did his feelings toward Yamamoto improve and this was largely because Yamamoto did not have a deep-seated dislike of Hara and was already pro-Seiyūkai. He joined that party in 1913.[20] As president of the Hypothec Bank of Japan, Yamamoto brought with him an impeccable reputation and contributed much to the spread of Seiyūkai influence in big business.

In the fall of 1911, however, Hara was convinced that Yamamoto was "against party government."[21] From the outset Yamamoto rejected Hara's positive policy and urged a general tightening of the belt: the budget must be balanced, taxes reduced, expenses cut, imports curbed, and currency strengthened abroad. Funds for all new projects would be curtailed, the loan for the railroads stopped, and the railroad budget for the year reduced by ten million yen. Yamamoto's position, furthermore, received unequivocal support from Genrō Inoue and business leaders which was voiced in the "Inoue memo" of November 20, 1911. Administrative expenses, the memo argued, had risen sixfold since the early 1890's and at least twofold since the early 1900's. The burdens on the populace were "excessively great," while the economy remained in a slump. To correct the situation, Japan must expand cautiously: all borrowing from abroad must be postponed and spending at home sharply reduced.[22]

The Seiyūkai argued the opposite. Rather than reduce expenditures, it would have the government spend more: interests on foreign loans would be paid off with profits from the railroad and more loans floated. After reading the "Inoue memo," therefore, Hara noted angrily that it was full of "anachronistic arguments" and that retrenchment was "extremely passive" and even "infantile." [23] Moreover, as the comments of both Inoue and Yamamoto were identical, he suspected that Yamamoto was an agent of Inoue. Strongly against outside interference in the cabinet, Hara further distrusted Yamamoto.

The dispute between Hara and Saionji was resolved by Saionji in favor of Yamamoto. In a letter of December 23 Saionji formally asked Hara to surrender his positive policy: "Aside from those projects that have been agreed to in the past, all new projects must wait until after the retrenchment." [24] Hara bitterly complained that the cabinet had discarded the most basic of all Seiyūkai policies, and that this was a breach of faith with his party. Aware that it was precisely his pursuance of the positive economic policy that gave him his raison d'être in the party, he would not be responsible for its discontinuation. To accept Saionji's request without modification, therefore, was tantamount to "loss of pride" for himself, and "harmful to the cause of constitutional government and for the forthcoming elections." [25] Leaving Saionji's letter unanswered, he submitted his resignation the next day.

Saionji's response was conciliatory: Would Hara remain in the cabinet if railroad expansion, at least, were carried out in a positive fashion? Hara hesitated, but decided to "endure" the situation. He agreed not to float any foreign loans until after 1913; in turn, Yamamoto conceded to Hara his sixty million yen for railroads. "At any rate," Hara wrote, with a feeling of triumph, "aside from a reduction of a few kilometers on the projected lines, my plan was agreed to as I had wanted." [26]

Excluding railroads, then, general retrenchment would be carried out. In late December 1911, an emergency committee on retrenchment was established; it set as its rough goal a decrease in the budget of forty million yen — each ministry being expected to reduce expenses by anywhere from nine to fifteen percent. Tax relief was to follow accordingly.

The Hara-Yamamoto controversy had settled an important issue for the Seiyūkai: a passive policy would be adopted temporarily. Because of this, the party would oppose increases for "unproductive" military expenditures. At the same time, Hara's defense of railroad development left no doubt in the party that the positive policy was still basic. Discussing railroad development and the national economy, one party leader reflected this feeling: "Toward financially unproductive enterprises I am completely passive. To administrative retrenchment I give my full support. But with regard to the matter of the economic development of the people, I believe in a thoroughly positive policy." [27]

Because the positive policy still remained basic to the party, the settlement in favor of retrenchment created an unmistakable feeling of impatience in the party that had an important bearing on the events of late 1912. The assumption was that retrenchment would be carried out as quickly and as efficiently as possible, so that by 1913–1914 a full-scale positive policy could be resumed. Buttressed by the reality of partially completed projects, expectation was high that the Second Saionji Cabinet would continue until well after the positive policy had been resumed.

While the controversy over a positive policy and retrenchment was being resolved, the position of the army was becoming rigid. To party men, railroads were "productive" and military expenses "unproductive"; but Yamagata and army men believed just the opposite.

YAMAGATA AND THE ARMY'S DEMAND: WINTER 1911–1912

The basic position of the army was summed up in Yamagata's terse statement to Prime Minister Saionji at the height of their disagreements during the Taishō Political Crisis: "National defense comes first, a financial policy last." [28] Widespread feeling that the victory over Russia had erased Japan's defense problems was not shared by army leaders who feared Russian retaliation. Moreover, it was believed that, in the end, the West would turn against Japan. Yamagata was the arch example of those who feared this: unlike Itō and Mutsu Munemitsu, who developed a sense of confidence in their dealings with the West, Yamagata was distrustful, predicting that Japan's alliances with the West would be "blown away like bubbles and Japan will suddenly find itself isolated . . ." as a result of the West's "rejection of different races and religions." [29]

The main concern was China, where complete political disintegration had become imminent. Should the Western powers gain control over China, it was feared that Japan would be alone against a hostile and (toward Japan at least) united combination of powers. The military solution was to establish the army in Korea and southern Manchuria securely and pre-empt other key areas as well. It was in accord with this line of thinking that the army, with imperial sanction and approval by the First Saionji Cabinet, launched a plan in 1906 to add eight new divisions. Four were to constitute "phase one." Of these divisions in "phase one" two were immediately established, but the other two were postponed because of a lack of funds. Each year thereafter, the army demanded the addition of these two divisions. With the annexation of Korea in the fall of 1910 and, above all, the Chinese Revolution of October 1911, the army's demand became strident.

Perhaps the most cogent statement on behalf of the army came from General Tanaka Giichi: "Russia has made great strides toward increasing its military installations in the postwar period. . . . It is almost as powerful as Japan in actual numbers. . . . In the matter of railroads, too, the double tracking of Siberian lines will be finished in two years. By 1916, the Amur lines will be complete. As a result, Russia's carrying power will have doubled. . . . Add to this the conditions within China from last year on [October Revolution of 1911]. . . . China is an area that vitally concerns our security. Should China be subdivided into spheres of influence, how will Japan move forward? For Japan, China must remain independent. In sum, Japan's position in East Asia has become truly dangerous." [30]

In the months immediately following the Chinese Revolution, the army attempted to send troops to Manchuria. This course of action was explained by Yamagata in a memo of January 14, 1912: One or two divisions should be sent to Manchuria because there was a "breakdown of order" there, and, following this, an agreement should be reached with Russia over the future of Manchuria and Mongolia.[31] In mid-January 1912, Yamagata wrote to Katsura making it clear that the "time was ripe" to send troops to Manchuria.[32]

The Saionji cabinet, however, was concerned more with economic recovery at home than with happenings on the Chinese mainland. The cabinet hoped to pursue a policy in line with England's, which meant nonintervention in this instance. Under pressure from Katsura, it mouthed agree-

ment with the army but evaded sending troops and continued to play for time — or "dilly-dallied" (*guzu-guzu*),
as one of Yamagata's men put it.[33] Finally, in early February,
it decided firmly against sending troops.

On February 8 Katsura reported to Yamagata that he was
unable to persuade the Saionji cabinet to send troops to
Manchuria: "Members of the army ministry are not in agreement with those of the foreign ministry, and, generally, also
with those of the prime minister. . . . It appears difficult
to make headway." [34] Yamagata's reply was immediate and
angry: "A golden opportunity has been lost; it is truly beyond regret." [35]

Although a "golden opportunity" had been lost, there was
no doubt in the minds of army leaders that another such
opportunity would present itself. Thus, Terauchi wrote to
Katsura on April 6, 1912: "There is no prospect at all that
China will be brought under orderly control. . . . I believe
it more sound to assume that there will most certainly be
turbulence again." [36] Army leaders wanted the two additional divisions established before the "turbulence" occurred;
but contrary to the army's growing concern about the Chinese mainland the Saionji cabinet had decided, railroads
excepted, to adopt a retrenchment program. Two clearly defined and divergent positions had been formed, and failure
to reconcile them would cause the collapse of the Second
Saionji Cabinet. In retrospect, it seems that there might have
been an agreement had there been effective mediation. The
mediation traditionally provided by Katsura, however, was
conspicuously missing.

KATSURA'S "RETIREMENT": AUGUST 1912

Katsura's last years were not easy. They did not bring a
triumphant close to a career which, through 1910, had been
marked with spectacular successes. In his ambitious struggle
to adjust to the politics of compromise and ultimately over-

come Hara and the Seiyūkai, Katsura had to strike out on a new and unfamiliar course. He became alienated from the Yamagata faction. In the unfolding political drama he ran into repeated disasters, the first of these coming unexpectedly in August 1912.

Taking his close aides Wakatsuki Reijirō and Gotō Shimpei, and with imperial consent, Katsura set out on July 7, 1912, to tour Europe. The purpose of the trip was to talk with heads of state, to visit old friends — this was Katsura's fourth trip to Europe — and, it was widely understood, to study political parties there.[37]

The trip was ill-fated. On July 30 the Emperor Meiji passed away, and Katsura was forced to end his trip at Moscow and return immediately. When he returned to Tokyo on August 11 he was astonished to learn that retirement into the Imperial Household had been arranged for him. The scheme was sponsored by Yamagata, who had sent him off a month earlier with a flowery poem and words of gratitude for his consistently fine leadership,[38] and it had received close collaboration from others in Yamagata's coterie, notably Hirata Tōsuke. Saionji, who was prime minister, recalled his feelings on the matter: ". . . Yamagata had gotten a bit weary of Katsura . . . and they kept a respectful distance of each other. Thus, when Katsura entered the Imperial Household, I simply looked on. . . . In short, Katsura blundered when he left for Europe, thus leaving his home ground open."[39]

The public believed that Katsura's entrance into the Imperial Household, as chamberlain and keeper of the imperial seal, was a plot of the Yamagata faction to dominate the Imperial Household and establish control over the new Emperor.[40] Katsura, however, had not planned on retiring from active politics. Although positions in the Imperial Household were highly prized by aristocrats, he had not sought them. To those close to Katsura it was common knowledge that he had retired under duress and that he had been "rejected by the Yamagata faction." [41]

In the first place, Katsura had failed to persuade the Saionji cabinet to send troops to Manchuria. Both Yamagata and Terauchi had counted heavily on him: neither had written directly to Saionji or the foreign minister, but had always worked through Katsura. Because Katsura had brought the Saionji cabinet into existence, they had assumed that his influence in it was substantial. As it turned out, Katsura had proven ineffective on a matter that was of vital concern to Yamagata. [42]

The main reason for Katsura's estrangement from the Yamagata faction, however, was his tendency to act independently. Yamagata admitted later that Katsura did not discuss matters with him and that Katsura had "turned his back" to him. [43] Since 1905 Katsura had dealt with Hara and the Seiyūkai without consulting Yamagata. In Yamagata's eyes, the results were not all satisfactory: there had been the embarrassing mutual understanding of January 1911; following this, Katsura had begun to think of forming a party of his own, telling the press, for example: "I have found that the disregard for political parties and the maintenance of transcendental cabinets at this day and age are anachronisms — more than that, they are impossible. Unless the government relies on a powerful party, it will not be able in the future to manage the affairs of state." [44] Moreover, before resigning in August 1911, Katsura had told Yamagata and Terauchi that he wanted to spend the rest of his life as a party politician and not as a military man. [45]

Katsura had also responded positively to overtures from the reform faction of the minority Kokumintō (see Chapter 3 on the *gun* issue) to form a party against the Seiyūkai. From the time of his resignation, talks between him and the reform faction gradually took on concreteness.

First, leaders of the reform faction (Ōishi Masami, Kōno

Hironaka, Sakamoto Kin'ya, and Shimada Saburō) established contact with Katsura through the liaison of Katsura's
friend Akiyama Teisuke. These talks confirmed that Katsura
was eager to counter the Seiyūkai. Second, the Mitsubishi
clique of Toyokawa Ryōhei, which occupied a key position
in the reform faction, appealed to Katsura and those close
to him for a new party. Finally, negotiations for an alliance
with the Chūō Club, a Katsura-controlled government party
in the Lower House, were carried out in behind-the-scene
efforts of men like Kinoshita Kenjirō and Katō Masanosuke
of the reform faction. These maneuverings obviously could
not be kept secret; neither could the fact that Katsura had
shown interest in becoming the leader of a major political
party. By the beginning of the summer of 1912, Katsura's
plan to form a party had become, according to reform faction
men, "a public secret." [46]

These rumors of a new Katsura party were at their height
when Katsura decided to take his trip to Europe. The public
assumed that Katsura took the trip to plan for a party and
that he would execute this plan when he acquired the prime
ministership again. To prevent this, Yamagata skillfully retired Katsura into the Imperial Household, thus bringing
talks of a Katsura party to an abrupt halt. Yamagata did not
expect that his retirement of Katsura would cause much
complication, but in the dispute between the army and the
Saionji cabinet over the two divisions, Katsura's retirement
made negotiations between the Yamagata faction and the
Saionji cabinet difficult and confusing.

KATSURA AND THE COLLAPSE OF THE SECOND SAIONJI CABINET: DECEMBER 1912

Although Katsura's plan to form a party against the Seiyūkai had been temporarily blocked, his ambitions to return to
active politics did not subside; he did not expect, however,
that his retirement would end inside of a few months. The

disagreement between the army and the Saionji cabinet over the two divisions was rapidly reaching a critical stage.

Because of continued Seiyūkai domination of the Lower House, Hara anticipated a "direct conflict with the bureaucratic faction." [47] But he did not anticipate that the struggle would be with Katsura. In early August, he urged Saionji to seek Katsura's help in settling the dispute with the army: Hara had good reasons to suggest this, as Katsura had consistently restrained the demands of the military[48] and had come to a mutual understanding with the Seiyūkai; besides this, no one in Saionji's cabinet could deal with Yamagata as well as could Katsura. Katsura, however, refused to mediate and told Saionji (August 17) to deal directly with Yamagata.[49] Without mediation from Katsura, a settlement with the army was highly dubious.

Complicating the negotiations was Saionji's acceptance of the navy's ninety-million-yen expansion program. This was contrary to the cabinet's retrenchment program and it defied explanation. It could have been retracted with proper mediation, as in the past; instead, it caused unnecessary rivalry between the services. The army, controlled by the Chōshū faction, was sensitive to the threat from Russia and other powers in the Chinese mainland; with this as rationale, army leaders had pushed through the annexation of Korea in 1910. The navy, controlled by the men of Satsuma, contended that the main threat to Japan came from the United States in the Pacific — especially through the Panama Canal.[50] The navy, therefore, sided with Itō and Inoue and had opposed the annexation of Korea. To army leaders, Saionji's acceptance of the navy's plan and rejection of the army's indicated official approval of the navy's concept of national defense. Thus, when Saionji called on Yamagata at his Odawara villa on November 10, 1912, Yamagata warned: "To increase only the navy is clearly unjust. I feel this is an

extremely serious affair that can lead to grave consequences." [51]

At this meeting, Yamagata reiterated the army's demands:
the army wanted permission to apply its own retrenchment
funds to establish the two divisions. Army leaders claimed
they could save twelve million yen over a six-year period for
the two divisions, rendering the cost to the government
negligible.[52] Saionji rejected Yamagata's argument, stressing
that the army ministry could not be granted special privilege.
The army must comply with the decision of the rest of the
cabinet to postpone the two divisions for a year.

The meeting between Yamagata and Saionji came after
a series of desperate maneuverings by General Tanaka
Giichi, chief of general staff, to draw influential men to the
side of the army. In late October, Tanaka managed to gain
the support of Inoue, ironically the champion of retrenchment.[53] Inoue, in turn, arranged a meeting between Tanaka
and the Saionji cabinet. Finding the arguments of Tanaka
unconvincing, Saionji set out on November 10 to explain the
cabinet rejection of the army's plan to Yamagata.

While Saionji was in Odawara, Inoue called on Hara to
hear the cabinet's verdict. Hara explained the decision that
was being relayed to Yamagata and then suggested that the
cabinet was open to negotiation but that it would not submit
to the army.[54]

Hara knew that public opinion opposed the two divisions;
he also knew, however, that the prestige-minded army leaders would not submit without concessions from the cabinet.
Hara therefore again asked Katsura, his partner in compromise, to work for a settlement. "There is nothing as
mysterious as this two divisions problem," Hara told Katsura
on November 16; "public opinion is in an uproar and yet
Army Minister Uehara [Yūsaku] has said nothing to the
cabinet . . . isn't there some way to settle this issue?" Kat-

sura replied: ". . . in my present status, I cannot interfere." [55]

Katsura's position began to unfold with alarming clarity
to Hara. In the first place, Katsura was not interested in
helping the army, although he was being persuaded to do
so, because his relationship with the Yamagata faction was
strained. Secondly, Katsura was not interested in helping the
Saionji cabinet either, in spite of the mutual understanding.
Finally, because Katsura hoped to end his retirement in the
Imperial Household, he would remain passive. Fully aware
of Katsura's strategy, Hara wrote: "I realized that Katsura
had no intentions of bringing about a settlement to the
situation. I felt, in short, that Katsura and his backers hoped
to use this issue to topple the cabinet. Thus, I warned him
that on another day, a struggle beyond expectation might
develop between him and me." [56]

On November 30 the Saionji cabinet asked Army Minister
Uehara to resign. On December 2, Uehara submitted his
resignation directly to the Emperor although he had agreed
to consult with Saionji first. Army leaders then refused to
name a successor, making the cabinet incomplete. Three
days later the Second Saionji Cabinet resigned.

Without mediation by Katsura, a settlement proved impossible: neither Saionji nor Hara could deal effectively with
Yamagata, who tended to be reticent and noncommittal in
the company of those he disliked; Genrō Inoue, persuasive
on behalf of big business, was at best lukewarm in pushing
the army's demands; General Tanaka was vigorous, but
lacked prestige and was not taken seriously; Army Minister
Uehara was weak, ambivalent, and vague.[57]

Satsuma men were drawn into the picture: Tokonami
Takejirō, Hara's close aide, held talks with Army Minister
Uehara; Genrō Matsukata Masayoshi was persuaded, by
Yamagata's men, to work on the cabinet. But Tokonami
could not match the influence of the army general staff, and

Matsukata was too detached from the realities of the negotiations to be of much help; on November 24, for example,
Matsukata was writing, with the certainty of one ignorant
of the details, that all was well regarding the two divisions.[58]

Among Yamagata's men, Hirata Tōsuke was active but
ineffective. On one hand he agreed with Genrō Matsukata
that in case of a stalemate the army should reduce its demand to one division, and on the other he quickly admitted
to Yamagata that his plan was "completely erroneous" when
the latter rejected it.[59]

Practically everyone of political importance was involved
in the negotiations, but an agreement was not reached. The
incredible fact about the confused negotiations was that
neither Yamagata nor Saionji wanted the cabinet to collapse.
Even after Saionji had resigned, Genrō Yamagata and
Ōyama Iwao were arranging to have an imperial rescript
reinstate the Saionji cabinet.[60]

Yamagata had good reason to keep Saionji in power. He
was perfectly aware of the unpopularity of the demand for
the two divisions and did not want to be accused of destroying the cabinet. Thus, a memo originating from Mejiro
(Yamagata's Tokyo residence) in November warned Generals Tanaka, Uehara, and Katsura of the dangers of forcing
a cabinet breakdown: ". . . it is a foregone conclusion that
they [party men] will use against us convenient slogans such
as the army vs. the people, the ruling cliques vs. the people,
the bureaucrats vs. the people, and carry on this fight with
renewed vigor." [61]

As for the Saionji cabinet, it halfway wanted a rescript
from the Emperor so that there could be an honorable "out"
for both sides. Thus, Saionji recalled in his memoirs that
Yamagata could have settled the issue by appealing to the
Throne.[62] Hara also expected a rescript, saying to Saionji on
December 6, "If, by any chance, you should receive an imperial rescript commanding you to stay in office . . . it is

the wish of the party that you accept it.[63] And then — typical of Hara — he urged that this time the passive policy should be ended.

But the imperial rescript was not issued, although Yamagata had, in fact, asked Katsura to arrange for one.[64] It was not issued because, as Saionji put it, "Katsura's attitude remained ambiguous." [65] Although Katsura knew that the cabinet wanted an agreement and that the army did not want to destroy the Saionji cabinet,[66] he did nothing to bring about a conciliation because, in his view, it was not a vital concern of his. He was confronted with an onerous mutual understanding with the Seiyūkai and was already "estranged" from the Yamagata faction. Thus, although Katsura did not cause the breakdown of the Saionji cabinet, he let the conflict drift into crisis proportions, fully aware that only under such an emergency situation could he end his "imprisonment" in the Imperial Household and return to active politics.

With the collapse of the Saionji cabinet the issue of the two divisions was all but forgotten. In the words of Tanaka Giichi, it was "transformed into high-level politics." The next prime minister would be Katsura: having regained power, he would center his attention on finding a solution to his relationship with Hara and do nothing to push the army's demands; he would also demote Tanaka from chief of general staff to field general because of his zealous support of the two divisions. Thus confused and angered, Tanaka wrote that the "prestige" and the "honor" of the army had been impaired and that the "trust of the people" in the army had been sacrificed.[67]

The public was indeed distrustful of the army leaders, and, moreover, it was indignant over the circumstances leading to the sudden collapse of the Saionji cabinet. The atmosphere in society was tense — it was, in the somewhat exaggerated view of Hirata Tōsuke, "a time in which national disintegration is taking place before our very eyes." [68]

6

The Movement for Constitutional Government—
December 1912

The *fin de siècle* came after 1900 in Japan. It came in 1912 when "the splendor that was Meiji" [1] ended with the death of Emperor Meiji on July 30. Many were profoundly attached to the Emperor and to the culture of his period, believing as Natsume Sōseki did that "the spirit of Meiji began and ended with the Emperor." [2] Thus, the poet Yosano Akiko wrote from Paris: "Gone is our great and splendid Emperor — from this day, we are of times past." [3]

All through late Meiji, an uneasy feeling had spread through society that an era was swiftly coming to an end. Massive riots and strikes recurred on the late Meiji scene. The activities of socialists increased. A plot by anarchists on the life of the Emperor Meiji was uncovered in 1910, and twelve were executed. City youth seemed immersed in an unbridled pursuit of wealth (*haikin no fū*), and leading men wrote books telling them of the whys and wherefores of "success in life." The National Association of Commerce waged a vociferous annual campaign to abolish consumer taxes, and critics complained in bold language of excessive military spending as the cause of a chronic economic slump.

The death of the Emperor Meiji only served to emphasize

the feeling of uneasiness in society. A somber and foreboding mood fell over all classes that extended beyond the burial in mid-September and on into the December that would bring the "first year of Taishō" to its end. It was in this atmosphere that the Second Saionji Cabinet suddenly collapsed, boding ill for the new reign of Taishō. The immediate public response was that Yamagata and Katsura, the leaders of clique government, had committed an outrage against the Emperor Meiji just deceased and against the new Emperor Taishō as well. This feeling of moral indignation spread. It led to public disturbances that shook the land and made it appear that society verged on political upheaval. Katsura, however, was eager to launch his challenge against the Seiyūkai and therefore failed to gauge the emotional undercurrent that made the public highly susceptible to agitation. As the political crisis continued unresolved the public supported the majority Seiyūkai, giving that party a political significance that had not previously been possible in the framework of compromise.

The public, however, was moved by moral reasons that were obscure and not concretely political, and at best was only vaguely aware of the nature of the struggle taking place. Thus, while large crowds were swayed by party men to riot against Katsura because clique government did violence to the spiritual bond between Emperor and people, the struggle of politicians continued to be rooted in the realities of economic gain, factional dispute, and power struggle.

RESPONSES FROM THE SEIYUKAI

The first important response to the collapse of the Second Saionji Cabinet came from the Seiyūkai party branches throughout the country. Beginning in late November 1912, resolutions poured into central headquarters with a speed and unanimity of purpose that indicated a remarkable degree of structural development: "By December 14, Seiyūkai branch offices throughout the entire nation, without exception, were like caldrons seething in opposition to the two divisions, urging the destruction of clique government, and guaranteeing full support to party headquarters. It was truly an unprecedented phenomenon." [4] Coming within a few short weeks and through a recognizable and nationwide structure, these resolutions brought to the political scene a sudden and dramatic display of regional Seiyūkai solidarity.

Regional rallies held before Diet sessions came later than usual in 1912 — late November and early December — and they were clustered together in a period of several weeks. The rallies seem to have been hastily arranged. They were not large regional affairs with party leaders taking part; they were prefecture-centered, with about fifty to one hundred persons attending to telegraph resolutions to Tokyo. Almost without exception the "bureaucrats" and the "militarists" were denounced and pledges were made "to protect constitutional government." But, more than indicating a commitment to political principles, these resolutions were direct responses to a crucial political fact: Seiyūkai loss of power.

In agreeing to a policy of retrenchment, the Seiyūkai had understood that the positive policy would be resumed after a short one-year postponement. Retaining power to continue this policy was essential to the party. Thus, although the resolutions denounced the ruling cliques and urged a few structural reforms, such as making the military ministers civil administrators and opening up the bureaucracy to party men, the main concern of regional leaders was the effect that the loss of power would have on local economic development: "We recognize the recent cabinet change to be a threat to constitutional government. Consequently, the Akita Seiyūkai branch resolves to defend constitutional government to the limit. . . . We resolve that subsidies from the national treasury be granted for the development of the Funakawa port . . . that the Uetsu coastal and the Riku-u inland lines be completed quickly . . . that the development of the Sandai River in this prefecture receive national subsidy immediately." [5] Power had suddenly been lost; and local party leaders immediately assumed, without prompting from above or long deliberation below, that every effort should be made to regain it. The resolutions of party branches "to protect constitutional government" was a demand for rapid recovery of power; the "establishment of a cabinet based on public opinion" unmistakably meant the establishment of a cabinet dominated by the Seiyūkai. [6]

In Tokyo, Seiyūkai Diet men were confident. They believed their party had become sufficiently strong to control the cabinet and coupled this belief with the opinion that the strength of their traditional enemies, the ruling cliques, was rapidly waning.

Partly out of personal conviction and partly to convince local politicians of the changing times and the shifting power relations, Seiyūkai leaders had made a point of cultivating a feeling of confidence and trust in the party. Thus, while Hara and Matsuda were aware of the realities of power distribution, they spoke with unhesitating certainty of ultimate Seiyūkai victory. On June 22, 1910, while at Niigata, Matsuda said: "The growth of our party's strength has not been limited to this prefecture alone. Especially since the Russo-Japanese War, the growth of our party throughout the nation has been conspicuous. . . . Cabinets controlled by the ruling cliques are basically not responsible cabinets. And, because of the changing times, it will be impossible for them to perpetuate their old dreams much longer." [7] And from a speech at a Tokyo rally by Hara on September 31, 1909: "You are no doubt all aware, as I am, that there are many who seek to establish what is, in fact, a despotic state under the veneer of constitutional government. Because of this, we will suffer a variety of obstructions, but it is essential that we be prepared to fight against these. It is already a thing of the past for cunning politicians to succeed in establishing a despotic state . . . the worldwide trend is such that this will not be permitted. It is clear that whatever the country, government will be . . . run on the strength of majority opinion." [8] Spurred on by speeches such as these and by evidences of party growth as well, confidence in the party swelled.[9]

While party leaders spoke of eventual dominance, how-ever, they made compromises with "cunning politicians" such as Katsura — those who, presumably, were being swept away by the changing times. The effect of this was confu-sion in the party rank and file regarding a program of action.

On one hand, there was growing conviction among party men that the Seiyūkai need no longer compromise or share power with the likes of Katsura. Behind this conviction was the idealistic desire to establish party cabinets as well as a wish to control the entire pork barrel. No one in the party disagreed with this view, but a few took a seemingly un-compromising position in defense of it. Their most eloquent spokesman was Ozaki Yukio. Below him were younger Diet men such as Takekoshi Yosaburō, Uzawa Sōmei, Hayashi Kiroku, Fukuzawa Momosuke, Koyama Kango, Kinoshita Seitarō, Kikuchi Butoku, and Horikiri Zembei, many of whom had just begun their political careers. They were called the "hard faction" of the Seiyūkai.[10]

On the other hand, party men realized that compromises were favorable to the party and that the foundations of party power had been built through compromises. Aside from an insignificant minority, all Diet men, including the "hards," depended on party influence to preserve their electoral bases. Leaders such as Ōoka Ikuzō, Motoda Hajime, Noda Utarō, and, of course, Hara, formed the nucleus of those who, more consistently than others, argued the merits of advancing toward party government through political compromises.[11]

A majority of the party membership agreed with both positions. Sentimentally, everyone in the rank and file shared the view of the hard faction; but, more often than not, they were compelled by political reality to support the group that urged compromise.[12] In the immediate context of early December 1912, Seiyūkai Diet men exhibited a powerful display of party unity because power had been lost. Together they resolved: "The reign of Taishō has just begun and the nation is still in a period of mourning. Still, the bureaucratic faction has arbitrarily plotted a change in government and seeks to completely undermine constitutional government. This abusive condition must not be tolerated. Therefore, we pledge to rise resolutely to the occasion to uproot clique government, and, on this basis, realize constitutional government." [13]

It appeared that the Seiyūkai had decided to reject compromises with Katsura. This unity of the "hards" and the "softs" continued as long as the relationship between the cabinet and the majority Seiyūkai remained uncertain. Because of this uncertainty, the Seiyūkai effort to regain power became part of a larger effort: the Movement for Constitutional Government. Because the Seiyūkai controlled the Lower House and its members were active on a national scale, Seiyūkai participation was crucial to the movement. The originators of the movement, however, were not primarily Seiyūkai Diet men.

FROM THE FIRESIDE OF THE KŌJUNSHA

The beginnings of the Movement for Constitutional Government have been described in different ways, but they are generally variations of this description by Kojima Kazuo, a supporter of Inukai in the Kokumintō: "It began with talks in smoke-filled rooms by some regulars at the Kōjunsha. . . . As a spark touches off a blazing fire, the talks that began by the fireside soon became a joint Seiyūkai-Kokumintō rally." [14]

The Kōjunsha was an association with headquarters at Kyōbashi in downtown Tokyo. Its members were largely Keiō University graduates; many were top-ranking business leaders, and their ties were strongest with the Mitsui firm and with the Seiyūkai. The Kōjunsha had been established by the great Meiji intellectual and founder of Keiō University, Fukuzawa Yukichi, in January 1880, "to exchange ideas and discuss political affairs." [15] Although it remained active as a political group throughout the 1880's — for example, drafting a liberal constitution in 1881 called the "Kōjunsha plan" [16] and taking part in the movement to establish the Diet — it gradually ceased to function as a political organization. By the late 1890's it had evolved into a social club.

Since Kōjunsha headquarters was located in the heart of downtown Toyko, Keiō alumni in business, as well as newspaper reporters, gathered there for lunch, a game of pool, and the latest political gossip.[17] It was here, at some unspecified date in early December, that talk began to develop about organizing a movement. Most of those taking part were young men in their thirties and forties, graduates of Keiō University. Some had traveled or studied in Europe, some were reporters, and others were Diet men.[18]

These men held a formal meeting at the Kōjunsha on December 14, to discuss the political situation, and decided to launch the Movement for Constitutional Government. The first rally was set for December 19 at Kabukiza in Tokyo. A planning committee was chosen and its headquarters was opened at the Kyōbashi office of a Seiyūkai Diet man and a leading planner, Kikuchi Butoku.

The men at the meeting decided on two popular phrases for the slogan of the movement — "protect constitutional government" and "destroy clique government" (kensei yōgo, batsuzoku daha).[19] Both of these phrases stemmed from the widely held view that the entire nation was one before the Emperor: that there was an undefined but nonetheless vital relationship, or a harmony, existing between sovereign and people. Belief in such a relationship permeated the political thought of the time, and speeches and writings of leading politicians and critics frequently referred to it. For example, one leading critic and firm supporter of the Movement for Constitutional Government argued for party cabinets by saying: "The soul of the people is the soul of the Emperor. . . . Therefore, it is natural that the leaders of the majority party in the Diet, which represents the people, should organize the next cabinet.[20]

To the educated elite, constitutional government meant party government patterned after the West.[21] They were basically unconcerned with mystical ideas of imperial sovereignty; contrary to what was widely taught, they understood that the Emperor's powers were limited by laws and institutions.[22] They flatly opposed the existence of special imperial advisers such as the Genrō who perpetuated rule by a narrow elite, or clique government. Instead, they wanted the majority party in the Lower House to control the cabinet, an arrangement not specifically proscribed by the Meiji Constitution. They believed that such a system fulfilled the ideal of the constitution. Thus, party government was best for Japan because it would be, as Ozaki Yukio observed, a "systematic method to ascertain the will of the people and thereby bring about a union between Emperor and people." [23]

But whether one interperted "constitutional government" as party government or as Emperor-people harmony or as a mixture of both, since these two notions actually overlapped, the common enemy was clique government. Clique government was a barrier in the people's relationship with the Emperor and a block to the establishment of party cabinets. "To protect constitutional government," therefore, involved a negative act — "to destroy clique government." The two phrases were opposite faces of the same coin.

The planners at the Kōjunsha selected an excellent slogan. There was good rhythm to it, and, furthermore, the phrases were well known. "Destroy clique government," in particular, had a long tradition behind it that began with the party movement in early Meiji. "Protect constitutional government" went as far back but began to gain currency in more recent times, especially after 1905. It was not as well known and certainly not as fully understood, but made perfectly good sense in terms of "destroy clique government." Above all, the slogan had an emotional quality that appealed immediately to the feeling of resentment that swept through society against clique government.

Having selected a good slogan and having been assured of financial support from business leaders of the Kōjunsha,[24] there remained the task of finding suitable men to lead the movement. All agreed on Inukai Tsuyoshi of the Kokumintō and Ozaki Yukio of the Seiyūkai for this role. These two men had the widest popular appeal, and, from early Meiji, they had been famous as champions of constitutional government.

THE GODS OF CONSTITUTIONAL GOVERNMENT

Because of their leadership of the movement, Inukai and Ozaki were called "gods of constitutional government" (*kensei no kami*). Their backgrounds were similar: both had studied under Fukuzawa Yukichi at Keiō University; both belonged to the Kōjunsha; both began their political careers in the early 1880's in the same faction of Ōkuma Shigenobu's Kaishintō. By the late 1890's they had risen in the party to the rank from which cabinet ministers were picked.[25] By that time, too, they had become widely known as outspoken advocates of representative government.

Although similar in background, their personalities were

different. Ozaki was a brilliant public speaker; he dressed meticulously, most often in Western clothes; he loved Western literature, from which his metaphors were drawn. Inukai disliked public appearances and stressed the importance of the less flamboyant, heart-to-heart "sincerity" (*seii*) among men; his dress was subdued in tone and tended to be traditional; he loved Chinese literature and was a master at calligraphy, and his metaphors were often drawn from Asia.[26]

Ozaki was perhaps the greater critic, but the lesser politician. In September 1900, he left Ōkuma's party to join the Seiyūkai.[27] By joining the party alone, he surrendered his factional backing and for the next decade sank into obscurity. He resigned from the Seiyūkai in 1902, only to rejoin it in late 1909 — again alone. As a Diet member and as mayor of Tokyo, positions he held jointly between 1902 and 1911, he did not distinguish himself;[28] in part this was because he was as strongly egocentric as he was ambitious, "finding it distasteful," as he put it, "to lower my head to anyone." [29] Unable to subordinate himself in the framework of a political party, Ozaki drifted from one small splinter group to another. Throughout his long and, at times, brilliant political career he remained, as one critic described him, "an orphan of the political world." [30]

Inukai was a strategist, closely attached to political maneuver.[31] Unlike Ozaki, who, though an "orphan," remained self-reliant, Inukai could not have been satisfied as an independent political critic or a party unto himself. Throughout his political career he aspired to become the leader of a popular party; thus, he could not leave his factional support and join the Seiyūkai as did Ozaki. But with the traditional notion of a "union of people's parties" (*mintō gōdō*) as pretext, he schemed to combine his faction with the Seiyūkai.

Because of their contrasting temperaments and strategies, Ozaki and Inukai could not cooperate over an extended period — a serious drawback to their leadership of the Movement for Constitutional Government. Their differences were already evident in their responses to the planning that went on at the Kōjunsha.

For complicated tactical reasons, Inukai saw immediately that his political future rested on the success of the movement. He saw major political realignments taking place and realized that by strategic use of this movement to defeat "clique government" he would prove untenable the position of his opponents, the reform faction in the Kokumintō who sought a coalition with Katsura. He would emerge victorious in the intraparty struggle which was becoming an open and bitter affair. From Inukai's letter of December 5: "Regarding this recent cabinet change, Sakamoto [Kin'ya] has begun once again to urge the usual line of giving support to Katsura . . . and he has been openly urging party members to support a Katsura party . . . I know that if Katsura were finally to step out into the political arena, our party will be thrown into confusion once again. In other words, I will be attacked from all sides. But there is hope for certain victory." [32]

Inukai was sure the next prime minister would be Katsura: "round and round the nomination will go, but in the end Katsura will be named again," [33] but this time — judging from the utterances of the reform faction — he believed that Katsura would not turn to the Seiyūkai for a compromise agreement. Instead, Katsura would draw on the support of the reform faction and try to split the Seiyūkai, thwarting a Katsura-Hara mutual understanding. Faced with these divisive tactics of Katsura, Inukai was convinced, the Seiyūkai would come to him for assistance. Inukai felt that here was the key to "certain victory." Thus, he wrote to his aides (Kojima Kazuo and Aijima Kanjirō) taking part in the planning at the Kōjunsha: "Find out at the next meeting if there are men in the Seiyūkai who are working to split it as well as other groups on behalf of the bureaucratic faction. If this is the case, then fine. It will be all the more convenient for us." [34]

With support from the Seiyūkai, Inukai would be assured of the passage of a no confidence vote against Katsura. The latter would then retaliate with a dissolution of the Diet, and a battle at the polls would follow: the parties against Katsura, Home Minister Ōura, and the bureaucracy. In this situation Inukai felt he could negotiate a permanent union between his party and the Seiyūkai; and once inside the Seiyūkai he believed he could rise to a position of power unequaled by Hara himself. Many Seiyūkai leaders (for example, Matsuda and Sugita Teiichi) were his friends and would support him, and so would the hard faction which shared his political views. He therefore saw the rapid turn of events in December as providing the once-in-a-lifetime opportunity for him to assume the leadership of the powerful Seiyūkai itself.

With these realistic objectives in mind, then, Inukai — like the reform faction — set out to prevent a Katsura-Hara rapprochement; but while the reform faction would use this breakdown of compromise to form a new party around Katsura against the Seiyūkai, Inukai would use it to penetrate into the upper ranks of the Seiyūkai and defeat the Katsura-reform faction entente. First, he tried (without success) to persuade Hara, who distrusted Inukai, and Matsuda to lead the movement with him, for this would eliminate the possibility of a compromise settlement. [35] Then, this time successfully, he made certain that the platform of the movement would explicitly interdict compromise with Katsura. He gave this command to his aides at the Kōjunsha: "The revision of the phrase 'anti-compromise' in tonight's resolution to read 'protect the constitution' on the basis that the latter already presumes rejection of compromise is actually a device to leave leeway for compromise. At tomorrow's planning committee, the words: 'Compromise will absolutely not be made' must be explicitly included." [36] The clause rejecting compromise under any circumstances was included in the platform, and this temporarily satisfied Inukai. Firm agreement with Hara for a union could be postponed, for Inukai was convinced there would be plenty of opportunities in the near future to realize this objective.

Unlike Inukai, Ozaki did not envision a radical change in the political situation and at first took a dim view of the movement. He suspected that a compromise would be reached between the Seiyūkai and Katsura and that the leaders of the movement would be left stranded. He argued that the total rejection of compromise was tactically unsound. Earlier, in 1902, Ozaki had taken a strong stand against compromise, had been defeated, and had subsequently had to leave the party: "I always tend to overstep my bounds and have run into disaster. This time, I'd like to take a careful attitude. . . . I must have learned from the experience of having had to leave the party." [37]

However realistic, Ozaki's exercise of caution was only momentary. On firm, but entirely hasty, assurances from Hara's close friend Okazaki Kunisuke that Hara and Matsuda would agree to the movement's refutation of compromise, Ozaki decided to join the struggle with Inukai.

Seen together, the contrasting personalities of Ozaki and Inukai strengthened their appeal. Ozaki, impeccably dressed, was full of histrionics; he reflected the views of the liberal press and called for structural reforms: abolition of the Genrō Council, the opening-up of the bureaucracy to party patronage, and the establishment of party cabinets. He deemphasized the idea of a "union of people's parties" and stressed reform of the structural foundations of clique government: "Two parties have met here as one. This is the chance to destroy clique government. But let me make it perfectly clear to you that without the system, clique government cannot maintain its position. . . ." [38] He especially urged the revision of the civil service appointment act (*bunkan nin'yō rei*) to open up for party men fifty to one hundred positions in the bureaucracy at each cabinet change.[39]

As if by way of rebuttal, although for the most part not received as such, the austere and less flamboyant Inukai de-emphasized the problem of structural reforms and, true to his political strategy, emphasized the need for unity among the parties: ". . . a few minutes ago, Ozaki suggested the revision of the civil service appointment act as a means to destroy clique government. But that is not such a difficult matter . . . as long as the political parties exterminate clique government, that obstacle can be broken down. The destruction of clique government and the protection of constitutional government are not controversial matters. I am asking that the barriers between all party factions and all personal feelings be done away with." [40] Or: "The broad objectives of the two major parties in the Lower House, the Seiyūkai and Kokumintō, are not significantly different. Still, due to their history and the emotions of their members, they have come to take opposing views on relatively minor problems thus making it impossible to take united action. For this reason . . . it has not been possible to destroy clique government." [41]

In the political context of December 1912, the differences between Inukai and Ozaki were minor since neither man was interested in presenting a reasoned platform for political reform: both were primarily concerned with arousing public sentiment and prolonging political unrest until power was surrendered to them. This was the tactic to destroy clique government and specifically Katsura, who, as Inukai had expected, was named to form his third cabinet on December 17.

THE RE-EMERGENCE OF KATSURA

The Genrō had not met to select a prime minister since the establishment of Katsura's first cabinet in 1901. With Katsura retired and Saionji just resigned, the Genrō Council was summoned. Yamagata, Inoue Kaoru, Ōyama Iwao, Matsukata Masayoshi, and Katsura met on December 6 and daily over the next ten days, desperately seeking a successor to Saionji. The mood at these meetings was one of indecision and dislike for the task assigned.[42] Public displeasure mounted steadily and rumors were rampant of an assassination plot against Yamagata.

Genrō Matsukata was named first. Fellow Satsuma men urged Matsukata to accept, but after accepting halfway he declined. General Terauchi Masataka, Hirata Tōsuke, and Admiral Yamamoto Gonnohyōe were each named in turn, but none accepted. Finally, Yamagata was convinced that only Katsura or himself could bring about a political settlement. The Genrō picked Katsura: "I felt that there was no one except Katsura and myself. I was being considered by party men as the main person to have destroyed the cabinet, and it was being demanded that I be destroyed. . . . Should I take the reins of government, this would needlessly compound the disturbances, but the continuation of chaos was inexcusable to the previous and present Emperors, and to the people. . . . I decided to accept the responsibility of establishing order . . . and contribute my services to the Imperial State. Thus, I explicitly asked the Genrō to select either Katsura or myself, and the Genrō then decided to pick Katsura." [43]

Thus, as Katsura had hoped, he was asked on December 17 to end his retirement in the Imperial Household and form the next cabinet. Katsura had attended the Genrō conferences but had not taken an active part. Immediately following the collapse of the Saionji cabinet, however, his supporters in the Kokumintō had begun rallying support for him. By December 14, three days before his appointment was announced, Katsura had already chosen his cabinet members. This is clear from Gotō Shimpei's letter to Katsura on that date: "I considered the possibility of spending the rest of my life as a critic, but I will be most pleased to join the cabinet and contribute in any way I can. . . ." [44]

The activities of Katsura and his supporters invariably made their way into the newspapers and became known throughout the political world. Men in Yamagata's faction, for example, were clearly displeased at Katsura's rumored re-emergence on the active political scene and warned Yamagata, as Kiyoura Keigo did, of the dangers of a return by Katsura: "For some reason, newspapers such as the *Jiji shimpō* are reporting as if it were absolutely certain that Katsura will return again. I believe this is completely unfounded, but if by any chance this were to happen, it will be deeply regrettable as regards the important responsibility of serving the Emperor as well as for Prince Katsura personally. . . . Regardless of who organizes the next cabinet, he must be prepared to face a tempestuous political situation." [45]

This warning reflected what was being said generally of Katsura: He had entered the Imperial Household in August 1912 to establish the control of Yamagata's faction there; on the basis of his influence in the Imperial Household, he had destroyed the Second Saionji Cabinet and then had issued an imperial rescript to himself to become prime minister for the third time. [46] To worsen matters, on December 21 Katsura issued an imperial rescript to Admiral Saitō Makoto commanding him to accept the post of navy minister in the new cabinet. Katsura had agreed to postpone the army's two divisions as well as the navy's six-year expansion program, but navy leaders objected to the postponement and refused to accept the navy minister's portfolio, thus threatening to destroy Katsura's cabinet at the outset. This led Katsura to issue the rescript.[47]

His movements in and out of the Imperial Household as well as his issuing of rescripts made Katsura highly suspect and coincided with the widespread belief that clique government acted as a barrier between the Emperor and the people. Widely unpopular already ("at that time, all classes, from the Genrō to business leaders, were saturated with feelings against Katsura" [48]), his re-emergence from the Imperial Household to form his third cabinet was deeply resented by the public.

THE MOVEMENT AND SEIYŪKAI STRUCTURE

On December 19, two days after Katsura had been officially appointed prime minister, the Movement for Constitutional Government was launched at Kabukiza in Tokyo. Leaders of the Kokumintō's reform faction were conspicuously absent, as were Hara and Matsuda of the Seiyūkai. But the press and three thousand belonging to both parties attended, while outside several thousands more caused a stoppage of the streetcars. Seki Naohiko, an Inukai supporter, recalled the emotionally charged atmosphere in this way: "The first notes of that [movement] were sounded at Kabukiza. The top leaders were Ozaki Gakudō of the Seiyūkai and Inukai Bokudō of the Kokumintō. I was vice-speaker of the Lower House at that time and so I was considered one of its leaders. . . . The audience came from everywhere and overflowed the hall. In front of the hall, several thousands more had gathered, and the flow of streetcars was forced to stop. As for the order of speeches — Seki Naohiko opened the rally, and then Sugita Teiichi was made chairman for the evening. . . . Gallant heroes rose to speak one after the other, each making fiery speeches. At the end, Inukai and Ozaki rose in turn to the podium. Voices cried out 'the gods of constitutional government! the gods of constitutional government!' . . . These first notes that were struck resounded throughout the country.[49]

The beginning of the movement was auspicious; it seemed that at long last the parties would rise in unison "to uproot clique government and protect constitutional government." [50] But underlying the color of public rallies — the stoppage of traffic, and the frenzied cries praising the "gods" — was the harsh world of political reality: of what the structure of the movement would be and what would be its power objectives. And the settlement of these issues was not in the hands of the "gods," but in those of Hara and the Seiyūkai.

Although Hara was not a participant in the initial phase of the movement, he saw that a strong movement was decidedly to his advantage should there be talks with Katsura. To preserve his tactical position he would not become directly involved himself. However, he had close associates take part in the planning that went on at the Kōjunsha, and he delegated Okazaki Kunisuke (who hated Katsura) to represent the executive staff in the movement. Like Inukai, in short, Hara recognized the strategic value of the movement in the context of the new political alignments taking shape.

On December 26, Hara supported plans to establish an emergency coordinating committee to act as liaison between the leaders of the movement and the Seiyūkai executive staff. On the next day, he gave assent to a decision to make the movement nationwide by using party structure, which meant primarily the Seiyūkai. Telegrams were sent to party branches throughout the country urging sponsorship of popular rallies (kemmin taikai) and re-election of present Diet members (that is, mostly Seiyūkai men) should there be dissolution.[51]

This development in late December pointed to several crucial factors of the Movement for Constitutional Government and of the Taishō Political Crisis in general: first, the movement was dependent on the national Seiyūkai party structure, through which local leaders had already begun to agitate in late November and early December because of the sudden loss of power; second, this structure was under the tight control of the party's executive staff — Hara, Matsuda, leaders of the eight regional groups — and not the planning committee of the movement; third, the Seiyūkai leaders at the branch offices were closely bound to local economic interests or to the positive economic policy, and not to the abstract notion of a unified popular party; and finally, although the movement had certain reforms as objectives it was primarily an affair of party politicians involved in a struggle against Katsura. This was evident in the pledge to re-elect the present Diet members if a dissolution were to occur, a clear indication of the use of the movement to preserve the existing Seiyūkai majority. And as rumors of a new Katsura party spread, indicating a Katsura-controlled election in the near future, the support of Seiyūkai men for the movement became even more enthusiastic. By late December, the pledge "to protect constitutional government" could just as well have read "to protect Seiyūkai power" (*Seiyūkai seiken yōgo*).[52]

Before the second year of Taishō (1913) had begun, therefore, the basic outlines of the Taishō Political Crisis had taken shape. The disagreement between the army and the Saionji cabinet had led to the collapse of the latter, and in its wake Katsura had formed his third cabinet. Meanwhile, a movement against clique government had begun to take concrete form in terms of structure and leadership. In late December, this movement was strongly oriented to the impending power struggle between the majority Seiyūkai and Prime Minister Katsura. In view of this, the nature and course of the movement and of the political crisis as a whole hinged on two crucial considerations.

On one hand, if Katsura intended to continue the mutual understanding with Hara, the future of the Movement for Constitutional Government was pessimistic: Hara, in all likelihood, would agree to a compromise and withdraw the Seiyūkai majority in the Lower House and the party's national organization from the movement. On the other hand, if Katsura formed a party and rejected the mutual understanding, Hara was willing, although he had never had occasion to do so before, to throw the weight of the entire party organization behind the movement and come into direct conflict with Katsura. This was the crux of the struggle in the political crisis that ushered in the new reign of Taishō. Events in January clearly defined what course the struggle would take.

7

Katsura and the Formation
of the Doshikai—
January 1913

Of the men in Yamagata's faction, Katsura had the
clearest understanding of the main political developments
of the day. First, the systematic expansion of Seiyūkai power
had resulted in the steady erosion of the bases of the ruling
cliques. And second, this growth of the Seiyūkai had made a
multiparty system in Japan a practical impossibility. He
therefore no longer subscribed to Yamagata's scheme of
having a "loyalist" or "government" party which would control the balancing votes, as was often the case in the multiparty situation in the German Imperial Diet. Through first-
hand experience, Katsura knew the Lower House could not
be manipulated at will from above if one party maintained
a constant majority in that house. Consequently, unless the
ruling cliques could match their commitment to the principle of transcendental government with realistic strategy to
counter the Seiyūkai, that party's pre-eminence in the
political order was a foregone conclusion.

Nevertheless, Katsura did not draw from this assessment
the conclusion made by many party men that Japan must
have a two-party system — he believed in a one-party system. To accomplish this he would, if necessary, sacrifice his

personal ties with Yamagata and form a powerful coalition consisting of men with different backgrounds and interests — businessmen, bureaucrats, peers, Diet men — to attract all political groups, including the Seiyūkai, into this new union of parties. Only with a pragmatic strategy such as this, Katsura was convinced, could the principle of transcendental government be preserved.

Katsura was quite right in his belief that the ruling cliques needed a new approach to control the Lower House, but he was far from correct in assuming he could undermine Hara's leadership of the Seiyūkai and draw the rank and file to himself.

In January 1913, Hara waited for Katsura to make overtures for compromise. Although Katsura let rumors spread that he planned to form a party against the Seiyūkai, hoping to lure Hara into an awkward first move, Hara simply bided his time. Having a popular movement as a weapon, he could wait for Katsura to initiate negotiations. He permitted the political crisis to deepen, the government to come to a standstill. He remained passive as the Seiyūkai rank and file, already apprehensive and impatient, sponsored rallies and made strident speeches.

Then Katsura acted. He would depart radically from previous patterns and form a party to end Seiyūkai domination in the Lower House. Only if Hara came to him would he agree to a compromise settlement. The lines of battle were now drawn: in refusing to seek an understanding with Hara, Katsura must meet this astute tactician on his own grounds. The political future of Katsura — general, Genrō from Chōshū, ostensibly underling of Yamagata — now hinged on his tactical skill as party politician.

KATSURA TARŌ: PARTY POLITICIAN

As an ambitious young political figure at the turn of the nineteenth century, Katsura's attitude toward the parties had been one of contempt. In 1898 he had threatened to wreck the Ōkuma-Itagaki Cabinet by resigning as army minister because it was a "party cabinet" and violated the principle of imperial rule. Itō, responsible for the formation of that cabinet, had managed to stop Katsura by appealing to the throne; but, undaunted by imperial reprimand, Katsura had intrigued with other Yamagata men to cause the collapse of the "party cabinet" inside of four months. Again in 1901 Katsura had resigned from Itō's cabinet because it was a "party cabinet" and contrary to the ideal of transcendental government.[1] He had intrigued to obtain party support for Yamagata (as in 1898), but had refused party leaders their share of cabinet posts and had done nothing while Yamagata erected legal barriers against those parties with whose leaders he had just dealt. To Katsura, political parties had to be manipulated for the cause of "impartial government."

This attitude underwent change when Katsura encountered Hara. Here was a party leader who could not be manipulated, who was persuasive in his own way, and who bargained sharply on a concrete give-and-take basis. Katsura came to realize, at the time of the mutual understanding of January 1911, the need for a powerful party. This change in view did not mean that he intended to discard his belief in transcendental government: it was in fact to preserve this ideal that Katsura decided to form a party.

Although the details of Katsura's views on party government are difficult to define because he left no commentary on the matter, the basic outlines are clear. Party politicians from the reform faction of the Kokumintō were convinced that Katsura believed in the idea of party government, and his enemies in the Yamagata faction were similarly convinced. But Katsura left a different impression on those close to him, like Gotō Shimpei, his friend and adviser: "From the point of view of theory, he was not an exponent of the

English political party system. He believed in the Emperor-centered idea of the constitution and . . . was opposed to the majority party organizing the cabinet. To him, a political party was no more than a device to run the Diet smoothly." [2]

Katsura held to the belief that government should be run by men exclusively loyal to the Emperor (*kinnō*). This meant government by an impartial elite, or transcendental government. Katsura, however, accepted the idea of a political party because he believed that the ideals of loyalty to Emperor and transcendental government could best be preserved by establishing a party of his own that would unite all political groups in society. In grandiose fashion, Katsura planned for a party that would embrace both the Lower House and the House of Peers. He would name his party the "United Constitutional Party" (*rikken tōitsutō*),[3] and it would establish harmony throughout the political structure, making it possible, as he informed Yamagata, to achieve not part but all of the political goals Katsura and Yamagata had in mind.

Yamagata had strong misgivings about Katsura's formation of a party, saying of his ambitious goals, "How proud he is";[4] he correctly predicted that Katsura would be forced to relinquish his ideals. As one of Yamagata's underlings expressed it, rather than correcting the evils of parties Katsura would in the end "be consumed by those very same evils." [5]

The reality of growing Seiyūkai power, however, dictated that Katsura form a party of his own. Like Genrō Inoue, Katsura saw the growth of Seiyūkai power as the proliferation of "party evils" (*tōhei*). The Seiyūkai, to use his words, "placed the party first and the nation second." [6] Katsura reported to Yamagata that the need for a political party "is not a matter of principle, platform or scholarly arguments." [7] And by this he meant that the compromise relationship with Hara — the mutual understanding — had to be ended, for it had enhanced the position of the Seiyūkai at his expense.

To Katsura, the Seiyūkai had prevented a vigorous China policy, undermined the purity of regional "self-government," and, above all, led to the creation of a basis of power that could potentially ruin him. Thus Gotō Shimpei described Katsura's attitude toward the Seiyūkai in these moralistic and indignant terms: "It [Seiyūkai] urged on the one hand, a retrenchment policy, while on the other, it planned expansionistic projects. . . . It forced the union of prefectural governors to the party and satisfied its interests as it pleased. It sought to convince the virtuous people to believe that its party was more powerful than the government. . . . In the case of expanding railroad lines throughout the country, it said, without any sense of responsibility, that nothing can be accomplished unless the Seiyūkai was relied on, and stretched out its tempting hands everywhere. Are these not truly treasonous to the cause of constitutional government, and should they not be despised?" [8] Intimately familiar with the policies and tactics of Seiyūkai party expansion, owing to half a dozen years of negotiations with Hara, Katsura now turned to defeat that party.

KATSURA PREPARES TO FORM A PARTY

Becoming a party politician was a complicated matter for Katsura: it involved detaching himself from the Imperial Household and retiring from the army; it meant ending the mutual understanding with Hara and projecting to the public the image of a reformer; and finally, it meant trying, in a painful and awkward manner, to explain his actions to his mentor, Yamagata. Yamagata did not, or perhaps could not, understand Katsura during these months, and a virtual severance of ties between the two resulted. As the leading figure in the Yamagata faction, Katsura's act of disloyalty or "turning his back" [9] caused Yamagata a shock from which he did not fully recover.

Since those on the active military list were barred from

joining a political party, Katsura appealed to the throne in early November 1912 to be retired from his rank as general in the army. Katsura wrote Yamagata on November 1 of his intention to spend the rest of his life as a civilian politician and his trust that Yamagata would not interfere in this plan through a counter appeal to the throne.[10] Katsura was officially retired from the army on November 28. At that time, he was alleged to have said: "I have at last been placed on the reserve category. This makes it clear that my ties with the army have ended. . . ."[11] A week later the Second Saionji Cabinet collapsed and Katsura gave up his cloistered position in the Imperial Household to re-enter the political arena legally free to become a party politician.

On December 17, the day on which Katsura was named to form his third cabinet, he broached to Yamagata the subject of organizing a party. Yamagata agreed to a small "loyalist" party led by someone other than Katsura. Katsura, however, advanced a different plan, beginning a discord in dialogue between mentor and protégé: "If a political party is to be organized, it will not succeed if left to Ōura or Gotō. If there is a need, I will undertake the task myself."[12]

Katsura tried to indicate to Yamagata, who remained remarkably impervious to Katsura's reasoning, that he had already decided to form a party. Thus, even though he had promised Yamagata he would not mention the subject to anyone else, Katsura could not keep his plans secret. Yamagata, caught unawares, recorded these events confused more than angry: "On the evening of the 18th, Katsura told Ōura [Kanetake] that he intended to organize a party and, moreover, that I agreed to his plan. From the beginning, I did not strongly encourage him to personally organize a party. And, after promising me [on the 17th] that the time was not ripe and that he would keep the matter absolutely secret, on the following day he told Ōura of his decision — it is truly difficult to understand the circumstances of what went on.

I think he foolishly underestimated the gravity of the task and dogmatically concluded that if he personally organized a party, party men throughout Japan would flock to him." [13]

Despite Yamagata's feelings, Katsura began to rally support. In late December 1912 he offered reforms and power to the minority Kokumintō: he would end the political importance of the Privy Council, revise the civil service appointment act, place civilians as military ministers, and grant Kokumintō men three cabinet posts.[14]

He took similar steps to gain support in the House of Peers and, quite interestingly, promised the same reforms that he offered the Kokumintō. He summoned Den Kenjirō (January 8), a leader among the peers, and asked that Den persuade the peers to support the new party: "Katsura explained the general points of his platform to me, including his plans for financial retrenchment and national defense. Then he turned to the central matter of the functioning of constitutional government in the future. *He explained the necessity of reforming the present political parties and organizing a new party, as well as his firm determination to undertake that task himself. He then stated the need to reform the rules on the army and navy ministers so that they be civilian administrators.* . . . I expressed my support to him and agreed to act on his behalf in the House of Peers." [15] (Emphasis mine.)

To Saionji and to the political world in general, Katsura made it clear that his assumption of power meant the end of Genrō influence in politics: "As a by-product of this present situation, I have arranged it so that the Genrō will not be able to interfere henceforth." [16] And he reportedly said: "The next time I return, I must somehow or other force people like Yamagata to retire. Otherwise, I won't be able to manage things." [17]

Katsura made these statements partly to project a favorable image to the press, but he genuinely believed that the

Genrō should retire and directed the members of his third cabinet to act without heed to them. From a draft of his speech, dated late December: ". . . up to now, the custom in politics has been total compliance with the advice of the Genrō outside the cabinet. . . . On the one hand this had a baneful influence on the Genrō, and on the other, it led ministers to forget their responsibilities. With the advancement of time, I ask, is it necessary to perpetuate this custom? . . . When I [literally Tarō, referring to self] assumed this post, I reflected on this problem and I appealed to the intelligence of the various Genrō how I sincerely felt . . . and the Genrō pledged that this evil should be destroyed." [18]

Katsura's statement to Saionji and message to his cabinet regarding his rejection of Genrō influence made its way into the press, throughout the political world, and finally to Yamagata, who at first refused to believe that Katsura would willfully retire him. But Katsura indicated his intent in a statement recorded by Yamagata himself: "Inadequate though I am for the task, I shall handle the affairs of state. I will not cause you great anxiety. Hence, although it may be lonely for a while, I beg that you happily rest your spirits and . . . pass your time peacefully at your villa." [19]

This was as straightforward as Katsura could get and not be completely discourteous to Yamagata. On January 12, Katsura wrote Yamagata that while he would follow the "charge-the-enemy" (tokkan) policy strongly supported by Yamagata and involving a dissolution of the Diet, the formation of a political party was still necessary for the nation's future.[20] Through Katsura's messenger Sugiyama Shigemaru, Yamagata began at last to recognize Katsura's plan of action: "Sugiyama said that Katsura's plan of action was either to reach an agreement with the Seiyūkai or else, destroy it and build a separate party, and that Katsura had already decided to organize a party immediately himself." [21]

Yamagata tried to dissuade Katsura, writing him (January

14) that rumors of a Katsura party were creating unnecessary disturbances throughout the country and that Katsura
should, therefore, "charge the enemy" to stop the agitation
of party men.[22] Yamagata's warning went unheeded. When
contacted again, on January 19, Yamagata was informed
that the formation of a party would be announced publicly.

A sudden or complete disruption of ties did not occur
between Yamagata and Katsura; but the exchange of messages between them left no doubt that by mid-January 1913
their relationship was strained to a breaking point. Yamagata,
who welded his faction together with ties of loyalty, could
not understand Katsura's decision to form a party against
his advice and attributed Katsura's independence to extreme
arrogance.[23] Faced, however, with the complicated task of
solidifying his political position, Katsura found little time to
debate or fully explain the situation to Yamagata. The Seiyūkai had not remained idle: by mid-January it was prepared
to force Katsura to form his party and dissolve the Diet or
else come to the Seiyūkai for an agreement. This, plus the
fact that the Kokumintō was on the verge of division,
prompted Katsura to proceed with the announcement of his
party.

THE BREAKDOWN OF COMPROMISE BETWEEN KATSURA
AND THE SEIYŪKAI

Fully aware of the views being expressed at the rallies
and in the newspapers on the evils of clique government,
Hara believed that, short of political suicide, Katsura would
come to the Seiyūkai for assistance. Hara disclosed his
strategy to Saionji: "At present [December 17], the popularity of the Seiyūkai throughout the country is at its height.
We will sacrifice this popularity . . . if we should casually
compromise or do some such thing. . . . Should Katsura
call, therefore, we should neither commit ourselves to give
him support nor should we sever our ties with him. More-

over, in dealing with him, it is best that he propose the two divisions to us. It is not a wise tactical move to reject the two divisions at the outset thus causing him to withdraw the plan." [24]

By permitting public protests against Katsura and the army to grow, Hara hoped to weaken Katsura's position and then drive for a hard bargain. The circumstances duplicated those that had led to the mutual understanding in January 1911, except that in this instance Katsura would have to explain to Hara his lack of concern regarding the collapse of the Second Saionji Cabinet in spite of his mutual understanding with the Seiyūkai. Hara's bargaining position was strong and he could afford to wait for Katsura's expected call.

Contrary to Hara's expectations, and breaking previous patterns, Katsura evaded direct contact with Hara and dealt with Saionji. Katsura requested of Saionji that the Seiyūkai retain cordial relations with him, but made no mention of wanting a meeting with Hara for a political agreement. Because of this, Hara concluded that Katsura "is preparing to do battle with our party," [25] which meant Katsura would form a party, dissolve the Diet, and use Home Minister Ōura, whose dislike for the Seiyūkai was common knowledge, to win decisively at the polls at the expense of the Seiyūkai. Under these conditions, Hara could not take the initiative and seek an agreement, even though this was being urged by influential men such as Genrō Inoue.

On January 16, at Saionji's Tokyo residence in Surugadai, Hara groomed the Seiyūkai for political battle ("Surugadai conference"). First, all specific planks would be removed from the Seiyūkai's platform, making the party less vulnerable in an election campaign. Second, the argument that constitutional government was a legacy of the Emperor Meiji would be made explicit, drawing the support of the public. Third, Seiyūkai men would be given complete freedom to participate in the Movement for Constitutional Government, encouraging agitation against Katsura at public rallies. Fourth, a moderately phrased questionnaire would be submitted to Katsura when the Diet reconvened on January 21, ostensibly to give Katsura an opportunity to explain his usage of the imperial rescript but actually to indicate a flexibility in the Seiyūkai position. Fifth, if Katsura still showed no signs of wanting to reach an agreement, then, as a last resort, a resolution of no confidence would be issued against him. Finally, while a union with Inukai was tactically unsound, close ties would be maintained with him through Okazaki Kunisuke.

The rest of the party leadership was informed of the plan. The questionnaire and vote of no confidence were drafted, Hara dictating and Motoda Hajime recording. Motoda would submit the questionnaire and, if necessary, Ozaki would deliver a speech of no confidence. Complete secrecy was to be maintained to prevent foreknowledge by Katsura.[26]

As was often the case in Japanese politics, conferences carried out in strict secrecy were almost instantaneously known — content included — throughout the political world. The first meeting at Surugadai on January 16 drew swift responses. Through the rank and file, word was rapidly spread that the executive staff had unconditionally approved public demonstrations against Katsura.[27] In Katsura's quarters news that Seiyūkai leaders had agreed to go through with a no confidence vote had already been received on January 16.[28] The following morning, Katsura sent Gotō Shimpei to Saionji demanding that agitation against him be stopped; Katsura had good reason to make this demand of Saionji since the latter had urged a seemingly reluctant Katsura to step out of the Imperial Household and form his third cabinet. Saionji recalled: ". . . when he [Katsura] re-emerged, I exerted myself somewhat. Since Katsura seemed hesitant about moving from the Imperial Household to form a cabinet, I told him he need not have such fears. . . . I explained that such and such examples could be found in the West. . . . Katsura was quite pleased and said: 'I feel reassured to hear you say these things to me.' " [29] Saionji was now caught in a moral predicament which Messenger Gotō was prepared to capitalize on.

Gotō reminded Saionji that Katsura had entered the Imperial Household under duress, and that Saionji (then prime minister) had approved of Yamagata's plot to retire Katsura. Furthermore, when Katsura re-emerged from retirement to organize his third cabinet, Saionji had again fully approved. Having refreshed Saionji's memory on these points, Gotō demanded that Saionji tell the Seiyūkai that Katsura had no intention of using the Emperor and that he, Saionji, was involved in Katsura's entry and re-emergence from the Imperial Household, thus rendering the vote of no confidence groundless.[30]

Saionji admitted that he had encouraged Katsura, but noted that he had done this without foreknowledge of Katsura's schemes against the Seiyūkai. Furthermore, Saionji pointed out that the final decision had been made by the Genrō Council and that the Genrō, therefore, should be held responsible for Katsura's re-emergence. Saionji was technically correct, but his ambiguous comments to Gotō reflected the weakness of his moral position. Although fully aware that the party was already drafting the resolution of no confidence, Saionji told Gotō in perfectly bewildering fashion: "I do not believe that the Seiyūkai will present a vote of no confidence — but this does not apply if something unexpected happens. . . . Although party men are working vigorously to have a resolution of no confidence submitted, I have not incited them, nor have I tried to suppress them." [31]

Although Katsura had good reason to prefer working with Saionji than Hara, this choice was a mistake. Unfamiliar with the ways of frank political give-and-take, Saionji was indecisive and vague, and he failed altogether to present the Seiyūkai's position to Katsura. For example, he misled Katsura into believing that the Seiyūkai leadership was completely opposed to compromise with him. He did not tell Katsura that the main objection of Seiyūkai party men was his plan to form a party against them; he failed to make clear to Katsura that under no circumstances would the Seiyūkai surrender unconditionally; and he failed to warn Katsura that if the new party were formed the Seiyūkai was determined to submit the no confidence vote and engage its entire powerful organization in an all-out battle against him.

Katsura interpreted Saionji's equivocal statements simply as verification that the Seiyūkai completely opposed an agreement with him. Although uncertain of the determination of Seiyūkai men and of the Seiyūkai's organizational strength, Katsura decided, on January 17, to continue his plans for forming a party. In taking this step he was encouraged by developments in the minority Kokumintō. The reform faction, which had always (in the words of Inukai) "sought to establish an alliance with the Katsura faction and sell our party unconditionally," [32] was now preparing to take that decisive step.

THE DIVISION OF THE KOKUMINTŌ

Inukai had retained his leadership over the minority Kokumintō only because Katsura, although receptive to overtures from the reform faction, had chosen the more practical alternative of compromise with Hara. This control of power by Katsura and Hara kept alive Inukai's insecure leadership over the Kokumintō and, at the same time, left that party's rank and file weak and dissatisfied. Inukai was an obstacle to the emergence of a strong second party because he excluded all "bureaucrats" from the Kokumintō, which robbed that party of men with influence, and because his commitment to a union with the Seiyūkai resulted in little more than buttressing that already vastly more powerful party. When Katsura disrupted his relations with Hara, it was inevitable that Inukai's shaky leadership over the Kokumintō would end because a merger between Katsura and the reform faction was a foregone conclusion.

The reform faction sought an alliance with Katsura because it would lead to expanded opportunities to acquire power. Unlike Inukai, they rejected the idea of union with the Seiyūkai and, instead, were intensely opposed to that party. Apart from this tactical difference the reform faction was united by a passionate dislike for Inukai because of his sarcastic tongue and dogmatic methods.[33]

But, in spite of some unifying factors, the reform faction was not held together by a common political idea or reform program. Some, such as Kinoshita Kenjirō, supported Katsura's plan for a one-party system: "In organizing a new party, we did not have in mind the assembling together of the Kokumintō and small factions. We had as our ideal the creation of one huge party, including the Kokumintō and Seiyūkai, under the leadership of Prince Katsura. We even had the name United Constitutional Party picked. It was the same as the one-country, one-party idea." [34] Others, such as Taketomi Tokitoshi, saw the alliance with Katsura as a temporary weapon to be employed against the Seiyūkai. They were not motivated by a desire to form a permanent second party; the idea of "devotion to party" remained foreign to them.[35]

Another, and perhaps the most important, group, including such men as Ōishi Masami (the recognized leader of the reform faction), Kōno Hironaka, and Shimada Saburō, saw a new party under Katsura as a permanent countervailing force against the Seiyūkai. These men accepted the existence of the Seiyūkai and looked toward the establishment of a two-party system. According to their view Seiyūkai domination had led to excessive abuses and corruption: the remedy was another party of equal strength which would act as a corrective force to the Seiyūkai and represent the public more adequately. This group further reasoned that a two-party system was compatible with the Japanese political climate because there were no radical differences of opinion between groups which could cause political discord; from this they came to the realistic and logical conclusion that the key political issue was the acquisition of power to compete against the Seiyūkai. The Kokumintō would not increase its political strength by joining the Seiyūkai on the "academic argument" of a popular united front against clique government. Ōishi refuted Inukai's ideals in terms reminiscent of Hara: ". . . as long as the essence of politics is power, what good is it to be detached from it and founder hopelessly in academic arguments. . . . Those who avail themselves of the trends will win; those who oppose the trends will lose." [36]

United above all else by this realistic commitment to power, the reform faction planned from the outset of the Taishō Political Crisis to establish ties with Katsura and form a coalition against the Seiyūkai. Thus, when Inukai joined the Movement for Constitutional Government, the reform faction was cold to the idea: in their view the movement was, or would inevitably become, a Seiyūkai affair. The duration and actual content of the movement and the nature of the settlement were in the hands of Seiyūkai leaders. The reform faction predicted that, when the movement came to its end, the Seiyūkai would be as preponderant as ever and the minority Kokumintō would have very little to show for the effort.[37]

But because Inukai believed these considerations to be unimportant — feeling that the political crisis could be used to hasten a union of the minority Kokumintō with the Seiyūkai — a decisive intraparty struggle between the Inukai and reform factions was inevitable. When the breakdown of the Katsura-Hara relationship became imminent, Inukai wrote, "The activities of the enemy will become vigorous — not a few will be taken captive." [38] Inukai was right. Before his struggle with the reform faction was over, he would lose one-half of his party of eighty-eight Diet men to Katsura.

The final struggle was triggered on January 19 at the annual Kokumintō party congress. The reform faction prepared a platform that was silent about destroying Katsura and clique government, and instead denounced the Seiyūkai. Inukai hastily drafted a platform of his own strongly endorsing the movement against Katsura. Then, with the support of a slim majority, he rejected the platform of the reform faction in an atmosphere of near riot. Taking full advantage of his slight majority, Inukai ousted reform faction men from key party posts and turned to expel some of them from the party in the same way that the reform faction had tried to expel him in 1908.[39]

The reform faction was not prepared for Inukai's sudden counteroffensive. It had expected that there would be ample time to dissolve the party and regroup, minus Inukai, to join Katsura with as strong a contingent as possible to support its bargaining power vis-à-vis Katsura. Rather than taking issue with Inukai, however, five leaders of the reform faction resigned, forcing the Kokumintō to split. These leaders — Ōishi Masami, Kōno Hironaka, Shimada Saburō, Taketomi Tokitoshi, and Minoura Katsundo — had not worked out their terms for joining Katsura, but as Kōno Hironaka explained: "We were already quite certain of Katsura's decision and planned to move when the time was ripe." [40]

KATSURA FORMS THE DŌSHIKAI

While the Kokumintō was in the midst of disorder, Katsura informed Yamagata (January 19) of his decision to proceed with the formation of a party. "This will be no more than an announcement of my desire to form a party," he told Yamagata.[41] But at a press conference on the following day,

Katsura left no doubt that more than an announcement of desire was involved, clearly indicating his plan to depart from the previous pattern of compromise and form a party of his own. Having committed himself, he could not retreat from a struggle with the Seiyūkai without tremendous loss of prestige. However, with much arrogance (as Yamagata had noted), Katsura believed that his announcement of a party would suffice to draw to him politicians of all shades and from all groups throughout the land.

Katsura met with leaders of the House of Peers on January 17, begging them to join his party; his aide Ōura Kanetake did likewise, trying to persuade Yamagata's closest supporters, Komatsubara Eitarō and Hirata Tōsuke.[42] Although Katsura's invitation was actively debated, in the end no one joined him. Even Den Kenjirō, who earlier (January 8) had agreed to support Katsura's cause in the house, refused to join him.[43]

Despite Katsura's arguments, the rest of the Yamagata faction refused to sacrifice the sanctity of the House of Peers. Hirata Tōsuke informed Yamagata on January 19 that he and his friends — everyone of influence in the house — were strongly opposed to Katsura's plans and would not permit the peers to join Katsura. Yamagata approved: "The House of Peers exists in a transcendental position, apart from political parties, and it should exercise its authority accordingly." [44] On January 20 Hirata reported again, convinced that "the purity of the House of Peers will be preserved." [45] Late January did not bring a weakening among the peers; on the contrary, contempt for Katsura grew, for to them Katsura had corrupted himself: "Katsura's plans for a political party will not reach a satisfactory conclusion because Katsura has blundered in using the defecting Kokumintō group as the nucleus for his party . . . and inevitably, he will be ruined by the defectors, that is, Ōishi's group. . . . If Prince Katsura has agreed that his future will be based on a political party, he has indeed discarded his basic principles of transcendental government and surrendered to public opinion." [46]

In overestimating his influence in the House of Peers, Katsura suffered the first of several setbacks. He was forced to give up the idea of a "united constitutional party" and agree to something less pretentious: "The Constitutional Association of Friends," or the Rikken Dōshikai. Rebuked by the peers, Katsura shifted his focus to the reform faction of the Kokumintō, meeting with its leaders on January 27.

True to the predictions of men in the Yamagata faction, Katsura was forced to compromise on his ideal of the Emperor-cabinet system — that is, transcendental government. In the course of the negotiations, Katsura replied to questions asked of him as if he were committed to the idea of party government. He stated that he would resign or dissolve the Diet if a majority in the Lower House opposed him; he claimed that he would step down as prime minister if he lost an election. Katsura made it clear, furthermore, that not even an imperial rescript, presumably one originating from Yamagata, could stop him from becoming a party politician: "Regardless of an imperial rescript, I believe that it is my duty, in the years that remain, to establish a new party. Moreover, I believe that working toward constitutional government means rendering service to the Imperial State. Thus, in that event [receiving a rescript] I am prepared to discard my title of Prince . . . to serve the nation as commoner Katsura Tarō." [47]

Leaders of the reform faction found Katsura's statement on party government reassuring and agreed to join the new party. After their decision was reached, the rest of the Kokumintō had to decide whether to stay with Inukai or follow Ōishi and others into Katsura's Dōshikai. A total of forty-four joined the Dōshikai. [48] Through vigorous action Inukai managed to keep the rest of the party with him, but he had lost the more important half to Katsura. Among the defectors — "every one of them distinguished men," Inukai admitted — were the men with wealth and influence who had sustained the party: "We have been reduced to 44 members, but I believe we will be able to gain some back after the election. However, we will suffer from one thing — lack of money. . . . Most of my friends in the business world are now allied to the new party.[49]

Besides capturing from the Kokumintō what strength it had, Katsura set out to gain the backing of groups which Inukai had either shunned or not represented adequately. As expected, Katsura gained the full support of the thirty Diet men of the "government party," the Chūō Club. Leaders of this club, Ōura Kanetake and Adachi Kenzō, were influential in the bureaucracy and the House of Peers and close to men in the Yamagata faction. Katsura drew the solid backing of Katō Kōmei, Kataoka Chokuon, and Sakamoto Kin'ya and the powerful Mitsubishi *zaibatsu* behind them. Through Gotō Shimpei, Akiyama Teisuke, Wakatsuki Reijirō, and (again) Katō Kōmei, he attracted a number of young talented bureaucrats to join or become affiliated with the Dōshikai. These were the "up-and-coming" by Hara's definition: Hamaguchi Yūkō, Nagashima Ryūji, Egi Yoku, and Shimooka Chūji.[50]

The growth of Katsura's new party was not assured by any means: personal rivalry among the leaders was keen and in some cases bitter. For example, Gotō detested Ōura for his tendency to rely on police tactics and also disliked the Mitsubishi group and Katō in particular, whom he described as one who "does not understand the recent progressive developments in Japan and believes in the old and harmful opinions of the English." [51] Furthermore, it was not clear how much of the leadership in the Dōshikai would be shared by such men as Ōishi and Kōno of the reform faction as well as bureaucrats like Egi and Hamaguchi.

Regardless of this uncertainty over the future leadership

of the party, Katsura's formation of the Dōshikai was an extremely crucial event. Katsura decisively ended the tie with Hara that had dominated politics since 1905, an alliance that had provided a working relationship between the major centers of power — the House of Peers, the Lower House, and the bureaucracy — and had stymied the growth of a second party. With the breakdown of that key relationship, groups previously separated from each other could now minimize their differences and work together against the Seiyūkai. Exactly how this new party would influence political alliances was still open to speculation. For example, it was still unclear how it expected to establish a working relationship with the Yamagata faction. But without doubt permanent shifts in political alignments were taking place, and in this process the second party, the Dōshikai, stood to make substantial gains.

In the immediate context, the formation of the Dōshikai was above all else directed as a challenge to the Seiyūkai. It was part and parcel of Katsura's strategy to destroy that party, knowing as he did that the threat of dissolution caused intense fear in the Seiyūkai rank and file. He formed the Dōshikai expecting that whole factions from the Seiyūkai would defect to him to avoid facing almost certain defeat in a Katsura-controlled election. Furthermore, he believed, as did many others, that the Seiyūkai depended solely on intimate contact with the government for its existence, and that without nourishment from government funds it would soon capitulate.[52]

With this strategy in mind, Katsura postponed the opening of the Diet for fifteen days beginning January 21, expecting during this two-week period to split the Seiyūkai. In his calculation, with enough money distributed to key persons in the various regional groups a substantial segment of Seiyūkai Diet men was sure to bolt and join his new party.[53] In late January it was rumored that more than fifty "anti-

executive staff" (anti-Hara) Seiyūkai men were indeed prepared to join Katsura's party. With a minimum of fifty Diet
men from the Seiyūkai, another forty from the Kokumintō,
and thirty from the Chūō Club, Katsura could count on one
hundred twenty Dōshikai men in the Lower House. The
Seiyūkai would still have about one hundred sixty Diet members, but the difference could easily be made up in an election.

The rumors and Katsura's expectations proved illusory
— the Seiyūkai did not split. There were good reasons for
Katsura to end his ties with Hara and form a party, and his
decision to do so was of great significance: although his
plans for a one-party system had proved overly ambitious,
he had brought together men of diverse backgrounds into a
pragmatic coalition against the Seiyūkai, thus quickening the
pace toward a two-party system. But in the context of January 1913 his decision turned out to be a gross tactical blunder.
Thus, in trying later on to explain Katsura's decision to
struggle against the Seiyūkai when he did, Gotō (Katsura's
trusted political adviser — but trained as a physician)
pointed with subtle cunning to medical and not political
reasons: "Actually, Katsura had been ill for quite some time,
and during his third cabinet was already suffering from brain
disease. This explains why he was so completely different
from the Katsura of old." [54]

8

The Taishō Political Crisis at Its Height—
February 1913

The Taishō Political Crisis came forty-five years after the Meiji Restoration of 1868, roughly midway in Japan's determined march toward wealth and power. It marked the turning point into the period between the "splendor" of Meiji and the militarism of Shōwa. It began the period of "Taishō democracy."

Men active at the time of the Meiji Restoration, such as the Genrō Yamagata and Inoue and party leader Kōno Hironaka, were still active on the political scene in 1913. At the same time, a younger generation that had not experienced the Meiji Restoration, nor the "splendor that was Meiji," was making its way onto the political stage. Kita Ikki, a patron saint of the ultranationalists in the 1930's, launched his career at this time. Socialists Ōsugi Sakae and Katayama Sen led strikes. Yoshino Sakuzō, leading exponent of democracy after 1915, was finishing his studies in Europe when the Second Saionji Cabinet collapsed. Nakano Seigō, journalist and radical democrat, published his maiden work in 1913. A few of these men, such as Ōno Bamboku, even survived the Pacific War to continue their political careers into the 1960's.

Katsura and Hara belonged to a generation that fell between these two sets. Neither were men of the Meiji Restoration, as were Yamagata and Inoue. Neither had imbibed the
new and highly diversified ideas of late Meiji, as had Kita
and Yoshino. The Taishō Political Crisis was their struggle.

Both Katsura and Hara sought to revise the political arrangement. Katsura would end the politics of compromise
to draw the parties toward the ruling cliques or, broadly
speaking, the exponents of transcendental government; he
would overcome the Lower House. Hara would preserve
the politics of compromise to draw the ruling cliques toward
the parties; he would overcome the House of Peers. The
test of strength was to see who would have the determining
voice in the nature and course of party development.

Katsura had formed the Dōshikai. The Kokumintō had
split, and the Seiyūkai seemed on the verge of dividing. The
peers had withheld their support, but if Katsura succeeded
in his struggle against the Seiyūkai they could be expected
to reconsider. Against this, Hara had his party, its organization, and its supporters throughout the country. He must
preserve party unity at all costs and gird himself for a Katsura-controlled election.

SEIYŪKAI UNITY UNIMPAIRED

The prospect of dissolution and a bitter struggle against
the bureaucracy at the polls caused widespread fear among
Seiyūkai Diet men. The task of party leaders was to prevent
this fear from leading into unbridled defection from the
party, and to transform it instead into party esprit de corps
against Katsura.

Unlike critics of the Seiyūkai, Hara was generally optimistic about his party's strength, because he believed that Katsura's tactical position was basically weak and that his announcement of a party was a desperate act. He therefore

saw no call whatsoever to approach Katsura for a humiliating compromise.[1]

In spite of this confidence, Hara knew that utmost vigilance was needed to prevent Katsura from splitting the Seiyūkai. He worked out defensive measures with other party leaders, notably Matsuda, and also with leaders of the eight regional groups. The latter were important because they maintained communication between central headquarters and the various regions and, under Hara's firm leadership, also maintained party unity. By restricting the number of major factions in the party to these eight easily definable groups and distributing patronage on the basis of leadership in them, Hara was able to maintain a high degree of party unity. In mid-January he met daily with leaders of these regional groups to hear reports on pro-Katsura activities in the party and to remind them that the Seiyūkai was indestructible: "We cannot at this stage openly act against public opinion, and even if we are reduced to a minority, there will be a road to recovery if we are determined."[2]

Constant vigilance and personal encouragement were matched by efforts to stir up popular support for the Seiyūkai: "In view of the fact that the situation was leading inevitably toward dissolution of the Diet, we decided to dispatch party men to the various regions to explain the political situation."[3] In a familiar pattern, Seiyūkai Diet men toured the country and, at "popular prefectural rallies" that were part of the Movement for Constitutional Government, urged the re-election of Seiyūkai men in the event of dissolution. (See Appendix C.)

Seiyūkai Diet men took with them henchmen who could arouse and, if the occasion called, pacify crowds. Some of these "professional rooters" were employed temporarily; others were full-time staff members of the Seiyūkai. The latter held the cumbersome title of "non-Diet personnel" (*ingaisha* or, the group as a whole, *ingaidan*), to distinguish them from elected Diet men. They had a special room at party headquarters and gained membership by a special letter of introduction. Able-bodied members served as body-guards (*sōshi* or *mosaren*), and weaker and more gifted ones accompanied candidates on election tours and made speeches.

These men were conspicuously present at all the major rallies in Osaka and Tokyo — the two main coordinating centers of the movement — in which as many as ten thou-sand were said to have participated.[4] They cleared passages in the crowds for leaders like Matsuda and for the main attractions at all these rallies, Inukai and Ozaki, now at their apogee in popularity. They led miniature rallies outside the main halls, circulating leaflets, recruiting supports, making inflammatory speeches, and directing skirmishes against the police.[5]

The massive rallies and the myriad of little ones — all passing the same resolutions with monotonous regularity — had the combined effect Seiyūkai men desired. First, they bolstered the feeling of esprit de corps among Seiyūkai Diet men, preparing them for the confrontation with Katsura in the Diet and at the polls; second, they had a cumulative impact on Katsura, shaking his confidence. To Katsura the ex-general, the rallies seemed like the beginnings of a dreaded invasion. They reminded him of the Sino-Japanese War (1894–1895) when a surprise attack on a cold winter night had caught him in a drunken stupor, shocking him into insomnia and total avoidance of alcoholic drink from then on. Now Katsura saw in the uproar the approaching enemy over the windswept plains — "Rallies . . . have been constantly growing in force. With each day, the power of the enemy grows more violent, reminding me of Manchuria." [6] Consequently, when the Diet reconvened on February 5 Katsura was no longer confident of his position, while the Seiyūkai was united and in high spirits.

The session of February 5 began with an interpellation of Katsura regarding his reply to a Seiyūkai questionnaire presented to him on January 20. Although Katsura's written reply was adequate on financial policy (he supported retrenchment) it was completely inadequate on the key points of the questionnaire. For example, he had said in private (as to Den Kenjirō) that the restriction of military ministers to generals and admirals on the active list would have to be changed; yet, in his reply to the questionnaire on this point, he seemed irresponsibly unconcerned: "I have not yet witnessed the rule to be particularly obstructive to the function of constitutional government." [7] Moreover, he refused to disclose the source of the imperial rescripts that had ordered him to form his third cabinet (December 17) and had commanded the naval minister to remain in office (December 22). He lamely argued that he was not responsible for them because imperial "messages," unlike rescripts, did not require the signature of the prime minister. But Article 55 of the Meiji Constitution reads: "All laws, public ordinances, and imperial rescripts, of whatever kind, that relate to the affairs of state, require the countersignature of the minister of state." [8] Katsura's argument was obviously evasive, leaving him wide open for scathing attacks.

In assailing Katsura, Ozaki pointed out that all imperial rescripts, whatever their nature, had to be countersigned to relieve the Emperor of the burden of political responsibility. In an atmosphere of near riot because he had mentioned the Emperor, and with an emotional verve which he later admitted was excessive and uncontrolled, Ozaki uttered his famous tirade against Katsura and his supporters: "They always preach loyalty, as if they alone know the meaning of loyalty to the Emperor and love for the country, while in reality, they conceal themselves behind the throne and snipe at their political enemies. Do they not indeed seek to destroy their enemies by using the throne as a parapet and imperial rescripts as bullets? . . . We will begin to see the role of imperial adviser fulfilled only when we can have a person whose character is impeccable, whose morals are beyond reproach, and whose every act is an adornment of the Emperor. Does Prince Katsura have even an iota of these qualities? Owing to his insatiable ambitions, he has executed his duties by using the throne. . . . He gave free rein to his wily stratagems while the entire nation was still mourning the death of the Emperor Meiji. Thus, he deliberately caused unnecessary discord throughout the land.[9]

Ozaki's speech, described by one of his supporters as "the first and probably the last" of its kind in Japan,[10] had a telling effect on Katsura. According to one account: "His face turned deathly pale. I am certain his hands and feet were trembling. His facial expression was like one being sentenced to death. I had never seen such a pitiful figure. I can still vividly recall Katsura on that day." [11] Before a vote of no confidence could be taken, Katsura, armed with a rescript he had drawn up beforehand, postponed the Diet for another five days.

Hara had won a major battle. Knowing everyone in the party by name, he had painstakingly seen to it that the Seiyūkai was represented en masse against Katsura at this Diet session. The party had responded to his summons and he was pleased: "Aside from Itō Yōzō, who was away because of illness . . . all 214 members were present. Even Haseba [Junkō] and Sugawara [Den] and a few others who were ill were present. It was thrilling!" [12]

Reassured of party unity, Hara attended his first public rally that evening. There would be "continued vigilance" [13] exercised through leaders of the eight regional groups, but there was an unmistakable ring of optimism in his diary entries. If Katsura wished a settlement at this stage, Hara could demand far-reaching concessions from him (most certainly he would have demanded that Katsura dissolve the Dōshikai and hand power over to him). If Katsura would save himself from such an embarrassment and continue his struggle he must face a united Seiyūkai and an indignant public behind it. In either case, Katsura's position was weak.

Katsura misjudged conditions when he expected the Seiyūkai to split easily and submit to him. Realizing now the strength and determination of the Seiyūkai, he decided against dissolving the Diet and sought instead a belated settlement with that party. In dealing with Hara, however, he knew he had to gain the upper hand. In his desperation he turned, with disastrous consequences, to make strategic use of the Emperor.

KATSURA, SAIONJI, AND THE IMPERIAL MESSAGE

It was obvious to political observers that the strength of the Seiyūkai had prevailed over Katsura. Even Yamagata, observing from his villa in Odawara, saw that Katsura's position was serious: "The situation . . . is not at all favorable to the government. Although the Diet has been . . . prorogued, it seems that Seiyūkai predominance still cannot be destroyed." [14]

Realizing this, Katsura sent messengers surreptitiously to establish contact with Hara and those close to him. Hara's response to these overtures from Katsura was self-assured. Fully aware of Katsura's desperation, and thriving in the excitement of political maneuvering, Hara was alleged to have said: "Interesting, getting to be very, very interesting!" Then he sent his messenger (Fukui Saburō) to probe Katsura further: "Where I come from there is the story of the boy who upset his stomach by eating too many eels. Nothing could cure it. After trying a variety of remedies, he got well by eating another charred eel. Katsura's predicament — the uproar in society — is precisely the case of one eel too many. The cause of this entire matter was the imperial rescript. . . . Do you follow me? Tell this to Katsura." [15]

The parable in the message was clear. Katsura had gotten into his "predicament" by using too many imperial rescripts. There was only one remedy — another rescript. Although for tactical reasons Hara did not say precisely how a rescript was to be used, he had in mind one that would reinstate the Katsura-Saionji relationship — in short, Hara's mutual understanding. Because Katsura had gotten into his present difficulty when he disrupted the mutual understanding, such a rescript would restore order for him and permit the smooth transference of power back to the Seiyūkai. It meant victory for Hara.

Regardless of how desperate his situation was, Katsura could not concede to Hara. In not dissolving the Diet immediately he had in effect admitted the tactical weakness of his position. And, like Hara, he knew he had to turn to the Emperor to restore his position; but contrary to what Hara had in mind, Katsura decided to use the Emperor to command the Seiyūkai to surrender. In this final attempt he again avoided the confident Hara and worked through Saionji, who proved once more to be unpredictable and inept.

Katsura had considered using Saionji to restrain the Seiyūkai as early as January 24. Sending the record of the Gotō-Saionji talks to Yamagata, he suggested the following plan of action: first, the Seiyūkai would be allowed to submit the resolution of no confidence; second, Katsura would resign; and third, Saionji would be employed to recommend him once again to the Emperor.[16] Yamagata rejected Katsura's strategy as unscrupulous and dangerous since Saionji was not obliged to agree to his plan. Instead, Yamagata, using typical military verbiage, urged: "It is time to stand before your enemy!" by which he meant that Katsura must "charge the enemy" — dissolve the Diet and strike a vigorous blow at the Seiyūkai, using the bureaucracy.[17] Katsura agreed with Yamagata but made it clear that his tactical position against the "enemy" was deteriorating. The events of February 5 convinced Katsura that he must use Saionji in spite of Yamagata's warnings to the contrary.

Saionji was the obvious person for Katsura to use against the Seiyūkai: he had admitted recommending and encouraging Katsura to form his third cabinet (Gotō released the record of this admission to the press on January 30), and this admission was clear evidence that Katsura had not machinated his own re-emergence from the Imperial Household. Since Saionji was as deeply responsible for the situation as Katsura himself, he would be obliged to deliver an imperial message to the Seiyūkai on behalf of Katsura.[18]

Details were worked out through the mediation of Katō Kōmei. Katō had returned in late January from his post as ambassador to England to take up the position of foreign minister in Katsura's third cabinet. He agreed that under the circumstances an imperial rescript or message should be used to declare a moratorium to the political dispute. Katō argued from no less than English precedent, in which a royal message was successfully used (May 1910) to establish a temporary rapprochement between the House of Commons and the House of Lords on the death of Edward VII; a similar plan of action could be taken now because Japan was still in mourning for the Emperor Meiji.[19] Katō called on Saionji and, although Saionji could have refused, he agreed to a meeting for February 8.

Katsura was forceful on February 8, Saionji pliant. Katsura first asked if Saionji had designs on reacquiring power, and the latter's reply was negative. Katsura proceeded to remind Saionji that he, Saionji, had advised Katsura to form a third cabinet, and that therefore, as president of the

Seiyūkai, he should command party men to stop their agitations against Katsura. Katsura then suggested an imperial message which would help Saionji do this. Saionji was not obliged to agree; yet, curiously, he did not veto the plan.

Whether Saionji in fact opposed the usage of the Emperor against the Seiyūkai is moot. When Hara and Matsuda rejected Katsura's plea to withdraw the vote of no confidence, both feeling the position of the Seiyūkai could not be reversed at that late stage, Saionji failed to inform these two men that Katsura would then proceed with an imperial message commanding the Seiyūkai to submit. And when Katō asked him again if he disagreed with the use of an imperial message, Saionji once more did not veto the plan; in fact, he left Katō and Katsura with the distinct impression that he would cooperate with them in this course of action.

On February 9 Saionji was duly summoned by the Emperor, who commanded him to have the Seiyūkai retract the vote of no confidence against Katsura. Having received the imperial message, he told Katsura that if he failed to carry out the command he would resign as president of the Seiyūkai, and that if this had been a day in the past failure would have involved death at one's own hands — a supreme way of declaring total commitment to an obligation. Thus, Saionji announced, in good spirits, that colleague Katsura could soon be festive (*ōi ni ogori tamae*) because victory was about to be his.[20]

Judging by Saionji's words, Katsura had every reason to feel confident that he had won over the Seiyūkai. He sent a telegram to Yamagata optimistically predicting the withdrawal of the vote of no confidence[21] and openly told his friends that he had won: "At noon, we lunched together before proceeding to the Diet. Just before entering the lunch room, Katsura smiled and said: 'There is no doubt that Marquis Saionji will transmit the imperial command in good faith. If the party does not obey him, he will have to resign as president of the party — he clearly said so himself before he left yesterday.'"[22] But the day proved to be disastrous for Katsura. Intense resistance in the Seiyūkai against surrender to Katsura, plus injection of Satsuma intrigue into the political scene, combined to turn apparent victory for Katsura into sudden defeat.

FEBRUARY 9: SEIYŪKAI RESPONSE TO THE
IMPERIAL MESSAGE

Major party decisions in the Seiyūkai were made by the executive staff and were then discussed by the board of councillors. About twenty, or two-thirds, of this board were elected by the eight regional groups; the rest were appointed by the president. The decisions of the executive staff were revised and elaborated but were almost always upheld by the board of councillors. The general party congress, in turn, simply ratified what had been decided by the executive staff and board of councillors. Perhaps the only exception to this general pattern came on February 9 and 10 during the height of the Taishō Political Crisis.

The executive staff met at Saionji's home on the evening of February 9 to discuss the imperial message that Saionji had just received. Nine men were present.[23] Existing evidence does not tell us what precise conclusions were reached; it is clear, however, that while everyone present agreed that Katsura's strategy was distasteful and highly irregular only Ozaki and Inukai, when the latter had joined the meeting later in the evening, unequivocally opposed submission, contending that Saionji's acceptance of the imperial message should not interfere with the party's right to decide for itself on the matter.[24] Yet even Ozaki believed that the struggle had ended in defeat for the Seiyūkai. He left early, admitting later that he wanted to avoid meeting Inukai in the hour of defeat. Phone calls from Ozaki's friends and supporters urging him to show up at party headquarters to give the rank and file moral support were to no avail because he had concluded that the situation was hopeless.[25]

In the rank and file, however, feeling was definitely against the decision of the executive staff. At about midnight, Hara went to party headquarters to persuade leaders of the regional groups to accept the imperial message and was surprised to discover that the party was in no mood to submit. The party had had a taste of victory on February 5 and this had caused much excitement. Hara's persuasiveness notwithstanding, the leaders of the regional groups could not be made to submit to the imperial message, leading Hara to believe erroneously that their reaction was Ozaki's doing. Hara left feeling he could settle the matter at the board of councillors meeting on the following day.[26]

On the morning of February 10 the rank and file still strongly opposed submission to the imperial message. Ozaki observed that "quite a few had spent the entire night there and were bleary-eyed — some were weeping." [27] Moved by this emotional display at party headquarters, Ozaki decided to renew the fight against Katsura that he had just given up the night before. That same morning, Admiral Yamamoto Gonnohyōe arrived at party headquarters and unwittingly bolstered the already strong current of resistance in the party to the imperial message.

YAMAMOTO GONNOHYŌE AND SATSUMA INTRIGUE

One of the immediate repercussions in power relations that followed the breakdown of the Katsura-Hara ties was the attempt by the men of Satsuma to seize this opportunity to regain their former power and status. Like the reform faction, the Satsuma group had played a subordinate political role on account of the Katsura-Hara compromise relationship. When this tie was ended the reform faction fastened itself to Katsura to rival the Seiyūkai, while the

Satsuma faction, although in less binding fashion, allied itself with the Seiyūkai to strengthen its position vis-à-vis the Chōshū or Yamagata faction.

The Satsuma faction was one of the ruling cliques and had once rivaled the Chōshū faction. From the mid-1890's on, however, it steadily declined in power. The last Satsuma cabinet was under Genrō Matsukata in 1896. Since that time this faction had sought, without success, to bring one of their leaders into political prominence. In early December 1912, when the Second Saionji Cabinet collapsed, Satsuma men actively backed the aging Genrō Matsukata and then Admiral Yamamoto to succeed Saionji. When Katsura's third cabinet verged on collapse, Satsuma men again plotted to seat one of their men at the helm of the government.

On February 9, Tokonami Takejirō (a close supporter of Hara and also a Satsuma man) called on Hara. They discussed the political situation and then, according to Hara, Tokonami left with the vague comment that he would appeal to Admiral Yamamoto and others to bring about a settlement.[28]

At eight o'clock on the morning of February 10, Yamamoto called on Katsura and demanded that Katsura shoulder the responsibility for the disturbances and resign. Katsura explained to Yamamoto that Saionji was not interested in the prime ministership and that he was holding on to it only because no one else was available: in this Katsura was the victim of his own erroneous supposition that the exchange of power was restricted to himself and Saionji. Confident that victory was his, Katsura blundered, as he admitted later in the day.[29] Not even stopping to consider that Yamamoto might have ambitions of his own, Katsura told him that the job was his if Yamamoto wanted it.

Borrowing Matsukata's automobile (a means of transportation still rare in those days), Yamamoto went directly to Seiyūkai headquarters to inform Saionji that he, Yamamoto,

was available for the prime ministership if the Seiyūkai
would support him. Yamamoto then called on Katsura again
at about eleven A.M. This time the usually amiable (*niko-
pon*) Katsura angrily told Yamamoto that his meddling was
highly irregular because Saionji was about to deliver an
imperial message to the Seiyūkai that would solve the present political crisis. Admitting his error, Yamamoto had a
telephone call placed to Saionji with the obscure message
that their talks should be nullified. When Saionji took the
phone to find out precisely what aspect of the talks was to
be nullified, Admiral Yamamoto had discreetly disappeared
from Katsura's residence.[30]

Yamamoto later claimed that he had acted unselfishly[31]
— obviously a falsity. Prodded by other Satsuma men, he
had set out on the morning of February 10 to gain the prime
ministership. It does not seem that he consciously sought to
undermine the imperial message, but since he claimed to
have acted without awareness of the message he was either
poorly informed, terribly naive, or a liar.

The motives and plans behind Yamamoto's activities on
February 10 are questionable, but the fact remains that he
led Seiyūkai men at party headquarters to believe that the
collapse of the Katsura cabinet was imminent and that a
change in government was in process. This meant that a
dissolution of the Diet and a possibly ruinous election would
not occur as had been feared. Under the circumstances,
yielding to the imperial message meant granting victory to
Katsura by default. Already strongly opposed to submission,
the consensus of opinion within the party now overwhelm-
ingly veered toward proceeding with the no confidence vote
against Katsura.[32]

FEBRUARY 10: AN IMPERIAL MESSAGE IS REJECTED

An hour after Yamamoto had left Seiyūkai headquarters,
the board of councillors met. Hara and Matsuda urged the

board to agree to another postponement of the Diet for several days. This was intended to give Hara and Matsuda time to negotiate an exchange of power with Katsura and bolster Saionji's precarious position. The two party leaders were voted down: "It was explained to me that before the board of councillors met, the leaders of the regional groups had resolved to go through with the scheduled plan at all cost, that is, to submit the vote of no confidence at today's Diet session." [33]

Hara and Matsuda's failure at the board of councillors forecast Saionji's defeat at the general party congress. The rank and file of the party was in a highly emotional state and was less pliable than the smaller board of councillors, but in an unusual and desperate move the acceptance or rejection of the imperial message was left for the party congress to decide.

The meeting began shortly before noon. Saionji relayed the imperial message, telling the Seiyūkai it must retract the no confidence vote against the government and reestablish order. Saionji concluded: "I have already received the message from the Emperor. As his retainer, I must obey his command. As representatives of the people, it is understandable that you should hold strongly to your views. But for the sake of the party, and for the nation, I hope you will exercise restraint and not let momentary passions get the better of you." [34] There was no debate following Saionji's speech. A member of the hard faction (Tomizu Kanjin) moved that the Seiyūkai proceed with the no confidence vote, and a deafening chorus of "ayes" greeted the motion.

A command from the Emperor had been disobeyed. The general opinion was that the Emperor and Saionji had both been deceived by Katsura, hence it was specifically Katsura who was being defied and not the Emperor. Still, the rejection of the imperial message buttressed the view already widespread among politicians that a clear separation existed between the spiritual realm of the Imperial Household and the mundane one of actual politics. It served as a warning to those who headed subsequent cabinets: never again would a prime minister use the political prerogative of the Emperor against a party in the Lower House.

Despite justifiable moral and tactical reasons to reject the imperial command, Saionji's failure to relay the message effectively was fundamentally inexcusable. Some claimed that Saionji was not forceful when delivering the imperial message; others said that rarely had he been so earnest; still others suggested that he seemed earnest because he was pale and trembling, but that he was actually inaudible through much of the speech. Had Saionji been a persuasive speaker he might have impressed the party with the grave nature of the imperial message. But the real reason for his failure was not lack of eloquence. Armed with a command from the Emperor, yet hesitant about suppressing his own party, the trembling and almost inaudible figure on February 10 was the unhappy convergence of Saionji as both Genrō and party president.[35]

Saionji was close to Katsura as a Genrō and quite apart from Hara, Matsuda, and the world of party expansion: it was this Saionji who led both Katsura and Katō to believe that he would not fail, short of political suicide, to execute the imperial command. On the other hand, as president of the Seiyūkai he was genuinely proud that his party was standing firm against Katsura's divisive attacks. He told the rank and file on February 8: I decided to sit in with you today to express my gratitude. The recent posture of our party has been exemplary to our country and to the world as well. There is nothing that can surpass my feeling of honor and pride in being your president." [36] Had Saionji understood clearly where he stood, he certainly could not have acted as he did. Leading Katsura to believe one thing and his party another, he fell victim to his own ambivalence.

The Seiyūkai was out of the control of its leaders. At both the board of councillors meeting and the party congress, the position of the executive staff was rejected. Hara, however, shrewdly yielded for the time being to the decision of the party and was said to have led the Seiyūkai march to the Diet that afternoon. To Hara what had just happened was an irreversible fact. He could not afford to let this rejection of the executive staff's decision by the rank and file interfere with party unity. Thus, he made it explicit to Katsura (via Katō) that there could be no further dialogue between them: "We have severed all ties with the cabinet. Whether you decide to dissolve or prorogue the Diet is no concern of ours. Saionji will submit his explanation to the Emperor, but other than that we have no connections whatsoever with you." [37]

His only other words to Katsura, again through a second, were, "I am deeply sorry for what happened; the very best of luck to you." [38] The course of action for Hara was clear: he must restore control over the party, a formidable task as he saw it. Yet, he had cause to be optimistic for, unlike Katsura, his maneuverability had not been completely undermined.

For Katsura the rejection of the imperial rescript was a staggering personal defeat. His political position was damaged almost beyond repair. He could not turn to Yamagata nor could he use the Emperor and Saionji again, and Hara would not talk to him. Had Katsura decided to reach an agreement with Hara a month earlier he could have done so; had he used the imperial rescript in the way Hara had suggested he could have avoided the excruciating events of February 10. In either case Hara would have retained the upper hand, but Katsura's political image would not have been so badly impaired. Some of his aides wanted him to continue the struggle against the Seiyūkai by dissolving the Diet and using force at the polls,[39] but he was no longer confident of victory at the polls even with the use of the bureaucracy. Given Seiyūkai unity and an indignant public, Katsura might indeed have believed, as Hara did, that a Katsura-controlled election would have given rise "to truly revolutionary disturbances." [40] Grasping at the highly unlikely possibility that the Genrō Council might reinstate him, he chose not to dissolve the Diet but to resign and concede defeat.

The epilogue to Katsura and his short-lived (two months) cabinet was written by Yamagata himself. Left completely uninformed of the details of the last few days of the Katsura cabinet, Yamagata wrote this scathing denunciation of his protégé: ". . . due to Katsura's deranged feelings, complete chaos resulted and . . . the foundations of the state have been jeopardized. Although he knew the situation to be truly difficult regarding the protection of the Emperor, the establishment of administrative order, and the restoration of the social structure, he acted without consulting the various Genrō and . . . he went ahead and submitted his resignation on his own personal judgement. He must be judged as being unfaithful to the state and of having left things undone. This was due to the extreme arrogance with which he judged the affairs of state." [41]

In Yamagata's eyes, Katsura was "unfaithful" because in conceding defeat to the Seiyūkai he had failed to accomplish the most important task of all — restoring order in society. The rallies that had been building up from December — which had prompted Katsura to say "with each day the power of the enemy grows more violent" — reached their peak in early February, and on the afternoon of February tenth exploded into riots.

THE RIOTS "TO DESTROY CLIQUE GOVERNMENT"

Mass demonstrations were a late Meiji or post-1905 phenomenon, and began specifically with the demonstrations against the Portsmouth Treaty in September 1905. "It is an undeniable fact," wrote Hara, "that today's situation reflects the gradual transformation of popular feeling since the end of the Russo-Japanese War when it was then believed that Katsura had taken a mistaken policy." [42] The demonstrations were sudden, explosive and brief; they were highly nationalistic and moralistic in tone. They were against the defacement of national honor: for example, the protests against the Portsmouth Treaty in September 1905 and against the violent treatment of Japanese nationals in China in September 1913. They were against unscrupulous politicians such as Katsura during the Taishō Political Crisis, and against corrupt navy leaders in the Siemens Incident during the winter of 1913–1914.

The mass demonstrations during the Taishō Political Crisis, therefore, were one in a series of popular demonstrations. From December 1912, thousands turned out at rallies "to protect constitutional government." The majority did not come with positive political goals in mind; they did not come to affirm the Diet system. They came with a sense of protest against clique government and with a strong tendency toward violent action.

On the afternoon of February 10, a multitude of people surrounded the Diet building. Similar crowds had also gathered on January 21 and February 5 when the Diet had been scheduled to reconvene. The crowd on February 10 had come to witness Katsura's defeat, and it was in good spirits and spoiling for excitement. Organized sections chanted: "Will he advance and do battle? Will he retreat and lay plans? Is it dissolution? Is it resignation?" [43] Diet men supporting the Movement for Constitutional Government wore white roses in their lapels, and the crowd exuberantly cheered these heroes as they approached the Diet building.

When news spread that the Diet would not convene after

all the crowd rioted, demolishing and burning police boxes throughout Tokyo and turning on the newspaper firms that supported the government — Hōchi, Yomiuri, Miyako, Kokumin, and Yamato. At Tokutomi Sohō's Kokumin, the crowd was well organized with leaders ("professional rooters") up front sounding the attack and retreat against the editors inside the building armed with swords and pistols. This went on for six hours.[44] Before the riots throughout Tokyo could be quelled, over two thousand policemen and three companies of mounted soldiers were employed. A few rioters were killed, scores injured, and several hundreds arrested.[45]

In Osaka, a rally on February 11 celebrating the twenty-fifth anniversary of the Meiji Constitution was suspended by police order, triggering riots. Again police boxes and pro-government newspapers were stormed. Residences of Kokumintō men who had joined Katsura were also attacked. Two days later, in nearby Kōbe, a rally of some five thousand in an open field on the outskirts of the city "to protect constitutional government" turned into a riot involving many thousands more and lasted three days. Disturbances of a similar nature also broke out in Hiroshima on February 16 and in Kyoto on February 17.[46]

By this time, however, the riots had lost political significance. When Katsura resigned the major political issue had been settled, and the crowds were suddenly left without leadership and organization. Aware of the power of the masses, Hara once wrote: "Not only in elections but in other matters as well . . . those who stir up the masses will always win." [47] But Hara also saw in the actions of the demonstrators blind resentment rather than a reasoned drive toward political goals. Without party leadership, he was convinced, the crowds could not carry on a sustained movement of political importance: he concluded that the masses should not be provoked needlessly.[48] In this instance, Hara's reasoning was correct. Moved toward violent action but only vaguely aware of the nature of the conflict, the masses had spent their energy by mid-February.

The problem that now loomed largest was the nature of the political settlement. Hara and the Seiyūkai executive staff had temporarily lost control over the party rank and file regarding acceptance of the imperial message. The hard faction could take advantage of this "anti-executive staff" atmosphere. But there were powerful factors working for Hara and the party leadership. First, there was the backlog of achievement through the politics of compromise. Second, fear of dissolution and a battle at the polls was gone. With the latter fear out of the way, Hara and Seiyūkai leaders focused attention on reacquiring power. While the rioting went on, the forces at the center of the political arena were moving quickly toward a political settlement.

9

Compromise and Reform in the
Political Settlement

The Taishō Political Crisis gave rise to a mood of great expectation among party men — reforms were inevitable, sweeping changes would alter the government. Backed by the press, which publicized the Movement for Constitutional Government, party men had become intoxicated by their own speeches and believed the time was ripe for the establishment of a pure party cabinet. Because the Meiji Constitution did not specify the selection process for the prime minister, they believed that the precedent of appointing the prime minister from the majority party in the Lower House could be established now.

But beneath the euphoria of victory was the grim reality of having to maintain party strength. Seiyūkai Diet men needed a swift reacquisition of power to preserve their local bases of support; and, given the institutional arrangement, this reacquisition must again involve the pattern of advance through compromise. Concrete political problems had to be solved which the advocates of an immediate party cabinet had not considered seriously, which placed them at a disadvantage against Hara and the gradualists. For example, although the theme of the Movement for Constitutional Government had been "destroy clique government," no one had any practical recommendations on how this was to be done. There were no suggestions for revising the institutional position of the House of Peers and the Privy Council. As for the Genrō Council, there was widespread talk of assassinating its members but no alternatives of concrete value.

The leaders of the Seiyūkai made a balanced assessment of power distribution, taking into account the various centers in the government. In seeking a settlement they were especially concerned with the selection of a prime minister to succeed Katsura, in consideration of the fact that, despite the spirited demands for a pure Seiyūkai cabinet, the Genrō Council had already been summoned to select the next prime minister on behalf of the Emperor (this was an imperial prerogative which remained unquestioned by all, including the hards). But now Saionji, president of the Seiyūkai, was among the Genrō; and the leaders of the Seiyūkai aimed at maximizing this situation.

SAIONJI AND THE ESTABLISHMENT OF THE
YAMAMOTO CABINET

Immediately after Hara had heard of Katsura's resignation (the afternoon of February 10) he rushed to tell Saionji this pertinent fact. Saionji greeted Hara with the suggestion that Admiral Yamamoto be named as successor. Earlier in the day Saionji had assured Hara that he had not committed Seiyūkai support to Yamamoto, but it seems that he had reached an agreement by this time. Hara urged Saionji to take the cabinet, but Saionji firmly declined the prime ministership. Hara was not without ambitions of his own nor was he against the idea of a party cabinet, but he suspected that Yamagata and Katsura wanted another "bureaucratic cabinet" bent on destroying the Seiyūkai. This suspicion of his was not unfounded, for although the possibility of another Katsura cabinet was slim, an "anti-Seiyū" cabinet was entirely possible. Katsura had not named a successor. In the past, he had agreed with Hara that his successor should be Saionji; but this time he privately told the Genrō he wanted another anti-Seiyū cabinet under Katō Kōmei of the minority Dōshikai. Aware of these moves by Katsura, Hara agreed to work with Yamamoto but strongly warned Saionji to be wary at the Genrō Council and not make concessions detrimental to the Seiyūkai.[1]

The Genrō had not met for the better part of ten years while Katsura and Saionji had exchanged the prime ministership between them. But because the compromise relationship between Katsura and Hara had broken down, the Genrō were summoned twice inside of three months — in December 1912 and February 1913. On February 11, Yamagata, Ōyama Iwao, and Saionji met to choose the next prime minister. Each of them no doubt had candidates in mind, but, unlike the earlier December meeting when the Genrō freely offered names of likely prime ministers, they were hesitant and noncommittal. Finally, as a tactical move, Saionji suggested: "Henceforth, could not the system operate as in Great Britain, so that power is taken by the majority party?"[2] After this suggestion had been turned down by the other two Genrō, as Saionji had expected, he offered the name of Admiral Yamamoto of Satsuma. Ōyama, who was from Satsuma, agreed, and Yamagata did not object.

Saionji did not mention any other names at the Genrō Council. Many assumed that he would recommend Hara or Matsuda,[3] but he was certain the other Genrō would have vetoed them. Moreover, Saionji believed that the prime minister should be an impartial person selected by judicious advisers of the throne: his selection of Yamamoto was in keeping with this notion.[4]

Having successfully nominated Yamamoto, Saionji retired as president of the Seiyūkai. Hara pleaded with him to remain as nominal head of the party because his presence was needed for party unity: "Without a president the party lacks central unity. While the party is in power, there is no problem, but when the party goes out of power, division will be inescapable.[5] In spite of such pleadings, Saionji turned the party over to Hara and Matsuda on March 1. Alluding to his part in the rejection of the imperial message, Saionji told Hara and Matsuda that it was best for him to resign for the sake of the public, the party, and himself personally.[6] He urged Hara and Matsuda to help Yamamoto pass some reforms, but other than that did nothing to help the Seiyūkai reach a favorable settlement. Actually, Saionji had been waiting for a chance to leave the party: "I thought it was about time to let Hara take over. Besides, I had begun to feel somewhat weary of the presidency." [7] He went to Kyoto and for the next several years rarely returned to Tokyo.

It was fitting that Saionji should retire as party president after Katsura had discontinued the mutual understanding. His presence had been a front: as "Marquis Saionji" he had given prestige to the Seiyūkai in its dealings with the Yamagata faction, but when Katsura ended the compromise relationship that had marked the 1901–1911 period he was no longer needed. Hara's fears to the contrary, the party was hardly aware of Saionji's absence.

It remained for Seiyūkai leaders to work out the details of a settlement with Yamamoto and then persuade the party to accept it. The settlement would have to be based on an accurate assessment of their actual bargaining power and, at the same time, take into account the impatient and disappointed feelings of the rank and file. The purpose behind the compromise was, clearly, to reach a prompt settlement in order to steer the Seiyūkai, still united and strong, back onto the course of party expansion.

The process took nine days, and for a week Hara made no entries in his diary: "13th–19th: I have been extremely fatigued these past several days and have not had time to make any memos. I must enter from memory and, therefore, the times and dates will be uncertain. Generally, of course, there was utter confusion over the matter of organizing the cabinet." [8]

THE COMPROMISE WITH YAMAMOTO

Hara's opinion of Yamamoto as a political leader was not high. In fact, he distrusted Satsuma men in general, saying of them, "they seek only to enhance the prestige of their territorial area, not the cause of constitutional government." [9] The Satsuma faction, however, was weaker than the Chōshū or Yamagata faction; Hara, therefore, drew Satsuma men into the Seiyūkai — for example, Tokonami Takejirō, Anraku Kendō, and Yamamoto Tatsuo — by arguing that their faction was doomed unless it joined with his party. [10] In short, Satsuma men such as Admiral Yamamoto were acceptable because they could be exploited to help the Seiyūkai deal with the House of Peers, the military services, and the Privy Council. This was principally why Hara chose to work with Yamamoto.

The activities of the Satsuma faction at the time of Katsura's resignation confounded Hara, and as late as September 1913 he was still trying to piece together the puzzle of Yamamoto's ambiguous movements between February 9 and 11. [11] But quite apart from Satsuma intrigues and the merits and demerits of Yamamoto, Hara, as well as Matsuda and the other top-ranking leaders, had concluded that a Seiyūkai cabinet was not possible and that the issue at hand was reaching a quick settlement.

On February 12, Hara and Matsuda met with Yamamoto and presented him with five conditions: 1) three Seiyūkai men be included in the cabinet; 2) the remainder of the cabinet, excluding the military ministers, be supporters of the Seiyūkai; 3) the latter formally join the Seiyūkai; 4) Inukai of the Kokumintō be included in the cabinet; and 5) Yamamoto publicly announce his support of Seiyūkai principles. Yamamoto argued for two Seiyūkai men in the cabinet, Hara and Matsuda, and a free hand in the selection of the other cabinet members. Hara and Matsuda naturally found this unacceptable, and after five hours the discussion ended in a stalemate. Hara and Matsuda then threatened to decline cabinet positions of home minister and minister of justice respectively: under these circumstances, Seiyūkai support for Yamamoto would be tenuous. Yamamoto therefore revised his position, agreeing first to include three men in the cabinet who were Seiyūkai supporters and who would formally join the Seiyūkai, provided Makino Shinken, who was being considered for foreign minister, was not forced to join the party. Second, he agreed to include three Seiyū-kai men provided Inukai was excluded. Third, he agreed to state publicly his support of the Seiyūkai.[12]

Having gained these concessions from Yamamoto, Hara and Matsuda agreed to the compromise. They felt little need to quibble over Makino, who was the second son of the great Meiji leader from Satsuma, Ōkubo Toshimichi, and an intimate ally of Saionji, having served in two of his cabinets; he was also friendly to the Seiyūkai. They had misgivings over Inukai's exclusion because Matsuda felt obligated, as an ally and a friend, to include Inukai; Hara for reasons of tactic felt that "if Inukai were not included in the cabinet, the disturbances would continue." [13] But, in the end, they agreed to the inclusion of another Seiyūkai leader (Motoda Hajime, a supporter of Hara) in lieu of Inukai because Ya-mamoto had conceded that the three non-Seiyūkai men in the cabinet should be close supporters of the Seiyūkai. These three men were well-calculated choices to fit the needs of the party: Okuda Yoshindo was a legal scholar, a former supporter and friend of Itō, and influential in the bureauc-racy; the other two, Takahashi Korekiyo and Yamamoto Tatsuo, were members of the House of Peers and leading figures in the world of finance. Takahashi was a former president of the Bank of Japan and was extremely valuable because he subscribed to the Seiyūkai's positive economic policy. Yamamoto Tatsuo was a former president of the National Hypothec Bank and had been, ever since he had served in Saionji's second cabinet, a close collaborator with the Seiyūkai.[14] None of the three objected to joining the Seiyūkai, and by joining they emphasized the growing links between the Seiyūkai and the bureaucracy as well as the world of big business.

Hara and Matsuda, then, had reason to be satisfied with the compromise. They had established Seiyūkai control over the Yamamoto cabinet, assuring the continued advance of the Seiyūkai in the bureaucracy and local political bases that had been disrupted by the Taishō Political Crisis. Thus, they defended the compromise vis-à-vis the rank and file with confidence and without apology; and their arguments were difficult to refute.

First, Saionji's nomination of Yamamoto was fact, and there was no one to submit the name of Hara, Matsuda, or any other party leader for prime minister. This being the case, the wisest move for the Seiyūkai was to gain preponderance in the Yamamoto cabinet, a goal which they claimed had been achieved. Second, Saionji had to be upheld at any cost. Having the president of the Seiyūkai on the Genrō Council was an important advantage to the party. Moreover, failure to uphold Saionji's choice for prime minister would not lead to a Seiyūkai cabinet, but to an even less desirable "bureaucratic cabinet" or to a cabinet headed by a leader from the minority party which would be a contradiction of party government. Third, Katsura had been defeated, but, contrary to the wishful thinking of some, "clique government" had not been destroyed. In fact, the peers and the "bureaucrats" hated the Seiyūkai more than ever and were still plotting to undermine it. Under these conditions, there was no reason to assume that a Seiyūkai cabinet could deal effectively with the House of Peers and the Privy Council: compromise, therefore, was necessary.[15]

By working closely together, Hara and Matsuda prevailed over the doubts of Seiyūkai men. Hara was logical and effective. He analyzed the political situation, decided on a course of action, and pursued it relentlessly. "The cabinet has already fallen," he told the impatient hard faction; "without gaining control of the government, what do you expect to accomplish?"[16] Matsuda fully agreed with Hara, and although he demonstrated less logical rigor than Hara, he showed greater empathy for the frustration and ambivalence that tore the rank and file. With telling effect Matsuda contacted members of the hard faction personally and took part in some of their meetings. He expressed his commitment to the ideal of party cabinets, but went on to describe the details of the negotiations with Yamamoto and then urged acceptance of the compromise.[17] Thus, although there was an obvious contradiction between the goal to "destroy clique government" and the compromise with a member of the old ruling cliques, and although many in the rank and file "felt like fools,"[18] the desire to overthrow clique government with a single stroke was now being overshadowed by the need to acquire power. To a party convinced of the importance of strengthening its position through a positive economic policy, the realistic arguments of Hara and Matsuda held sway over the sentimental attachment to a pure Seiyūkai cabinet.

From the regional party organization came pressures on the rank and file to support the compromise and preserve party unity, buttressing the arguments of Hara and Matsuda. Party men could not openly flout the fact that their ties with local men of influence depended upon the flow of funds from above. From the branch office of Kōbe, for example, this statement was issued, refuting the arguments of those who opposed the compromise: "Presently, Kōbe receives subsidies for its waterworks and numerous projects connected with the government. In taking into account the welfare of the city, therefore, we cannot rigidly antagonize the compromise at this time." [19]

The inevitable "softening process" took place in the rank and file. Working through the eight regional groups, the bulk of the party had demanded on February 11 that talks with Yamamoto cease and that a pure party cabinet be established. By February 19, however, there was little doubt that the party would consent to the compromise even though it was still distasteful to many.[20]

Had there been effective leadership against Hara and Matsuda, it is conceivable that the protest against the compromise might have been more serious than it was. But without Katsura as a clear target of attack the opponents of compromise turned out to be weak and divided, a fact often overlooked by critics and historians.

THE PROTEST AGAINST THE COMPROMISE WITH YAMAMOTO

The movement to "destroy clique government" depended on continued public support to force the ruling cliques, which dreaded disorder, to concede to party cabinets and sweeping reforms. When Katsura resigned, however, the fear of dissolution was gone; and in spite of vigorous efforts by some, popular support quickly declined. Without Seiyūkai support the Movement for Constitutional Government, which had seemed so promising to many, was left structureless and became, as one active participant aptly described it, a "shriveled-up morning glory." [21] In the regions, the leaders of the movement were received coldly by local party leaders: "We held meetings . . . but were not able to convince anyone. . . . Everywhere we went, the situation was the same." [22] At Tokyo, the planning committee of the movement found its coffers empty. It sold gossip sheets featuring Inukai's fine calligraphy, but funds that once flowed from financial magnates at the Kōjunsha[23] now only trickled in, if they appeared at all. Hara's influence was obviously at work. He had many supporters at the Kōjunsha — by early 1914, for example, the majority of the members there backed a Hara cabinet — and he was constantly in touch with its leaders.[24] The Movement for Constitutional Government, then, was hobbled by certain crucial factors: popular interest had receded, it was left without a national structure, and it lacked funds. Added to these was the fact that cooperation between its two leaders, Ozaki and Inukai, did not continue.

Ozaki's tactical position was weak. He depended almost exclusively on the continuation of popular activity as his basis of power against the executive staff of the Seiyūkai, and when the inevitable "softening process" took place he was unprepared to give direction to the political settlement. His activities became confused, and he struck Hara as an opportunist. First, he campaigned among the rank and file for a Hara cabinet — a hasty act.[25] Next, he argued for a cabinet headed by an aging general from Satsuma, Takashima Tomonosuke. General Takashima was acceptable as opposed to Admiral Yamamoto because he was willing to join the Seiyūkai. Hence, a Takashima cabinet would be a "pure party cabinet." But Ozaki contradicted himself by rejecting men who would merely join the Seiyūkai as a condition for gaining cabinet positions. A cabinet such as this, Ozaki argued, could not be considered "pure."

At the general party conference of February 19, Ozaki desperately contested the compromise with Yamamoto, saying, "There is no need at all to speedily grab power now."[26] He asked for three days to negotiate for a "pure" party cabinet under General Takashima. Out of two hundred fourteen Seiyūkai Diet men, only thirty sided with him.

On the following day, Ozaki bolted from the party with twenty-five others, the nucleus of the hard faction. Their

"Seiyū Club" received much publicity, but in fact it was a half-hearted venture. They kept the name "Seiyū" because, for sentimental reasons as well as for economic benefits, they did not want to sever ties with the "mother party." [27] One of their leading spokesmen, Okazaki Kunisuke, for example, began negotiating his re-entry into the Seiyūkai only three days after he had left it. "Basically," Okazaki recalled, "taking part in a political movement was not my strong point, nor was it something I liked to do — rather, I disliked agitating among the masses." [28] And above all, Ozaki, who led the hards out of the party, was not interested in establishing a durable organization. Although he himself could never join the Seiyūkai again, he permitted over half of the group to slip quietly back into the "mother party," and the remainder, including himself, responded favorably to overtures from Katsura's men in the Dōshikai (for example, Nagashima Ryūji and Akiyama Teisuke).[29] But Ozaki's alliance with the Dōshikai was not firm. Although he joined that party's successor, the Kenseikai, in 1916, two years later he had resigned — still proud, widely known, and politically weak. In the context of spring 1913 his gravitation toward Katsura's Dōshikai alienated many in the hard faction and made impossible the continuation of the Ozaki-Inukai leadership of this faction.

The breakdown of cooperation between the two "gods of constitutional government" was apparent almost as soon as the Yamamoto cabinet was established. Ozaki recalled: "After the Yamamoto cabinet had been formed, Inukai and I simply could not keep in step with each other. Inukai's protection of constitutional government was a war of vengeance because half of his party had been stolen by Katsura." [30] They could not keep "in step" because Ozaki could move easily toward an "anti-Seiyū" or Dōshikai position, whereas Inukai could not. Although humiliated by being excluded from the new cabinet and offered, instead, the ambassadorship to China, which he of course turned down, Inukai could not join Ozaki in his protest against the compromise. To do so would mean drifting toward Katsura's Dōshikai, synonymous to Inukai with the Chōshū faction, and conceding defeat to his enemies of the reform faction.[31] Thus, although outwardly adamant in his opposition to compromise, Inukai took a permissive attitude toward the Seiyūkai executive staff and the compromise with Yamamoto, saying, for example, "Since I hope that we will once again act in unison, I do not intend to take a belligerent attitude toward the compromise now." [32]

Since Inukai could not join the Dōshikai, he remained committed to his impossible dream of taking over the Seiyūkai. A year later, in the spring of 1914, he was still saying: "A union between the Kokumintō and the Seiyūkai will not be accomplished easily . . . but with each day, my arguments spread among the healthy members in the party [Seiyūkai]. I imagine that the time to establish the union will be when they come to me for support in the next election. . . . From there on, the stage will be ours. Until then, there are only preparatory moves to make.[33] Politics for Inukai after the Taishō Political Crisis was a series of "preparatory moves." In 1925 he finally joined the Seiyūkai, when the president, quite ironically, was Tanaka Giichi, a Chōshū general.

Instead of providing an alternative political position for the hards, Ozaki and Inukai merely underscored the tendency of politicians to be drawn into one of the two rival party alignments — "Seiyū" or "anti-Seiyū." As the two "gods" drifted away from each other, the protest against the compromise became insignificant. Left without leadership and structure, the Movement for Constitutional Government became a small group affair with attention focused on such economic matters as tax reductions, rather than on specific political goals.[34] Thus, although the press and the hard faction viewed compromise as a defeat of principle, it was in fact a defeat of their unstructured tactic of total opposition to the government. In the aftermath of the Taishō Political Crisis this approach to politics, which had been steadily declining since 1890, was discredited. Never again would the hards manage to arouse the public "to destroy clique government." The Taishō Political Crisis was the final defeat of Ozaki, Inukai, and the hards, the exponents of total opposition.

Under these circumstances, Hara had good reason to conclude that the exclusion of Ozaki and Inukai from the cabinet had proved to be a wise decision — "there is no need to be concerned any more with the likes of Inukai and Ozaki." [35] The basic strategy of Hara and other party leaders, then, had succeeded. Yet, to assure continued support for their position, they had to take into account the demands of the rank and file for complete control over the cabinet: despite the overwhelming support of the compromise by the party, a feeling of frustration and impatience still pervaded the rank and file.

THE REFORMS

Although party men had not given serious thought to reforms because they had been engulfed by fear of a dissolution of the Diet, there was general agreement among them, as well as in the press, on the basic items for reforms: 1) administrative retrenchment; 2) revision of the law governing the appointment of civil servants; 3) revision of the rule on the selection of military ministers. [36]

Seiyūkai leaders turned to carry out these reforms. They did not see them as unreasonable, because party men were generally agreed on them; but above all, they were convinced that meeting these demands for reform was absolutely essential for the restoration of party harmony.

Of the three reforms, administrative retrenchment offered

the least problem. Arguments for it had gained considerable support beginning in 1905, and the Second Saionji Cabinet had collapsed defending this policy against the army. The Yamamoto cabinet was expected to resume the retrenchment policy, as it did with great dispatch. By the end of the year it had reduced administrative costs by about thirty-three million yen. It enforced retrenchment on the military to the sum of fourteen million yen. Besides this it released ten thousand employees to further curtail expenses, raising the total reduction of government expenses to an impressive seventy million yen.[37] The long overdue execution of retrenchment was well received, helping to improve the image of the Yamamoto cabinet. But of greater importance to party men and critics in the press than administrative retrenchment was revision of the two rules established by Yamagata against the parties.

In 1899 an imperial decree drafted under Yamagata's auspices (his second cabinet, 1898–1900) ruled that, excluding the prime minister and cabinet ministers, all positions in the bureaucracy from vice-minister down would be placed under the civil service examination system. Since this put high government positions beyond the reach of party patronage, opposition to the ruling by party men, including Hara, who had drafted a bill in 1911 to change it,[38] was strong from the outset.

Party men proposed a reform that would open positions in the bureaucracy to free appointment — the vice-ministers, chief secretaries, and councillors in the various ministries, and also the bureau chiefs of police and of legislative affairs. Hara had argued for the inclusion of all bureau chiefs on the free appointment list; he also proposed that graduates of private universities be given equal status with those of imperial universities whose graduates (especially those of Tokyo) were given preferential treatment and had come to dominate the bureaucracy. Both proposals were later retracted because the cabinet felt they were too extreme and hence detrimental to the passage of the main portion of the reform.[39]

Revision of the civil service appointment act required consultation with the Privy Council, whose president was Yamagata and whose members were under the control of his faction. The council held at least eleven special meetings, concluding against the proposed reform at each of these sessions. Hara and Yamamoto retaliated first by publicly announcing the reform plan and hinting that it was being blocked by the Privy Council; next, they threatened to disregard customary procedure and bypass the council completely; finally, they agreed that if the Privy Council continued its objection to the reform an appeal would be made to the throne to purge the council. Yamamoto duly informed Yamagata of this plan, and in late July Yamagata and leaders of the council quite unexpectedly endorsed the reform.[40]

The reform made an immediate impact on the bureaucracy. Vice-ministers who had risen through the normal bureaucratic channels were presented with the alternative of joining the party of cabinet ministers or facing replacement by those who would join. These high-ranking bureaucrats were given fair warning by Hara: "Rather than just being a bureaucrat," he told them, "it's time you started taking part in politics." [41] Within three months, seven bureaucrats of vice-minister rank joined the Seiyūkai. Their action forced bureau and section chiefs below them to consider commitment to a party. For each vice-ministerial position, there were half a dozen or so qualified bureau chiefs with similar education and experience; in other words, there was a surplus of personnel in proportion to jobs at the upper levels of the bureaucracy. Hence, when a vice-minister joined a political party, the pressure on bureaucrats at the lower levels to follow suit was felt immediately. The process was described by a member of the House of Peers: "On their own initiative, the vice-home minister and the chief of police have joined a political party [Seiyūkai]. . . . The influence of this is certainly not small. Because of their decision, bureaucrats in the various ministries are all confused as to what their course of action should be . . . unless they join a party, they will not rise to the level of vice-minister and not even to that of bureau chief." [42]

The reform did not mean that party men would now be appointed in great numbers to fill positions in the bureaucracy. Rather, the reform forced bureaucrats to join a party as a condition for upward mobility. It meant that their positions no longer depended on the patronage of the Yamagata faction, but on the parties. It hastened the fastening of links between party and bureaucracy which undermined the strength of the Yamagata faction, and thus it was a vital part of Seiyūkai expansion in the bureaucracy.

Like the civil service appointment act, the law on the selection of military ministers was established by Yamagata in 1899; this, too, had been by imperial decree and was intended to block the influence of the political parties. The law required that military ministers be generals and admirals on the active list. Because military men on the active list were forbidden by military code to join political parties, the ruling prevented military men who had ties with a party from becoming ministers.

The bone of contention regarding this ruling was that it gave the military what amounted to a special prerogative to determine the fate of a cabinet. Military ministers were under the directives of army and navy leaders, not under that of the prime minister. Hence, when the plans of a cabinet contradicted military policy, army and navy leaders could force their minister to resign and then refuse to select a successor. Under these circumstances the prime minister could take either of two courses, neither of which was satisfactory: he could resign as Saionji did in December 1912 to touch off the Taishō Political Crisis; or he could appeal for an imperial rescript as Katsura did in late December 1912 when he commanded the navy minister to accept the portfolio.

Early in March, Hara and Matsuda made it clear to Yamamoto that the reform of this ruling was necessary as a condition for compromise: "Following the cabinet meeting, Matsuda and I told Yamamoto that the restriction of military ministers to generals and admirals on the active list had to be revised since this revision was a *sine qua non* demand of the Seiyūkai as well as of public opinion in general." [43]

The revision planned by Hara and Matsuda was simple: the words "general and admiral on the active list" (*gen'eki shōkan*) were to be struck from the regulations. This meant that generals and admirals on the inactive list, who were not barred from having party affiliations, could now serve as military ministers. At first, there seemed little difficulty in establishing the reform. An admiral himself, Yamamoto had little trouble persuading the navy minister to agree to the reform. The army minister, General Kigoshi Yasutsuna, also agreed that the reform was "unavoidable." [44] His conciliatory position, however, was directly challenged by the army general staff. This became evident at the cabinet meeting of March 11 when Army Minister Kigoshi reversed his earlier position and cast a lone dissenting vote to the proposed reform.

Despite his dissenting vote, Kigoshi still leaned toward concession. On March 11, he appealed to Yamagata for support. In his letter he acknowledged the obvious reasons for opposing the reform — only an active general could control and unify the army effectively and prevent the leakage of military secrets — but went on to note that the army was the lone dissenter in the cabinet and that the army could not afford to cause another cabinet crisis. The avoidance of political conflict, Kigoshi suggested, was in the best interest of the army.[45]

Officers on the general staff strongly opposed the conciliatory position of General Kigoshi. In a manner reminiscent of their treatment of General Uehara during the struggle for the two divisions, these officers constantly prodded Kigoshi to take a strong position. Kigoshi refused to comply, and the general staff forced his resignation (June 24), bringing his career as a military leader to an abrupt end.

The officers then circulated a memo with the pretentious title "Concerning the protection of the founding principles of the imperial army." The memo defined the army's fundamental position in its relationship to the Emperor: the emperor was the ultimate source of power and "absolute submission" was due only to him. The authors of the memo pointed out that "politicians harboring the idea of party cabinets" were seeking to corrupt the army's special relationship with the Emperor by allowing the selection of reserve officers infected by the evils of "general politics." [46] Next, the army chief of general staff, with support from high ranking naval officers, appealed secretly to the Emperor. They presented the views expressed in the above memo with the further argument that it was treasonous to revise any law decreed by the Meiji Emperor.

In light of this concerted effort by army leaders in the general staff, Prime Minister Yamamoto was pessimistic and warned Hara to be prepared for failure. Hara, however, was adamant, telling Yamamoto that if the army could not be forced to back down under the present circumstances, there could be no hope in the future of ever bringing the army under civilian control. He thus prodded Yamamoto to take the only course open: make a counterappeal to the throne on behalf of the cabinet. On May 8, Yamamoto made his appeal. He asked permission to read the army's memorial and then, having read it, urged — successfully — that it be completely disregarded.[47] No doubt the fact that Yamamoto was an admiral with a meritorious past was crucial in countering the appeal of the army leaders. Certainly no party politician of the day could have matched the influence of Yamamoto in the obscure recesses of the Imperial Household.

Had Yamagata thrown his influence behind the army leaders, Yamamoto's counterappeal might well have failed. As it was, Yamagata remained acquiescent. Like Kigoshi, he opposed the reform but recognized the wisdom of avoiding another cabinet crisis. Although he did not stop the activities of men in the general staff he elected to remain passive, indicating, in effect, his acceptance of defeat.

The second of Yamagata's barriers against the political parties had been removed. The words "generals and admirals on the active list" were struck from the law. Retired generals and admirals with party affiliations could become military ministers. Party leaders, however, did not take advantage of this reform for the simple reason that a party-appointed military minister could not have influenced either of the services. The significance of the reform was primarily psychological and not structural. The reform created a position of strength for the parties against the army. It served notice to army leaders that they could not act with impunity in matters of cabinet policy. No party cabinet in the teens and twenties was forced to resign in the manner of the Second Saionji Cabinet.

Yamagata probably felt the impact most strongly. He had been responsible for establishing the two laws that underwent reform and yet, as president of the Privy Council and head of the army, he could not prevent the reforms. In his faction there was now disbelief and anger. There was also a feeling that Yamagata's influence was indeed coming to an end. General Terauchi wrote to Yamagata on June 20, 1913: "In a day, they have destroyed the administrative structure that you and your colleagues directed over the past decades. They have made bureaucrats seem like employees of party politicians. . . . Truly, there is no leadership over the state now. I fear greatly for what the future will bring. Even with regard to the army, an unexpected alteration has occurred. It seems that Kigoshi underwent a complete change of heart. . . . The army, too, has been under your direction over these years . . . and even this has been destroyed in a day. Indeed, the lifeblood of a hundred years is like the morning dew." [48]

SEIYŪKAI LEADERSHIP PRESERVED

In spite of the fact that army leaders had been placed on the defensive and that feelings of apprehension were widespread among Yamagata's followers, the significance of the Taishō Political Crisis cannot be judged by its impact on the Meiji constitutional order. This aspect was relatively minor because the Movement for Constitutional Government was not aimed at reform. The Taishō Political Crisis arose when the politics of compromise broke down, and the purpose of the struggle was to restore it. Hence, in the settlement, the precedent of party cabinets was not established, nor were sweeping reforms carried out to alter the political structure.

To Hara, the reforms were for objectives he had had all along — to break the influence of the Yamagata faction and preserve party unity. As a realist, he was willing to press only for those reforms which he thought could be effected and which would, at the same time, help achieve the above objectives he had in mind. The real issue of the Taishō Political Crisis, then, was the preservation of Seiyūkai power; thus, in the final analysis, it is the maintenance of this party's strength, rather than actual reforms, which must be the principal yardstick to gauge that crisis. It was the expansion of Seiyūkai power that drew the challenge from Katsura. In overcoming that challenge in the Taishō Political Crisis the Seiyūkai affirmed the indestructibility that Hara had so frequently mentioned. Seiyūkai victory over Katsura and over Yamagata with the reforms was a triumph for the politics of compromise.

Excluding Saionji, Seiyūkai leadership emerged from the Taishō Political Crisis intact. It prevented serious party division during the crisis and the period of settlement as well. Preservation of the party meant continuity in policies that had been temporarily disrupted.

Hara was again home minister. Members of his entourage were strategically placed in the central bureaucracy and throughout the land replacing those "who forgot their official duties and devoted their energies to Katsura's new party." [49] Furthermore, with the close cooperation of Finance Minister Takahashi Korekiyo, Hara drew up plans for a spending policy, attracting capital from private industrialists, to promote "industrial expansion in the northeast." [50] By mid-August 1913, he felt that the political situation in Tokyo was sufficiently under control to permit a tour of the countryside. With him he took Finance Minister Takahashi and Chief of the Railroad Bureau Tokonami Takejirō. In their speeches there were no apologies for the compromise, and they were well received wherever they went. From Hara's entry for August 20: "Set forth at 5 A.M. and headed for Akita with Finance Minister Takahashi. Arrived at 11 in the morning. . . . Toured the dredging of the Funakawa port, returned to Akita by car, and took part in a welcoming rally sponsored by officials and citizens. I delivered a speech on the completion of plans for the industrial development of the northeast and of administrative retrenchment and explained that hereafter, the positive policy will be resumed. . . . A program of bamboo and lights were shown for entertainment. It was exciting." [51]

By early fall 1913, the regions had sent in their resolutions expressing satisfaction over the reacquisition of power. The positive policy was supported and no more mention was made of protecting constitutional government.

10

Stemming the Anti-Seiyū Tide
(1913–1915)

The sustained growth of the Seiyūkai was the most significant political development of late Meiji and early Taishō. By 1913, friend and foe of the Seiyūkai and optimists and pessimists of party government were in agreement over this pertinent fact. With minimal competition from rival groups in late Meiji, the Seiyūkai extended its structural network into the countryside and spread its influence in big business and the bureaucracy. Then, in the Taishō Political Crisis, it resisted and overcame a challenge from Katsura, using party cadres to stir the crowds and exploiting men like Admiral Yamamoto in the political settlement that followed.

This ability of the Seiyūkai to maintain itself as a powerful group fostered an urgent need to counter and resist that party. And because it would take the strongest possible coalition to rival the Seiyūkai, a multiparty system — such as existed in France, Germany, and Italy in this same period — had become, as Katsura had concluded, a practical impossibility. A "government party" disappeared and groups of "independents," once numerous in the Diet, dwindled into insignificance as men with conflicting views and backgrounds now formed a pragmatic coalition to rival the Seiyūkai. Katsura, Ōura, Adachi Kenzō, and an array of lesser men who had close ties with Yamagata and his supporters in the House of Peers joined with leaders who hated Yamagata and his men — for example Katō Kōmei, influential liberal in the bureaucracy and business, and Ōkuma Shigenobu, the great party leader of early Meiji. The union even had the backing of Genrō Inoue, a founder of that very party the new coalition set out to undermine. The lines separating the ruling cliques from other political groups were being blurred, the exclusiveness of these cliques being undermined, as old Genrō, young bureaucrats, Diet men, military men, and ambitious peers of uneven quality were being drawn into the vortex of political rivalry between two competing party alignments. And as long as the Seiyūkai continued to meet the challenges of this new coalition, the tendency toward two major parties would persist.

HARA AND KATSURA AFTER THE CRISIS

Prior to the Taishō Political Crisis, Katsura and Hara acted as chief intermediaries in what was a single line or linear power structure extending from the Yamagata faction in the House of Peers and Privy Council at one end to the Seiyūkai in the Lower House at the other. But after 1913 the mediation that Katsura had provided for the Seiyūkai had shifted to the Dōshikai, bringing crucial shifts in political alignments.

By late May 1913 Hara had grasped the essentials of the new situation: as he saw it, the major threat to the Seiyūkai was no longer the Yamagata faction alone, but the new coalition centering on the Dōshikai. "Henceforth," he told Saionji, "the enemy will be the second party, even though it is being treated lightly by the public." [1] Convinced that an alliance between the Yamagata faction and the Dōshikai would be drastic for the Seiyūkai, he adjusted his tactics accordingly. His first of several critical plans was to prevent Katsura from restoring his badly damaged political position. Although

Katsura desperately sought his assistance, Hara remained cold, noncommunicative, and hostile.

Actually, time did not permit a political recovery for Katsura. By May he was critically ill, and was writing Yamagata with none of the recalcitrant overtones of his earlier letters. In subdued fashion he reported his daughter's marriage and his worsening physical condition.[2] Katsura was afflicted with cancer.

The last days of Katsura were pathetic. Yamagata urged him to disengage himself from the Dōshikai and return to an "appropriate status."[3] Katsura refused, unwilling to admit to Yamagata that he had been wrong. Through his close aides, however, he informed Hara that he had tired of party politics and wanted a rapprochement with him. Hara refused. Katsura must remain where he was — stranded with his party and disengaged from the Yamagata faction: "I explained [to Saionji] that at present, the best policy was to keep Yamagata and Katsura in their respective positions and that . . . to replace Yamagata in the Privy Council with Katsura was poor tactics."[4]

Realizing that Hara alone understood him and could restore his discredited image, Katsura anxiously sought a meeting with Hara for one final exchange of words; but up until the very end Hara was without pity, sending his good wishes to Katsura through his seconds. In Hara's eyes, there could be nothing between them: "Perhaps Katsura wants to see me — I can't tell. If he were not in the party [Dōshikai] it might be different. But given his present position, I cannot hastily pay a visit. There have been many rumors up to now about Katsura and me, but there is no special relationship between us. As individuals and between parties, there are no binding obligations whatsoever."[5]

On October 7 Hara paid his first personal visit to Katsura. By then, Katsura had suffered a paralytic stroke and had lost his speech. There was a firm clasping of hands and Hara gave words of encouragement. Three days later, October 10, Katsura was dead.

From 1905 through 1912, Hara and Katsura had held numerous and extensive talks which were the substance of the so-called "Katsura-Saionji decade." They had bargained and worked out compromises. Each had played on the other's ego: Katsura had lured Hara with the prospect of power while Hara had persuaded Katsura to awaken to the opportunities of a modern-type Genrō. But from the onset of the Taishō Political Crisis in December 1912 until Katsura's death in October 1913 there was not a single face-to-face exchange between them: during the crisis Katsura avoided Hara; afterward, Hara avoided Katsura.

Hara's ruthlessness toward Katsura reflected his uneasiness about the Seiyūkai's political position. Although he impressed others as certain that the Seiyūkai no longer needed Katsura and that it could withstand the strongest anti-Seiyū coalition, the image he projected was one thing, his actual apprehensions quite another. He was in fact deeply disturbed about the inevitable moment when the Yamagata faction, the peers, men of the Dōshikai, and Inoue and Ōkuma would all join to deliver a devastating blow against the party. To Hara's dismay, the opportunity for this came in early 1914, much before he had expected.

THE SIEMENS INCIDENT AND THE COLLAPSE
OF THE YAMAMOTO CABINET

According to a Reuters dispatch of January 21, 1914, from London, a trial in Berlin had uncovered instances of corruption in the Japanese navy ministry. A secretary for the Tokyo branch of the Siemens Munitions Firm had been convicted of smuggling company documents for purposes of blackmail against high company officials. Some of these documents showed that the Siemens firm had bribed Japanese navy officers to gain contracts for ammunition and wireless material. Tokyo papers printed the dispatch on January 23, and on that day Shimada Saburō of the Dōshikai, a politician noted for his oratorical skill, led the first in a series of heated interpellations in the Diet questioning the government and, more specifically, Prime Minister and Admiral Yamamoto on corruption in the navy.[6]

Although this was the incident that precipitated the collapse of the Yamamoto cabinet, the real reasons behind that collapse were more complicated than simply corruption. A special investigation committee uncovered only a few cases in which navy officers had accepted bribes from foreign and domestic firms; not enough, certainly, to cause a major political crisis. Thus, despite brilliant speeches by Dōshikai men and rallies sponsored by them, the Seiyūkai remained united to vote down the no confidence vote (February 10, exactly one year after Katsura's defeat) and restore order on the streets without any aid from the army, which had refused to give Hara assistance.[7]

Breaking previous patterns of behavior, however, the peers picked up the cudgel provided by the Siemens Incident. Under the direction of Yamagata's men — Hirata Tōsuke, Komatsubara Eitarō, Kiyoura Keigo — the peers vetoed the cabinet's budget. This tactic of disapproving the budget had been used in the 1890's by the Lower House against cabinets of the ruling cliques. Now it was being used by the peers against a party-controlled cabinet. In particular, the peers drastically cut the navy's allotment by seventy million yen.[8]

This move by the peers was decisive in forcing the cabinet to resign. Although the Seiyūkai, with help from Inukai and Ozaki, struck back, rejecting the peers' revision of the budget on grounds of political principle — that is, that control of the budget was the prerogative of the Lower House — the peers remained adamant. Even when a joint committee of both houses defeated the peers' budget by one vote, they would not concede. Unable to break the resistance of the peers, the cabinet resigned on March 23.

Hara and Yamamoto had hoped that the joint budget committee would accept the peers' revision to prevent a collapse of the cabinet. This would have given Yamamoto the chance he needed to clear himself of the charge of corruption before resigning. As for Hara, the possibility of Yamamoto's handing the cabinet entirely to him seemed excellent. Hara, in short, sought to use Yamamoto's predicament to gain the prime ministership before it could be taken by one of Yamagata's men. Yamamoto agreed to Hara's plan, as did Saionji, who telegraphed his approval.[9] Thus, although Hara and Yamamoto were unable to save the cabinet they agreed that it should be handed to the majority Seiyūkai, not to one of Yamagata's men. In submitting his resignation to the Emperor, Yamamoto recommended Hara as his successor, explaining that not only he but Katsura, too, had concluded that the era of transcendental cabinets was over; and that Hara, the successor to Itō and Saionji, was the logical choice for prime minister.[10] Hara was never closer to gaining the coveted prime ministership. Had this strategy worked, the task of defending his party in the Lower House would have been greatly simplified. But the strategy failed, as a result of the schemes of the Genrō Yamagata and Inoue.

Yamagata had anticipated the plan of Hara and Yamamoto. He therefore arranged a meeting of the Genrō to block Hara from heading the next cabinet. At this meeting Yamagata flatly rejected Hara's candidacy and presented a slate consisting of Kiyoura Keigo, Itō Miyoji, Ōkuma Shigenobu, and Katō Kōmei — two peers, two Dōshikai men — in that order of preference.[11] In the complicated process, the speaker of the House of Peers (Tokugawa Ietatsu) was first named in recognition of the peers' role in forcing the resignation of the Yamamoto cabinet. Then, after Tokugawa had declined as was expected, the Genrō picked Yamagata's first choice, Kiyoura Keigo.[12]

Yamagata's plan proved to be abortive. Kiyoura refused to restore the naval appropriations cut by the peers. The prospective navy minister (Admiral Katō Tomosaburō) then rejected the portfolio, threatening to duplicate the events that had touched off the Taishō Political Crisis. Rather than resorting to an imperial rescript, as Katsura had done against the navy in December 1912, Kiyoura declined the prime ministership on April 6.[13]

Although Yamagata had failed to have his choice become the next prime minister, his colleague, Genrō Inoue, would not fail: in separate negotiations Inoue was working out the details of yet another anti-Seiyū cabinet under Ōkuma. Thus, Hara's tactics notwithstanding, the Genrō saw to it that the next cabinet would not be under the control of the majority Seiyūkai.

THE EMERGENCE OF THE ŌKUMA CABINET, APRIL 1914

When the reform factions forced Ōkuma Shigenobu to resign as president of the Kenseihontō in January 1907, he did so with these words: "Politics is my life. Even if you should force me to leave the party, my area of activity is all Japan. I will not give up."[14] True to his words, Ōkuma remained politically ambitious; but, contrary to what he had implied, he did not set out to undermine the reform faction. By 1912 Ōkuma had come to accept the view of that faction that the enemy of the minority party was not clique government, but the Seiyūkai. He reasoned that the parties had been corrupted when party men joined with Itō, a leader of the ruling cliques, to form the Seiyūkai. Ōkuma, however, was inconsistent, concluding that the only hope for the minority party was to ally itself with a leader like Katsura, another

prominent figure in the ruling cliques, to crush the Seiyūkai.[15]

During the height of the Taishō Political Crisis, Ōkuma
encouraged the reform faction to join Katsura and kept in
regular contact with Katsura supporters. In March 1913, he
publicly endorsed the Dōshikai at a dinner held by that
party in his honor: ". . . if I support Katsura, the public
will say my action is tainted. But I do not care if this is said.
We must at all cost stand up against the Seiyūkai. . . .
Inukai too, will howl like a wolf . . . as he did against his
lifelong friend Ōishi. But after the storm has died down,
there will be clear weather. If the new party prospers, Inukai will join us." [16] No longer sharing Inukai's ideal of a
"union of people's parties," Ōkuma responded eagerly to
overtures from Inoue regarding the formation of an anti-
Seiyū cabinet.

Inoue had been one of the founding fathers of the Seiyūkai and had been Hara's sponsor in that party, but he strongly
objected to Seiyūkai policies and had become hostile to Hara
and his party. Inoue disapproved of the Seiyūkai's positive
economic policy and its party expansion schemes against the
bureaucracy; he disagreed with Hara's belief that the majority party in the Lower House should control the government;
and finally, he deeply resented the Seiyūkai's actions during
the Taishō Political Crisis. Overriding Inoue's plea, the
Seiyūkai had refused to reach an agreement with Katsura;
then, after having forced Katsura to resign, it had reached
an agreement with a leader from Satsuma. Inoue, a Chōshū
Genrō, took the compromise as a personal insult.[17] He now
lent his political weight to Ōkuma and the Dōshikai, not
because he stood for party government but because he despised the Seiyūkai.

Although Inoue and Ōkuma had been on opposite sides
of the fence for many years — Inoue as Genrō, Ōkuma as
party leader — they now adjusted their differences and

joined in a common effort to end "party evils." Ōkuma informed Inoue that he was in full agreement with Inoue on
all points; and, with mediation from Katō Kōmei (now
president of the Dōshikai) Ōkuma agreed to minimize fric-
tion between himself and the Genrō, especially Yamagata.[18]
On April 9, Inoue and Ōkuma met for talks that amounted
to a verbal agreement to destroy the Seiyūkai. As recorded
by Mochizuki Kotarō, Inoue's private secretary, the following exchange of words took place:

Inoue: "Party evils have extended beyond the central government into the regional administrative structure. It will
not be easy to bring this arrogant Seiyūkai under control."

Ōkuma: "The Seiyūkai is like a parasite — when it parts
with power, it will die. . . . I believe . . . we can destroy
it. . . . The Seiyūkai expanded its power by using government funds, and so, if it is not in power, it will fall apart.
. . . This is Hara's predicament."

Inoue: "Noda [Utarō, Seiyūkai leader] called this morn-
ing and said that Hara wanted very much to meet me. But
I refused a meeting. I told him I detested party politicians.
In short, I want you to deliver a crushing blow against the
Seiyūkai." [19]

On April 10, the other Genrō endorsed Ōkuma. Yamagata
was hesitant at first, but because his plans for a Kiyoura
cabinet had been thwarted he agreed with Inoue, who suggested that Ōkuma could be manipulated to defeat the
Seiyūkai and to establish the army's two divisions.

The public welcomed the Ōkuma cabinet with enthusiasm. Ōkuma was a historic figure of the early party movement. Now he had emerged from his retreat at Waseda, the
university he had founded, to bring new life to party politics. As a first step in this direction he invited Inukai and
Ozaki to join his cabinet. Inukai refused, observing that the
new cabinet was not what the public thought it was, but
in fact "the unadulterated revival of the Chōshū faction." [20]

Ozaki, however, agreed to be minister of justice and this was taken as evidence of the favorable turn in party politics.

But Ōkuma was not interested in bringing "new life" to party politics. He left no doubt in his public pronouncements that his central aim was the destruction of the Seiyū-kai.[21] And since it was evident, too, that he had the full backing of the Genrō Inoue and Yamagata, the enthusiastic reception of Ōkuma was indeed an illusion, as Inukai bitterly noted.

Hara's assessment was similar to that of Inukai. He saw the establishment of the Ōkuma cabinet as the beginning of a détente between the Dōshikai and the Yamagata or Chōshū faction. Sensing this, he began immediately to make countermoves of his own to prevent this détente from becoming a binding alliance between these two groups.

He started with a number of moves which proved ineffective. He sent messengers to the Satsuma Genrō, Matsukata and Ōyama, asking them to intercede on behalf of the Seiyūkai at the Genrō Council. Later, he personally tried to erase Matsukata's "misconceptions" about Seiyūkai expansion policies.[22] He also tried to dissuade Inoue from continuing his activities against the Seiyūkai, but Inoue remained implacably hostile; he died three months later (September 2, 1915) still bitter at Hara and the Seiyūkai.[23] In the end, the strategy that proved most effective for Hara was to establish direct lines of communication with Yamagata himself.

IN DEFENSE OF THE SEIYŪKAI: THE HARA-YAMAGATA TALKS, FALL 1914

Since Saionji's resignation, the Seiyūkai had functioned without a president. By late 1913, however, the succession problem was being resolved when Matsuda Masahisa, Hara's equal in status within the party, became critically ill. In January Matsuda was given the title of baron (*danshaku*);

on March 5, he was dead. Hara formally assumed the presidency of the Seiyūkai on June 18, 1914.

The beginning of Hara's presidency was inauspicious. Opposition to the Seiyūkai was nearing high tide. An anti-Seiyū pattern had begun with the House of Peers' rejection of the Yamamoto cabinet's budget and Yamagata's repudiation of Hara as successor to Yamamoto. It developed into the Ōkuma-Dōshikai cabinet backed by Inoue and Yamagata. Suppression of the Seiyūkai by this growing anti-Seiyū coalition appeared inevitable unless Hara could act quickly and effectively. This was his first task as party president.

The key to the survival of the Seiyūkai was the Yamagata faction. It was imperative that Hara gain the confidence of Yamagata, convince him of the necessity and indestructibility of the Seiyūkai, and pre-empt Dōshikai influence in his faction. Because of Yamagata's dislike of Hara and the Seiyūkai, however, establishing contact with him was a complicated affair.

Hara began at the perimeter. He cultivated a close relationship with Gotō Shimpei, formerly a Katsura man and a leading anti-Seiyū figure. Gotō's influence in the Dōshikai, however, had been surpassed by Katō Komei and Ōura Kanetake and he was now estranged from that party. Gotō was valuable to Hara because he had ready access to Yamagata and his close supporter, General Terauchi.[24] Hara also established close ties with Miura Kanju, a Chōshū general widely known for his independent views and love for political intrigue. It was said that only "Kanju" could speak his mind freely and with impunity to Yamagata. Another important ally was Tanaka Giichi, also a Chōshū general in the Yamagata faction, who from this time gravitated toward Hara.[25] Through these men Hara received in detail pertinent news about the Yamagata faction.

Moreover, Hara arranged meetings with leading men in

the Yamagata faction (for example, Hirata Tōsuke and Kiyoura Keigo, who were bitter antagonists of his). These men did not become close to him as did Gotō and Tanaka, but he used them to transmit his feelings to Yamagata. He told them: "At present, the Genrō, the cabinet, and the opposition party are all working toward the destruction of the Seiyūkai. In spite of some failures, however, the Seiyūkai has contributed significantly to the nation. . . . Until now, the party has taken a moderate position, but if the Genrō and those in office should not give recognition to that party and seek to destroy it, we will have no choice, but, as a matter of defense . . . take an extreme position regarding the abolition of taxes and revision of the press and election laws." [26]

The message was at once a threat and a proposal for talks. In his reply, Yamagata cited the reasons for his hostility to the Seiyūkai: its rejection of the two divisions, its secret dealings with Katsura, and its ties with Satsuma. Hara immediately sent a conciliatory note to Yamagata in which he denied strong Seiyūkai opposition to the two divisions and disclaimed the existence of a binding Seiyūkai-Satsuma relationship. Through these exchanges, Yamagata informed Hara early in July that a meeting with him might be useful to discuss their differences. This was an important breakthrough for Hara, and he waited for an opportune moment to make maximum use of a meeting with Yamagata.

In mid-July, Yamagata's attitude toward the Ōkuma cabinet cooled. Yamagata was piqued with Foreign Minister Katō Kōmei's handling of foreign affairs. Yamagata distrusted the West and believed that the ultimate political settlement in Asia would involve a racial struggle between East and West; Katō felt close to the West and envisioned continued cooperation with the Western powers. Moreover, Yamagata was an anglophobe and wanted a rapprochement with Germany; Katō was an anglophile and wanted Japan to side with England against Germany. Finally, and above all, Yamagata expected, as a matter of custom, to be consulted on foreign policy; Katō rejected Genrō interference in cabinet affairs.[27]

Fully informed of Yamagata's growing displeasure with Katō, Hara timed his meeting with Yamagata accordingly. On August 10 Hara received a telegram from party headquarters at his home in Morioka, where he was vacationing, to return immediately to Tokyo. Rumors were spreading that Katō was on the verge of committing a "gross blunder," that is, declaring war on Germany. This was Hara's opportunity, for Yamagata was reported white with fury over the foreign policy of the "Englishman." Hara arranged for a meeting with Yamagata to "ascertain" the political situation.[28]

On August 14 Hara met with Yamagata in what turned out to be the first of a number of lengthy discussions. The two men talked for three hours, spending a substantial portion of the time reviewing the details of the Taishō Political Crisis. Yamagata admitted that Katsura had expected the Seiyūkai to submit to him, and went on to say that his ties with Katsura had been strained to a breaking point. As for the reforms, Yamagata felt he had been "easily taken." [29] The importance of the talk, however, was not its substance: strategy-wise, Hara grasped what he most needed to know — Ōkuma had not succeeded in establishing close links with the Yamagata faction. Equally as important, Yamagata, known for his reticence in the presence of enemies, had carried on a lengthy and frank talk with him for the first time.

Hara had established rapport with Yamagata. Yamagata agreed that they should meet frequently to discuss their outstanding differences, and to keep the channels of communication open at all times between his group and the Seiyūkai. Hara had filled the gap left by Katsura, and had

seized the initiative from Ōkuma and the Dōshikai to establish close lines of communication with Yamagata. This did
not mean that Yamagata would yield to the arguments of
Hara as Katsura had, but Hara could now openly express
his views to Yamagata. Pleased with his accomplishment,
Hara recorded what were undoubtedly the most generous
words he had ever had for Yamagata: "Yamagata is not one
to reveal his true feelings completely, but . . . I was able
to read generally what he had in mind. He is the eldest of
the Genrō, but he is mentally the most sound." [30]

Hara called on Yamagata on at least four occasions and
relayed numerous messages through Gotō Shimpei, Tanaka
Giichi, and Takahashi Korekiyo, trying to dissuade Yamagata of his anti-Seiyū bias by arguing the merits of government by the majority Seiyūkai. He pointed out that the
assumption of power by the minority Dōshikai was irregular, particularly so because that party's sole intent was to
defeat the Seiyūkai. Hara maintained that participation in
government by the majority party was a permanent aspect
of Japanese politics; thus, even if Yamagata were to support Ōkuma's plan to demolish the Seiyūkai, the result
would not be a multiparty system as Yamagata expected
but simply the establishment of another majority party in
place of the Seiyūkai. Hara insisted, therefore, that it was
folly to destroy the Seiyūkai since nothing would be gained
and much would be lost in the process. More specifically,
Hara warned Yamagata that his continued support of
Ōkuma would force the Seiyūkai to oppose the army's second bid for the two divisions; he made it perfectly clear,
however, that this was a purely tactical maneuver and that
the Seiyūkai was amenable on this point if Yamagata would
make a firm commitment to transfer power to Hara and the
majority Seiyūkai.[31] He knew that Yamagata needed the
Seiyūkai's majority in the Lower House to approve the two
divisions, but he would not place his party at Yamagata's

disposal, in the same way that he had refused to do so with Katsura, unless an exchange of power was involved.

Yamagata, however, could not accept Hara's terms because granting the prime ministership to Hara would mean conceding to the principle of majority party control of the cabinet. He therefore informed Hara through his messengers that because he could not agree with Hara's idea of party government he would continue to support Ōkuma's plan to defeat the Seiyūkai at the polls. On December 25, the Seiyūkai retaliated by voting down the cabinet's bill for the two army divisions. Then, as planned, Ōkuma dissolved the Diet and scheduled an election for March 25, 1915.

Outwardly, nothing seemed to have been settled between Hara and Yamagata. Yet the events of the next several months were to show that Hara had laid a firm basis for the party's survival in his talks with Yamagata. As a result of these talks, furthermore, Yamagata would begin reluctantly to move toward a reconciliation with Hara's political views.

DEFEATED AT THE POLLS: MARCH 25, 1915

The attempts to destroy the Seiyūkai were direct responses to the continued successes of that party. The first of these attempts came from Katsura during the Taishō Political Crisis. The second came from Ōkuma in 1915.

Seiyūkai leaders were prepared to suffer heavy, but not decisive, losses in the election called by Ōkuma. When the Diet convened in December 1914, the Seiyūkai controlled two hundred five seats. Twenty-one of these defected to a "neutral" group, reducing the Seiyūkai to one hundred eighty-four before the election. With these weaker members out of the party, the most pessimistic estimate by Seiyūkai leaders was that another twenty or so Diet men would be lost at the polls, still leaving the party with a minimum of a hundred sixty seats in the Lower House.[32] In the election of March 25, however, the Seiyūkai's membership in the

Diet was reduced to one hundred four. Meanwhile, the Dōshikai rose from ninety-five to one hundred fifty and the total number of Ōkuma backers in the Diet to two hundred forty.

The election was one of the most corrupt ever held in Japan. Under Ōura, the police carried out extensive door-to-door canvassing and curtailed Seiyūkai rallies. There was large-scale purchasing of votes. It was estimated that during the two days before the election, 1.6 million yen was used for purposes of bribery.[33]

But even without extensive bribing and interference at the polls the Ōkuma cabinet would probably have gained a majority of Lower House seats. In the first place, the Seiyūkai compromise with Yamamoto was unpopular, and although the Seiyūkai had vindicated itself somewhat by a few reforms the Siemens Incident had wiped out those gains. By Hara's own admission, the compromise with Yamamoto "turned out to be extremely damaging to the Seiyū-kai." [34] Also, a general feeling prevailed that the time was ripe for the emergence of a party to rival the Seiyūkai. Aside from a few staunch Seiyūkai newspapers, the press in general was solidly behind Ōkuma. Ōkuma took advantage of his popularity and waged a spirited campaign. Graduates of Waseda University throughout Japan were mobilized to campaign for Ōkuma. Unprecedented techniques were used: speeches by Ozaki endorsing Ōkuma were recorded and played everywhere on phonographs; Ōkuma himself barnstormed the country, delivering numerous speeches from train windows and platforms. Finally, Ōkuma was in power, which in itself was a powerful drawing card and doubly so because Japan was involved in war against Germany.[35]

To guarantee a Seiyūkai defeat, however, Ōkuma closed his eyes to bribery and chicanery. The forecast for the election came in December when Ōkuma appointed Ōura Kanetake, formerly minister of agriculture and commerce, as home minister. A postelection trial revealed that in December alone Ōura had spent sixty thousand yen to bribe seventeen Seiyūkai men into defecting from that party. Evidences from the trial also revealed that Ōura had accepted money from timid candidates currying his favor.[36]

Hara estimated that there had been extensive bribery and interference at the polls in about one-half of the prefectures.[37] Generally, it was in strategic and hotly contested areas that intervention took place. For example, in the city of Kanazawa, where the Dōshikai candidate had won, a post-election trial uncovered bribery and strong-arm tactics by local police in which transparent ballots were used so that those who had accepted bribes could not conceal their votes. In the re-election, the Seiyūkai candidate won decisively.[38]

The uncovering of widespread bribery under Ōura's direction did much damage to Ōkuma and the Dōshikai. The Dōshikai suddenly appeared no better than the Seiyūkai. This development played directly into Hara's defensive strategy vis-à-vis Yamagata.

In his talks with Yamagata, Hara had tried to convince him that a majority party was a permanent feature of the political order; that destroying the Seiyūkai would only result in another majority party. In early November 1914, Yamagata had begun to see the bitter irony of "charging the enemy," about which he had been so fond of telling Katsura, by having to employ still another "enemy." He hinted at relaxing his position a bit. Hara noted: "Yamagata said that he did not wish the destruction of one despotic majority merely to build another in its place." [39]

By late January 1915, Yamagata had softened further. Now he did not believe the Dōshikai could be an improvement over the Seiyūkai. He admitted that although he had wanted the annihilation of the Seiyūkai at first, he now wanted that party reduced only slightly and was more interested in its reformation than its destruction.[40]

When the Seiyūkai was defeated at the polls, Yamagata's attitude toward it underwent almost complete change: from bitter hatred to sympathy and tolerance. Saionji reported to Hara, a month after the election defeat, "I talked with Yamagata in a leisurely manner. He seemed to feel that the blow delivered against the Seiyūkai was excessive. Moreover, he seemed sympathetic to the Seiyūkai." [41]

HARA AND SEIYŪKAI RECOVERY

Yamagata's remark that the Seiyūkai should not be destroyed meant that the anti-Seiyū tide had reached its limit and by the time of the March election had begun to recede. Therefore, despite defeat at the polls, Hara was optimistic regarding his party's recovery.

A few months after the election, Hara was confident in his dealings with Yamagata. He told Yamagata that Ōura, Yamagata's one solid connection with the now dominant Dōshikai, was an illiterate fool. He records the remainder of their meeting as follows: "I had heard of Yamagata's loyalty to Emperor and love of country, but since I was actually doubtful of it, I asked him for his view on one point: how was power to be exchanged after the Genrō were gone. The selection of the prime minister could not be made by the Emperor as in some other countries. Since this was the case, . . . who, I asked him, would advise the throne on the matter of exchanging power after the Genrō had left the scene? Yamagata did not have a definite, or even a tentative, plan. He said that men like Saionji would take over. I said that Saionji lacked the prestige of the various Genrō. . . . Yamagata's answers were obscure. To test him, I said that if politicians would, in good faith, hand power over to the opposition party . . . this custom would establish stability on that issue. I told him that if the incumbent gained the right to name the successor, he might recommend someone from his own party, thus establishing one-party monopoly over power. That party would then suppress other groups, and when the reaction took place, there would be revolution. I said that these matters required consideration and probed him with various hypotheses. Yamagata said only that the despotism of parties must be stopped and that if there was an extreme situation, there would be a road to a peaceful settlement — he has no sound views at all. . . . In these respects, he is vastly different from Itō and has not given deep thought to matters concerning the state and the Imperial Household." [42]

Still, before long, Yamagata was heard saying: "Hara's views and my own do not differ. It is only his idea of developing an absolute majority . . . that I oppose. Aside from this, we have no differences." [43]

Hara had persuaded Yamagata to believe that the only point dividing them was the idea of "developing an absolute majority." Indeed, this was the crux of all previous differences between Hara and Yamagata that the latter now chose to minimize. Yamagata had reconciled himself to the painful truth that the Seiyūkai could not be annihilated because this task involved building another "despotic majority," as he put it. Thus, although Yamagata had repudiated Hara's candidacy for prime minister in March 1914, within several years he was ready to agree to a Hara cabinet. Yamagata had in effect discarded the notion of a small "government party" controlling a multiparty system in the Lower House and had accepted the inevitability of a powerful party, under Hara, directing the affairs of state.

When Ōkuma attempted to establish a rapprochement between Prime Minister Terauchi Masataka (Terauchi Cabinet, 1916–1918) and the majority Dōshikai in the summer of 1916, he was too late. Hara had seized the initiative long before and had established his influence securely within Terauchi's entourage, even while believing that men in that group would soon "annihilate themselves." [44] Hara, however, did not commit himself to a mutual understanding with Terauchi as he had done with Katsura: he knew he could remain neutral and still be able to direct the Seiyūkai over a course of recovery. Gotō Shimpei, who was now a Seiyūkai supporter, was home minister in Terauchi's cabinet. Mizuno Rentarō, a member of the Seiyūkai and Hara's intimate friend, was vice-home minister. Seiyū governors were once again in office, and at the next election (April 20, 1917) the Seiyūkai regained its commanding position in the Lower House — the Kenseikai, the successor to the Dōshikai, held one hundred nineteen seats, the Seiyūkai one hundred sixty.

Under lesser leadership, the Seiyūkai might not have withstood the anti-Seiyū challenges and might have fallen into disarray. Under Hara, the Seiyūkai accepted the challenge from Katsura, overcame it, and then directed the settlement during the Taishō Political Crisis. In the aftermath of that crisis, Hara outmaneuvered the anti-Seiyū coalition and finally gained the sympathy, if not the full support, of Yamagata, his traditional enemy. All major obstacles seemed now to be removed; the politics of compromise would persist. In these crucial years between 1913 and 1915, then, the Seiyūkai had shown its ability to recover and continue its determined march toward domination of the political structure. And by surviving as the most powerful group in the political order, it continued to stimulate the growth of a rival anti-Seiyū coalition, deepening the grooves that directed Japanese politics toward a two-party system.

11

Conclusion

In our age of sharp ideological cleavages, we often tend to view the political processes in other nations in terms of an ideological spectrum ranging from democracy to totalitarianism. A closer examination invariably uncovers highly complex situations which, due to ethnic, religious, geographic, economic, and demographic factors, cannot be adequately explained by the framework of political ideas alone.

And if an ideological interpretation is inadequate in our age, then for an understanding of historical developments such a doctrinal framework is even more likely to lead to distortions of reality. A case in point, certainly, is the history of the rise and fall of the parties in pre-World War II Japan. Here, the ideology most publicized was one that urged total opposition (*daha*) to the government, an ideal professed by a handful of politicians referred to as the hard faction. Because these few were usually supported by a vociferous, if often unrealistic, press, the myth grew that they were the true democrats and that their method of total opposition was best for establishing political democracy. But for some members of this hard faction, as in the case of Inukai, the belief in political democracy and the realistic pursuit of power were so closely intertwined that they differed little from the mainstream of compromisers. More than this, the seemingly consistent stand of the hards against compromises with "absolutism" plainly reflected their inability to adjust to political reality. Their strategy of total opposition was discredited by many party men soon after the Meiji Constitution was established, and the bankruptcy of their approach to politics was clearly and dramatically shown during the Taishō Political Crisis. In the final analysis it was adherence to an ambiguous strategy of total opposition, not adherence to pure ideals, that explains the steady decline of the hards. Perhaps a convincing argument can be made that Ozaki and Inukai, leaders of this group, were more committed to democratic ideals than most party men. Still, to view the mainstream of parties chiefly from the writings and utterances of men such as Ozaki and Inukai, however brilliant and well publicized they were, can lead to distortion.

Critics and historians, however, have been swayed by the myth of the ideological integrity of the hards and have tended to view the broad spectrum of party history through the eyes of these few. In particular, Marxist historians — the most energetic and persuasive school of historians in Japan — have made this view dominant in their general studies of political history. The sentiment of "total opposition" happens to fit neatly with their view of an inflexible and "absolutist" government that was opposed to political parties, theoretically leaving the parties no real recourse but to struggle against it in vigorous fashion. In their analysis, the Meiji Constitution of 1889 was an illiberal document that established absolutist government, and this government persisted because the parties discarded their strategy of total opposition to it, becoming content with compromises instead. It is not surprising, then, that Marxist historians are inclined to see party history through the eyes of the few who adamantly opposed compromises, and that they cast forty years of party experience (1890–1930) in the light of a futile and debilitating process destined to end in the disasters of the 1930's and 1940's.

This pessimistic view of party history has been most ardently presented by Marxist historians, but it is not restricted to them by any means. Minus Marxist verbiage, non-Marxist historians have also argued in this same vein. Thus, previous studies have emphasized that the Saionji cabinets between 1905 and 1915 were not party cabinets but were tools of the ruling cliques. They speak of Hara's compromises as evidence of a basic flaw in his political character and in the entire party movement; they describe the frequent eruption of public demonstrations as mass risings against absolutism; they depict the "hards," the intellectuals, and the liberal bourgeoisie leading the masses for the cause of political democracy; they describe the Movement for Constitutional Government as a reform effort that was undermined, as were its leaders Inukai and Ozaki, by halfhearted party leaders who cast their lot against the forces of democracy. They conclude that the politics of the period betray the weak and capricious nature of the parties. In the long run, they add, it was this weakness that ruined the parties.

This view has a certain validity. Ozaki and Inukai were undermined, large crowds did riot against Katsura "to destroy clique government," and the Saionji cabinets were not party cabinets. The analytical weakness of the above view is its dichotomization of the political world into the forces of democracy (the masses, intellectuals, bourgeoisie, and hards) and the forces of absolutism (Katsura, the army, the ruling cliques, and party leaders). This picture does not allow a full or accurate view of the political dynamics of the time. It explains the actions of party men in an oversimplified ideological scale; it fails to point out the actual ineffectiveness of men like Inukai and Ozaki as party leaders; and it removes party men from the context in which they decided and acted, glossing over the growth of Seiyū-kai power as a syndrome of political and economic relation-ships conditioning the behavior of party men.

Is it particularly important, after all, that party govern-ment was not established at a certain point between 1905 and 1915? Is it especially startling that the Saionji cabinets were not party cabinets or that Hara compromised with the likes of Katsura and Yamamoto? Power did not come into the hands of the parties suddenly and totally — this was simply not possible. Power could shift only gradually to-ward the parties and always in relation to other groups, the most important being the Yamagata faction entrenched in the House of Peers, the Privy Council, the bureaucracy, and, to a substantially lesser degree, those groups in the amorphous world of the bourgeoisie, the intellectuals, and the demonstrators.

In light of this picture of the parties in the institutional setting provided by the Meiji Constitution, it would not seem entirely accurate to make a sharp ideological distinc-tion between Ozaki, Inukai, and the exponents of sudden party cabinets on one hand, and Hara, Matsuda, and the compromisers, or gradualists, on the other. The distinction between the two groups was one of method. Ozaki and Inukai strongly opposed compromises and urged the im-mediate establishment of party government; they contra-dicted themselves, however, by accepting the institutional framework of the Meiji Constitution. Hara and Matsuda urged compromises and the gradual realization of party government; they contradicted their position by occasion-ally fanning the flames of opposition to the ruling cliques with whom they made bargains. Hara and Matsuda, how-ever, were closer to reality because they acted in accordance with the basic fact agreed upon by everyone, including Inukai and Ozaki, that the Meiji Constitution provided the legal framework for achieving party government.

From the 1890's, party men had set out to expand their influence, convinced that the constitutional order gave them enough leeway to advance toward party government. Even nonparty men, such as Kuga Katsunan — friend and colleague of Hara — had concluded that, although the constitution granted sovereignty to the Emperor, the political nexus in the Meiji order would be reduced, in the end, to the relationship between the cabinet and the Diet. In 1914, the ideas of Kuga were expanded and made more explicit by Yoshino Sakuzō, the champion of "Taishō democracy": "It is natural . . . for political customs to be born within the limits of law. For example, it is a basic principle of the constitution that the right to appoint ministers resides with the Emperor. It is justifiable, however, for the custom of party cabinets to develop within the framework of that principle. . . . Our Emperor never appoints a minister on his own discretion. . . . It is here that leeway exists for the emergence of political custom. Party cabinets will not in any way be an infringement of the constitution."[1] As long as party men accepted the basic institutional framework of the Meiji Constitution — an acceptance that continued until after the World War I period — their focus naturally fell on struggles for power in that setting.

The sustained growth of the parties, then, reflected above all the successful adjustment made by most party men to the tactics of compromise within the political structure. Although this meant discarding the strategy of "total opposition," the "outsider mentality" was never completely suppressed because it gave party men psychological sustenance (as in Hara); but the central aim of the parties turned toward infiltrating, usurping, and broadening the avenues of access into the bases of the ruling cliques. It is in this context that we can best understand the probings of the Seiyūkai under Hara into those areas of the government that could be opened to party influence. The ramifications of these probes do not suggest that the constitutional order was moving inevitably toward political democracy as conceived of in some Western countries. Still, they were not insignificant by any means, for in their constant probings party men shaped an approach to politics of lasting importance, an approach which might best be described as systematic political pragmatism.

There was, in the first place, a tough and unequivocal acceptance of tactical flexibility over an intimate attachment to ideology or abstract principles. Unlike some parties in Europe (those in Germany, for example[2]) the parties in Japan instinctively understood the negative implications of a "religious" commitment to clearly defined ideologies. They saw that this kind of attachment restricted the possibilities of adjusting differences among party factions within a powerful and comprehensive structure, and that it tended to produce instead a diffusion of power among multiparties. They also understood, therefore, that the axiom "politics is power" meant precisely that the farther away a party was from the responsibilities of power, the more likely it would be for that party to divide along ideological lines; and that the opposite was equally true — the greater the potential of a party to seize power, the less likely its chances to splinter. Although there were no pragmatists like Disraeli in Japan, carrying out a "sewage policy" to preserve aristocratic dignity, still, as in Great Britain, it was the realistic pursuit of power within the legal framework that carried the day.

This was clearly reflected in Hara's observations that there were no predetermined principles operating in history and that the collective strength of the parties would prevail over "arguments" in deciding the course of history. And it was entirely consistent with this political attitude of men like him to aim at seizing the key centers of political influence. Thus party men sought control over the cabinet first of all. Armed with the legal privileges of interpellation and blocking government legislation, especially the budget, and also with the threat of stirring public demonstrations against the government, they struck realistic compromises with Katsura and the Yamagata faction as a substitute for a regularized procedure for exchanging power.

The key feature to stress about these negotiations is the explicitness with which party men voiced their irreducible demands — for example, control of the next cabinet and maintenance of the positive economic policy — while always leaving the door open for concessions. A good example was the mutual understanding of 1911 (Chapter 4), in which Hara gave to railroad developments a content and direction that meshed with Seiyūkai plans for expansion and diverged sharply from the aims of Katsura, Gotō, and military leaders. It was this flexible approach of giving here, taking advantage there, that gave continuity to Seiyūkai policies.

Tactical flexibility, however, was not synonymous with day-to-day opportunism (or *hiyorimishugi*, as this is referred to), in which policies were determined by the personal whims of a few ambitious men. It went hand in glove with a set of strategic priorities which were generally agreed upon by the party rank and file, giving this approach a consistent logical content. In the short run, the aim was party penetration of the government at all levels — trying to divide the House of Peers above and abolishing the *gun* below, and coordinating the control of government spending and of bureaucratic appointments with pressures from the party throughout the country. In the end, the expectation of party men was complete control of the centers of government. Hara and those around him were not flaming democrats as was Yoshino Sakuzō (see quotation above), but like most party men they accepted the idea of Lower House control of the cabinet. The different tactical moves, then, were stitched together by a set of strategic objectives which, while limiting the scope of political action for party men, gave consistency and continuity to the politics of compromise.

Directly related to the above, the uninterrupted growth of the parties after 1905 can be distinguished from earlier sporadic developments by a greater degree of structural unity in the parties. Clearly, the sustained growth of party influence depended to a considerable degree upon the ability of party leaders to construct a unified and durable party hierarchy — one which would encourage factions to adjust their differences on the basis of a realistic agreement that unity was the key to the satisfaction of political ambitions.

In the case of the Seiyūkai, substantial strides were taken in this direction. Greater regularity was established in relationships between the regions and party headquarters by satisfying local economic interests, thus strengthening vertical ties in the party. Again, it must be understood that gaining largesse to satisfy the public was not the primary end. The main objective here, as always, was the strategic use of money to consolidate the party: by using government funds via the bureaucracy, the party sought to stabilize electoral bases throughout the country, and, by remaining firmly united at the top, it forced Katsura to face the same majority with the same set of demands over an extended period. For these practical reasons, party leaders in the executive staff took great pains to prevent the growth of "a party within a party," carefully watching and coordinating the activities of the eight regional groups at party headquarters with branch offices at the regional and prefectural levels.

The development of a highly organized party structure of the sort that could sway the "impersonal" bureaucracy was viewed with considerable alarm by the Genrō and liberal critics in the press alike. For understandable reasons, they viewed with great concern the construction of a unified national organization by party men to manipulate the bureaucracy in pincer movements from above and below. This manipulation produced a massive interest structure in which local men of influence, governors and their staffs, as well as party men at all levels were interlaced from the local power base on up — blurring, especially at the local level, the division of labor between legislators and administrators, and fostering corruption on an unprecedented scale. But if this meshing of party and bureaucracy into an interest network was corrupt, in the sense that pork-barreling is corrupt, it was also crucial in buttressing the persistent growth of party power.

And finally, in a negative vein, although party structure was national in scope its base was narrow, its leadership elitist. Reminiscent of Michels' famous injunction regarding European parties that organization breeds oligarchy, we find with growing frequency in the press of this time commentaries on the emerging "party oligarchy" (*tōbatsu*). And the reasons for this elitist tendency are not hard to find.

Because party men were agreed that the survival of their parties as effective groups depended upon bargaining at close quarters near the top of the government, they agreed to orderly exchanges of power and rejected the strategy of staging anti-clique demonstrations each year. This concession, which men like Katsura insisted upon as a condition for talks, was also grounded in the belief that they could not integrate into their strategies the demands of the politically involved public for the immediate establishment of pure party cabinets and the sudden overthrow of the ruling cliques. With considerable justification, they viewed these demands as unrealistic and therefore restrictive of their flexible approach to power. Unlike England, where the demands of the public tended to be less extreme and, broadening the electorate and the party base gave greater flexibility to party leaders, in Japan it was precisely by restricting the size and quality of the base that party politicians maximized their negotiating strengths at the top.

They left their ties with the general public tenuous and vague, relying on it for political support only in such situations of dire need as the Taishō Political Crisis, when the politics of compromise had broken down. Generally they regarded the public — as Weber tended to[3] — as passive and inchoate, to be influenced and used as a means to power. Hence, they struck ties with men outside the main political structure only insofar as these ties had strategic value for their drives within that structure. And since the electorate was limited (its expansion was not a political issue at this time) it was quite natural that the attachments of party politicians to business leaders and local men of influence would be closer, their ties with the general public less binding. Indeed, for broad segments of society political loyalty continued to bypass the party-bureaucracy-Diet interest nexus, proceeding directly to the Emperor instead. Interest and loyalty, in short, never became one, and this no doubt reduced the role of the parties as a stabilizing force in a rapidly industrializing country.

But if the parties failed in this important respect, as many in Europe did also, they, and the Seiyūkai in particular, succeeded in another respect. They delivered a major impact on the ruling cliques above them, dramatically undermining their unity and convincing the best among them that the parties were unavoidable "luxuries" in the political order.

At every level of the political structure — from the central bureaucracy through the prefectural governments to the *gun* and on down to the local men of power — the Seiyūkai compelled men of influence regardless of political leanings to come to terms with it. Throughout the country, men in politics and business (many whose education and temperament made them more sympathetic to the "impartial" Genrō) were pressed to join the Seiyūkai, or to oppose it at great risk, or, at least, not to openly defy it. And above all, at the very top, it caused irreparable cracks in the once-solid bloc of Yamagata bureaucrats. The Privy Council and the army backed down before a strong show of party strength. Yamagata's most talented followers, meanwhile, became party men, Katsura, Ōura, and Gotō forming the Dōshikai in 1913 and Tanaka Giichi drifting toward the Seiyūkai in 1914 and becoming its president ten years later.

With each Seiyūkai advancement, the exclusiveness of the ruling cliques became less certain. It was neither death of the Genrō nor paucity of talent among their protégés that sufficiently explains their loss of immunity. By enhancing its power the Seiyūkai, in fact, from 1905 on, prevented this Meiji elite from perpetuating itself and the style of rule commonly called transcendental government. It was not an accident that men of Satsuma — Admiral Yamamoto Gonnohyōe and bureaucrat Tokonami Takejirō — gravitated toward the Seiyūkai. And it was certainly not by accident that men of considerable talent such as Generals Katsura and Terauchi Masataka, and Peers Kiyoura Keigo and Hirata Tōsuke — all protégés of Genrō Yamagata — were thwarted, without exception, in their ultimate political ambitions.

To some among the ruling cliques, their loss of unity was cause for great fear and resentment. This was perhaps less true of Yamagata, who reconciled himself in the end to the idea of a strong party directing the affairs of state, than of his underlings who clung to their positions in the House of Peers (their "isolated fortress," in Hara's words) waiting for the chance to purge the political system of party venom and restore the lofty principle of transcendental government. To others, this called for immediate and decisive countermoves against the parties, as, for example, the concerted efforts of the Yamagata faction to defeat Hara's plan to abolish the *gun* and to purge Seiyūkai affiliates from the House of Peers.

Above all, the countermoves against the Seiyūkai led willy-nilly to the formation of complicated political alliances around another party to constantly check and countercheck the Seiyūkai, further intensifying the involvements of all party men in a circumscribed arena of political struggle. This political situation was distinctive of Taishō Japan: it was a situation in which the growth of two rival party alignments, Seiyū and anti-Seiyū, had become the main focus of power relationships, pre-empting the possibility of multiparties. Unlike continental Europe, where, as Duverger reports, "multipartyism" was the prevailing tendency (with as many as six to ten bona fide parties in countries such as Germany, France, Italy, Holland, Denmark, Sweden, etc.),[4] in Japan a third, fourth, or fifth party — be it "socialist," "government," or "center" — was simply not possible. All political leaders, regardless of their ideological orientation, were agreed that the strongest possible coalition would be required to counter the Seiyūkai.

This dynamic tendency toward two parties, however, should not be taken casually as a development toward an orderly or "healthy" system of constitutional government. The history of the thirties has shown otherwise. Although there was great potential in this development in the sense that there were now two relatively clearly defined rival alignments seeking out policy alternatives in a competitive context, it was, at the same time, a development fraught with difficulties. In disrupting the unity of the ruling cliques, the parties jeopardized smooth political transitions under firm and consistent leadership. For tactical reasons, the rival party alignments were compelled to leave the limits of political change vague, intensifying, in the teens and twenties, the feeling of uncertainty among those in positions of responsibility — the "incumbents," including party men — as to where the limits should be drawn and, above all, by whom. Thus, as the Seiyūkai grew more powerful, the political alignments became that much more complex, the government that much more unwieldy. Not until the emergency of war beset Japan would the leaders of government act again with the swiftness and decisiveness of the narrow ruling cliques that fashioned the Meiji revolution.

It is these themes — Seiyūkai penetration of the governmental structure at all levels, the fear, resentment, and uncertainty it caused among the ruling cliques and the complex power alignments it produced — that the political developments between 1905 and 1915 take on their fullest meaning. And it is precisely in this context that the Taishō Political Crisis must be assessed: it was at this particular juncture that Katsura came to the realistic conclusion that he must break his entente with Hara and risk political conflict with him. Recognizing that the politics of compromise was detrimental to him and those behind him, Katsura launched his attempt to reintegrate all political groups into a united party based on the principle of transcendental government. This plan proved abortive, as we have seen, because in severing ties with Hara he became involved in a political struggle he could not cope with. The Seiyūkai met and overcame his test of strength, rallying party cadres throughout the country to direct public rallies and exploiting men like Admiral Yamamoto of Satsuma to preserve the policies of party expansion. As a result, Katsura suffered a staggering personal defeat, making decisions and promises that contradicted the very principle of transcendental government that he had set out to save.

But because Katsura disrupted the key tie with Hara, which had fostered the Seiyūkai and impeded the growth of a second party, his tactical move against the Seiyūkai brought into existence a new countervailing alliance which continued to resist the Seiyūkai. Despite Katsura's belief in a one-party system — a "united constitutional party" — or Yamagata's in a multiparty system, the trend persisted toward two parties as gravitational centers of power.

The central issue in the Taishō Political Crisis, then, was not a struggle between the "people," led by Inukai and Ozaki, on the one hand and "absolutism," represented by Katsura, on the other. In spite of his commitment to the ideals of party government, Inukai did not lead the Movement for Constitutional Government to spread political democracy. Like Hara, the movement was a strategic weapon, first against Katsura and the reform faction, and second to force the Seiyūkai into a union with him. His plan to discredit his enemies by gaining power through the Seiyūkai was at least as realistic as that of his rivals to join with Katsura against the Seiyūkai. As for Ozaki, his recognition of the need to use the movement for purposes of some reforms was offset by contradictory activities, ineffectiveness as leader of the hard faction in the Seiyūkai, and almost exclusive reliance on continued public demonstrations which was tactically unsound. Although both men were ostensibly the directors of the movement, and although there were sincere devotees of political democracy — intellectuals, students, men of the press — actually involved in it, the movement was, in fact, substantially a Seiyūkai affair.

This party gave the movement its structure and direction: it controlled the Lower House, and although men of the party were attached to the idea of party cabinets, their actions were conditioned more fundamentally by the specific struggle at hand and by the problems of increasing party influence. They feared a Diet dissolution because dissolution entailed a Katsura-controlled election. They were committed to recover power quickly because power, translated into economic benefits, guaranteed the security of their local power bases and the overall unity of the party as well.

Almost from the start, they set out to use the movement to preserve, not destroy, the politics of compromise. And so they did not engineer the settlement of the Taishō Political Crisis out of caprice, as is often suggested; they assessed power realities and negotiated it from a position of strength to preserve the policies of party expansion and, with it, a powerful Seiyūkai.

But the mistaken assumption that this crisis indeed involved such a revolutionary struggle between the "people" and "absolutism" led critics of the time and historians subsequently to judge that event in terms of exaggerated expectations for sweeping structural changes. In this way the Taishō Political Crisis was made to seem, as G. M. Trevelyan said of Europe in 1848, a turning point in modern history that did not turn. While the expectation of radical structural changes was unwarranted, still, in the context of political interactions made possible by the growth of the Seiyūkai, the Taishō Political Crisis was a critical turning point. In that party's show of strength, in Katsura's decisive move to form a party, and in the loss of cohesiveness in the Yamagata faction, the crisis of 1912–1913 dramatically reaffirmed the over-all trend of parties to move steadily into the mainstream of power relationships in the Meiji constitutional order.

The politics of compromise was intended to overcome the structural disadvantages of the Meiji political order and the Yamagata faction imbedded in it. There was more to the efforts of Diet men than an unbridled pursuit of power, although their actions struck observers to be indeed little more than that. Clearly, however, the quest for political power left indelible marks on the behavior of party men, a fact most readily apparent in the case of Hara Kei, the champion of party expansion.

Between 1905 and 1915 Hara was home minister three times. Without his vigilant and adroit leadership, the growth of the Seiyūkai is inconceivable. A person less attached to political reality and lacking his clarity of position and aims could not have succeeded against Katsura and Yamagata. Hara's position was not an easy one: facing him were the impeding factors of structure and power distribution, while below him was the party rank and file constantly pressuring him for more power and pure party cabinets. Hara's ability to stand in this position and steer the party over an expansive course made him a politician without peer in his day.

Hara transformed the Seiyūkai, divided and uncertain as to its future, into a powerful group. He worked faithfully to preserve party unity. He encouraged leaders of the eight regional groups to end their petty rivalries; he manipulated them. As party leader and then as president, he toured the countryside giving prestige to local Diet men and promising a positive economic policy to influential leaders. At the top, he negotiated firmly to gain power. He applied this power to further build the party; and, on the basis of party strength, he told Katsura and Yamagata that history was on his side, that the Seiyūkai was indestructible.

Hara was not creative; he was not a political leader with great vision. It would be erroneous to credit him with a more coherent system of political ideas than he possessed. Nevertheless, it would be unfair to paint him as no more than a skillful opportunist with reactionary tendencies. Hara was a strategist with conviction. He was genuinely devoted to his party and stubbornly opposed issues that might undermine the bases of the rank and file. Thus he defeated Katsura's plan for broad-gauge lines and kept railroad expansion on a "positive" basis during the Second Saionji Cabinet. He did not compromise his belief that ultimately the majority in the Lower House would control the Meiji political structure. From 1914 on, Hara knew that the one stumbling block to his prime ministership was his dedication to party. Inoue and Yamagata persuaded him that the coveted office was his if he would but surrender his commitment to party government. Hara refused and turned a lifelong friendship with Inoue into a bitter relationship.

Hara's rise as party leader, however, was rooted in the politics of party expansion. Because of this, certain patterns of behavior became ingrained in him and party men in general during this period. Prime Minister Hara in 1918 was still Home Minister Hara. Thoughts of structural reform and social legislation were, at best, secondary and tertiary considerations. During his ministry (1918-1921), Hara abolished the *gun*, established small electoral districts, launched a massive eight hundred-million-yen railroad expansion program, dredged harbors with unprecedental zeal, "promoted higher education" and tied it to the pork barrel, overrode objections from the army and opened top posts in Korea and Taiwan to party men, and, finally, weakened the House of Peers through his tough and persistent "House of Peers operations."

Meanwhile, "the trends of the time," to use Hara's own favorite phrase, had gone beyond "party expansion." The relative ideological homogeneity of the decade before 1915 had begun to break down due to the rapid influx of political ideas following World War I. The burning questions of the day were how and in what areas the parties would exercise their newly acquired power. The parties were ill prepared to solve these questions. By necessity, party men had committed their energies to the sharpening of techinques to seize power. Like Itō in the 1890's, Hara might possibly have responded to the new "trends" and provided the leadership being demanded in the post-World War I period. Regardless, the political foundations that he built between 1905 and 1915 were firm. Although not loved in his day, he was, like all politicians with extraordinary power, admired and envied by many, disliked by many more. His dominance in the political world was certain to continue well into the 1920's. Perhaps fate extended a kind hand, however, in ending his political career at the pinnacle of power.

On November 4, 1921, at the age of 66, Hara was fatally stabbed by a young ultrarightest in Tokyo Station. He had been on his way to a regional party rally in western Japan.

Appendix A

EXAMPLES OF TOKYO IMPERIAL UNIVERSITY GRADUATES WHO HELD THE OFFICE OF BUREAU CHIEF
OF REGIONAL AFFAIRS AND WHO AFFILIATED THEMSELVES WITH A POLITICAL PARTY

Name	Home prefecture	Graduated from Tokyo Imperial University	Previous position	Bureau chief of regional affairs	Party affiliation
Inoue Tomoichi	Hokkaidō	1893	?	1898–	?
Shibata Kamon*	Yamaguchi	1890	?	1899–1900	Dōshikai
Yoshiwara Saburō	Chiba	1899	Governor of Okayama	1902–1905	Seiyūkai
Tokonami Takejirō**	Kagoshima	1890	Governor of Akita	1906–1911	Seiyūkai
Mizuno Rentarō*	Tokyo	1892	Bureau chief of civil engineering	1911–1912	Seiyūkai
Yuasa Kurahei*	Fukushima	1898	Post in secretariat of home ministry	1912–1913	Dōshikai
Kobashi Ichita**	Kumamoto	1898	Bureau chief of sanitation	1913–1914	Seiyūkai
Watanabe Shozaburō	Okayama	1896	Governor of Tokushima	1914–1917	Dōshikai
Soeda Keiichirō	Fukui	1898	Governor of Yamagata	1917–1920	Seiyūkai
Tsukamoto Seiji*	Hyōgo	1902	Bureau chief of social affairs	1920–1922	Kenseikai-Minseitō
Ushio Shigenosuke*	Shimane	1907	Bureau chief of sanitation	1922–	Seiyūkai

* Appointed to House of Peers
** Elected to Lower House

Sources: Ijiri Tsunekichi, ed. *Rekidai kenkan roku* (Tokyo, 1925), pp. 111–112; Kuribayashi Teiichi, *Chihō kankai no hensen* (Tokyo, 1930).

Appendix B

Kawashima Junkan. Appointed governor of Shiga by Hara in January 1907 after having served in various minor prefectural posts. Transformed Shiga prefecture from a Kokumintō stronghold into a Seiyūkai-controlled prefecture. Suspended by Home Minister Ōura in 1913; re-appointed by Hara in 1913 to the governorship of Fukui.

Nakamura Junkurō. Appointed from minor prefectural posts to governor of Fukui prefecture in December 1907. In 1911 promoted to the important post of governor of Hiroshima, and in 1914 to the highly coveted post of chief administrator of Hokkaidō. (Each promotion was due to Hara.) Gained his reputation as a Seiyū governor with his extensive building projects in Hiroshima on behalf of the Seiyūkai.

Oka Kishichirō. Graduate of Tokyo Imperial University, 1891. Advanced steadily in the bureaucracy and finally became governor of Akita prefecture (1904) and then governor of Tottori prefecture (1910). Appointed by Hara in 1913 to police bureau chief and in 1918, again by Hara, to metropolitan police chief. Known for his dedication to Hara.

Hata Toyosuke. Graduate of Tokyo Imperial University, 1896. After various minor prefectural positions, appointed by Hara to governorship of Akita prefecture in 1912. Suspended in 1915 by Home Minister Ōura; turned to politics and was elected six times to the Lower House. A high-ranking Seiyūkai leader of the 1920's.

Andō Kensuke. Studied Russian at Tokyo Foreign Language School and French under Nakae Chōmin. Established Seiyūkai ties while governor of Ehime prefecture in 1904. In 1909 suspended by Home Minister Hirata Tōsuke. In 1911, appointed by Hara to the governorship of Nagasaki. In 1912 suspended by Home Minister Ōura. Reappointed by Hara to Niigata prefecture in 1913; suspended in 1914 by Ōura. An admitted Seiyū governor; carried on a bitter feud with Izawa Takio, an anti-Seiyū governor.

Kagawa Teru. Strongly committed to the Seiyūkai. Publicly asserted that a governor would not be able to carry out his job without a party affiliation. From a jobless condition, appointed governor of Fukui prefecture by Hara in 1913. Suspended by Home Minister Ōura in 1915; re-appointed by Hara in 1919 as governor of Okayama prefecture.

Minami Hiroshi. Graduate of Tokyo Imperial University, 1896. Entered the bureaucracy as a cabinet secretary and became chief cabinet secretary under Saionji in 1906. Appointed governor of Fukuoka prefecture by Hara in 1913 and suspended by Ōkuma in 1915. Under Hara's auspices, appointed to the House of Peers in 1912. Referred to as a "pure" Seiyū governor.

Kasai Shin'ichi. Graduate of Tokyo Imperial University, 1892. A Seiyū governor at Iwate, Shizuoka and Okayama prefectures. Well known for his strong-arm policies against Seiyūkai opposition, especially in Shizuoka prefecture during 1913–1914. Appointed to the House of Peers by Prime Minister Hara in 1918.

Mori Masataka. Graduate of Tokyo Imperial University, 1893. A Seiyū governor, notorious for excessively partisan policies — using development of roads, railroads, harbors, etc., for party expansion. A Hara appointee in 1907 from a minor prefectural post to the governorships of Ibaraki, Akita and Niigata prefectures. At these prefectures, especially at Niigata, Mori consistently pushed pro-Seiyukai policies, purged the local administration including school principals, and also terminated projects (especially schools) benefiting the minority party (Kokumintō), which led to bloody riots in the prefectural assembly. Suspended by Katsura in 1912, re-appointed by Hara in 1913 to Miyagi, suspended by Ōkuma in 1914, and re-appointed by Hara in 1916 to Shiga prefecture and then to governorship of Miyagi in 1918 during Hara's first cabinet. Finally, in 1921, appointed to the House of Peers by Hara.

Kawaguchi Hikoji. Graduate of Tokyo Imperial University, 1903. Promoted by Hara to a bureau chief in Ōita prefecture in 1906. Became a staunch Seiyūkai supporter during this period, and in 1913 was promoted by Hara to governor of Ōita. Expelled by Home Minister Ōura in 1914, appointed governor of Akita (1916), later governor of Kumamoto prefecture (1918), and then of Aichi — all through Hara's auspices. Opposition to the Seiyūkai was strong in each of these areas: Kawaguchi managed to force the local bureaucracy to join the Seiyūkai (for example, at Kumamoto even post office chiefs joined).

EXAMPLES OF ANTI-SEIYŪ GOVERNORS

Kurogane Taigi. Graduate of Tokyo Imperial University, 1896. Worked as anti-Seiyū governor in Ōita and Yamaguchi prefectures. Reduced Seiyūkai party to a minority status in Ōita by using economic pressures; for example, by favoring "anti-Seiyūkai" banks. Rose to rank of bureau chief in central bureaucracy, then ran for a seat in the Lower House (1920) as a Kenseikai candidate.

Kumagai Kiichirō. Graduate of Tokyo Imperial University, 1892. "Anti-Seiyū" policies led to suspension by Hara in 1908. Re-appointed shortly thereafter by Katsura to Yamagata prefecture (1909). Suspended by Hara in 1913. Re-appointed by Ōkuma to Ishikawa prefecture (1914). Treated post as a weapon to build the Dōshikai — for example, granting road and school projects on condition that the recipients join the Dōshikai. Actively interfered at polls in election of 1915 on behalf of the Dōshikai.

Shimooka Chūji. Graduate of Tokyo Imperial University, 1895. Appointed governor of Akita prefecture in 1908. In 1912, appointed by Katsura to bureau chief of agricultural affairs. Served as vice-home minister under Ōkuma in 1914 while his close friend and classmate, Hamaguchi Yūkō, served as vice-finance minister. The two ran successfully for seats to the Lower House in 1915 as Dōshikai candidates and became party leaders of the 1920's.

Izawa Takio. Graduate of Tokyo Imperial University, 1895. In first gubernatorial appointment under Katsura (1909) to Ehime prefecture, tried to "clean up" politics left behind by his predecessor, a staunch Seiyū governor, Andō Kensuke; in doing so came to be viewed as an anti-Seiyū governor. Suspended by Hara in 1911; re-appointed by Katsura in 1913 to Niigata again to "clean up" after Mori Masataka. Suspended by Hara in 1913; re-appointed by Okuma in 1914 to metropolitan police chief; in 1915 appointed to the House of Peers by Ōkuma. There continued "anti-Seiyū" and pro-Kenseikai activities together with Kamiyama Mitsunoshin and Yuasa Kurahei — two others with anti-Seiyū backgrounds.

Kubota Kiyochika.   Graduate of Tokyo Imperial University, 1895. A Hara appointee from prefectural bureaucracy to governor of Tochigi prefecture in 1906. Later through contacts with Gotō Shimpei (worked together on management of Manchurian railroad) rose to post of bureau chief of civil engineering in 1913. Promoted to vice-home minister during Ōkuma's cabinet (1914–1916).

Source: Kuribayashi Teiichi, *Chihō kankai no hensen* (Tokyo, 1930).

Appendix C

SEIYŪKAI MEN AT REGIONAL RALLIES OF THE MOVEMENT
FOR CONSTITUTIONAL GOVERNMENT, JANUARY–
FEBRUARY 1913

Location	Date	Seiyūkai representatives
Ishikawa	January 9	Ozaki Yukio, Matsuda Genji
Shiga	January 10	Motoda Hajime, Sugawara Den, Ogawa Heikichi
Kyoto	January 11	Ozaki Yukio, Ogawa Heikichi
Fukui	January 11	Sugita Teiichi, Sugawara Den
Osaka (general rally for western Japan)	January 12–13	Takekoshi Yosaburō, Ogawa Heikichi, Ozaki Yukio (also Inukai Tsuyoshi, Seki Naohiko of the Kokumintō)
Kobe	January 14	Ozaki Yukio (also Inukai)
Shizuoka	January 14	Ebara Soroku, Takekoshi Yosaburō
Iwate	January 14	Itakura Nakaba, Saitō Hanji
Gumma	January 15	Motoda Hajime, Kikuchi Butoku
Niigata	January 16	Tomizu Kanjin
Yamagata	January 16	Yamamoto Teijirō
Ibaraki	January 16	Sugita Teiichi, Matsuda Genji
Saitama	January 16	Ebara Soroku
Tochigi	January 17	Ōkubo Kishichi
Hokkaidō	January 23	Kinoshita Seitarō
Akita	January 25	Mito Chūzō, Mochizuki Keisuke

Aomori	January 26	Takekoshi Yosaburō, Mochizuki Keisuke
Saitama	January 26	Matsuda Genji, Koyama Tanizō
Nagoya	January 26	Ozaki Yukio, Nakamura Keiji
Gumma	January 27	Inoue Tokutarŏ, Shida Yoshio
Tochigi	January 28	Sugita Teiichi, Okada Taizō
Nagano	February 1	Kosaka Junzō, Okabe Jirō, Kazama Reisuke, Ozaki Yukio, Koyama Kango
Saitama	February 1	Tanaka Yoshitake, Takekoshi Yosaburō
Osaka (second general rally for western Japan)	February 1	Matsuda Masahisa, Matsuda Genji, Tsuruhara Teikichi, Ozaki Yukio (also Inukai of the Kokumintō)

Major Rallies in Tokyo

January 7, 11, 14	Rally of the 18 member groups of the Movement for Constitutional Government
January 16	Non-Diet party groups (*ingaidan*) of both parties (Ozaki and Inukai took part)
January 17	National Newspaper Reporters' Conference of 350 delegates (Ozaki and Inukai took part)
January 18	Informal speech rally (*konshinkai*)
January 19	Annual Seiyūkai and Kokumintō party conferences
January 22	Non-Diet party groups (*ingaidan*) of both parties
January 24	Second general rally of Movement (first general rally held in December)
February 5	"Rally of the White Mark" — a white rose symbolized the Movement
February 9	Bi-partisan speech rally
February 11	Rally celebrating twenty-fifth anniversary of promulgation of the Meiji Constitution

Sources: *Seiyū*, No. 149 (January, 1913), p. 70; also No. 150 (March, 1913), pp. 60–61. See also Ueda Sotoo, *Taishō no seihen* (Tokyo, 1913), pp. 75–76; Bokugaku Sanjin, *Taishō ishin seihen no shinsō* (Tokyo, 1913), pp. 107–113.

Notes

NOTES TO CHAPTER 1

1. Yoshino Sakuzō, *Gendai no seiji* (Modern politics; Tokyo, 1915), p. 62.

2. The first to receive this special commendation were Itō Hirobumi and Kuroda Kiyotaka in 1899. Subsequently, the following received the same recognition: Yamagata Aritomo, Matsukata Masayoshi, Inoue Kaoru, Ōyama Iwao, Katsura Tarō, Ōkuma Shigenobu, and Saionji Kimmochi. Shinobu Seizaburō, *Taishō demokurashii shi* (A history of Taishō democracy; Tokyo, 1954), I, 64.

3. Miyake Setsurei, *Meiji shisō shōshi* (A short intellectual history of Meiji; Tokyo, 1913), esp. pp. 14–24, 63–94; Ozaki Yukio, *Rikken kinnō ron* (On constitutional loyalism; Tokyo, 1918), esp. pp. 2–23; Nakano Seigō, *Meiji minken shi ron* (A history of the popular rights movement in Meiji; Tokyo, 1913), especially the general remarks on pp. 495–502, which explain the framework of his analysis of the parties in the Meiji period. (Nakano also contributed regularly to the journal, *Nihon oyobi nihonjin*, which was edited by Miyake Setsurei; any one of his articles in this period reflect these views.) Kunō Osamu and Tsurumi Shunsuke, *Gendai Nihon no shisō* (Thought in modern Japan; Tokyo, 1956), esp. p. 128.

4. Kunō and Tsurumi, *Gendai Nihon no shisō*, pp. 126–127.

5. Ozaki Yukio, *Nihon kensei shi o kataru* (Reflections on Japanese constitutional history; Tokyo, 1938), I, 456.

6. A stimulating discussion along these lines in Oka Yoshitake's *Yamagata Aritomo* (Biography of Yamagata; Tokyo, 1961), pp. 45–48, and his *Kindai Nihon no seijika* (Politicians of modern Japan; Tokyo, 1960), pp. 13–16. See also Ozaki, *Kensei shi o kataru*, I, 456–457; and Toyabe Shuntei, *Shuntei zenshū* (Collected works of Toyabe; Tokyo, 1909), I, 1–54, 154–155. Toyabe was a brilliant and prolific political critic at the turn of the 20th century.

7. *Hara Kei nikki* (Diary of Hara; Tokyo, 1951), VI, 285 (July 14, 1915).

8. Oka, *Yamagata Aritomo*, pp. 45–72. A typical example of a

staunch Yamagata follower was Kiyoura Keigo (1850–1942). Kiyoura began as a minor bureaucrat in Saitama prefecture in the mid-1870's. In the early 1880's he established ties with Yamagata, who promoted him to chief of police (1884–1891). In 1891 he was appointed to the House of Peers under Yamagata's sponsorship. In 1896–1897, he was minister of justice, in 1898–1900 home minister, and in 1901–1905 minister of justice. He became the leading figure in the Yamagata-controlled Kenkyūkai, the most powerful group in the House of Peers. From 1906 on, Kiyoura also served in the Privy Council. Oka, *Yamagata Aritomo*, p. 55; Rōjō Gakujin (Uzaki Kumakichi) *Batsujin to tōjin* (Oligarchs and party men; Tokyo, 1913), pp. 84–85.

9. The words of Gotō Shimpei, quoted in Irie Kan'ichi, *Yamagata Kō no omokage* (Biographical sketches of Yamagata; Tokyo, 1922), pp. 279–280.

10. Tanaka Giichi, for example, described Yamagata's strength in these words: "The Prince [Yamagata] was extremely stern in the presence of others, but on the other hand, he was very warm. Once he accepted the services of another, he looked after that person's welfare from then on — he was not one to discard [those who served him]. Once a person had close contact with the Prince he invariably worked for the Prince from then on. This was what sustained his [Yamagta's] power, and was, moreover, the basis for his success. In other words, the group that surrounded the Prince never suffered from frequent splits." (Quoted in Irie, p. 228.)

11. This was O-Koi, a former geisha who became Katsura's favorite. Her two-volume memoir is a treasure of interesting anecdotes of Katsura and other leaders of the time. Andō Teru, *O-Koi monogatari* (Memoirs of O-Koi), and *Zoku O-Koi monogatari* (Sequel to the memoirs of O-Koi; Tokyo, 1927).

12. Maeda Renzan, *Rekidai naikaku monogatari* (A chronological account of cabinets; Tokyo, 1961), I, 65–67. The election was held under police control — this included censorship of the press, control over travel, and prohibition of public meetings. Directing the affair were Yamagata's men: Home Minister Shinagawa Yajirō, Vice-Home Minister Shirane Sen'ichi, and Chief of Police Komatsubara Eitarō, and directly under him, Ōura Kanetake.

13. Oka, *Kindai no seijika*, pp. 15–16 and the entire section; Oka, *Yamagata Aritomo*, pp. 52–85.

14. Ozaki, *Kensei shi o kataru*, I, 436–449.

15. *Hara nikki*, II sequel, 411 (Dec. 4, 1906).

16. *Hara nikki*, III, 294–295 (Apr. 7, 1909).

NOTES TO CHAPTER 2

1. I am indebted in this and the next two chapters to Professor Mitani Taichirō's valuable study on Hara's leadership, "Seitō seiji kakuritsu katei ni okeru seiji shidō to sono jōkyō, Hara Kei o chūshin to shite" (Political leadership and conditions in the emergence of party government, with special emphasis on Hara Kei); *Kokka gakkai zasshi* (The journal of the Association of Political and Social Sciences), 78.5 and 6: 1–34 (November 1964); 78.7 and 8: 1–66 (February 1965); 78.11 and 12: 64–118 (July 1965); and 79.1 and 2: 93–125 (September 1965). These articles are from Professor Mitani's doctoral dissertation (Department of Legal studies, Tokyo University, 1963) which he kindly permitted me to read in the fall of 1963. Since my manuscript went to press, these articles have been published in book form by Tokyo University Press as *Nihon seitō seiji no keisei: Hara Kei no seiji shidō no tenkai* (The formation of party politics in Japan: The development of the political leadership of Hara Kei; Tokyo, 1967).

2. Hara's feelings regarding the so-called "loyalists" in power are expressed in "Kinnō no setsu" (The theory of loyalism) written for the December 8, 1881, issue of the *Yūbin hōchi* in *Hara Kei zenshū* (Collected works of Hara) ed. Tanaka Asakichi (Tokyo, 1929), I, 42–45. In it he sharply criticizes those who boast of being "loyalists" and at the same time "violate the wish of the Emperor" and "act contrary to the will of the people."

3. See Oka, *Kindai no seijika*, pp. 95–97.

4. *Ibid.*, pp. 97–98; also, Maeda Renzan, *Hara Kei den* (Biography of Hara; Tokyo, 1943), I, 128–161.

5. The issue that led to Hara's expulsion was this: A group of 17 students, largely from northern Japan, petitioned for the abolishment of board expenses. Hara was not part of the group but was expelled anyway for arguing that, while he would obey the rules, he could not agree, as a matter of personal conscience, to "submit to authority."

With regard to his having to leave the *Yūbin hōchi:* In 1881, Ōkuma Shigenobu's faction, including Yano Fumio, Ozaki Yukio and Inukai Tsuyoshi, resigned en masse from the government. This group took over the *Yūbin hōchi* and Hara was forced to leave. For a discussion of the above events, see Oka, *Kindai no seijika*, pp. 97–100; Maeda, *Hara den*, I, 128–168, 181–184.

6. Hara entered the bureaucracy in 1882 through the auspices of Nakai Hiroshi (whose daughter he married), a close friend of

Inoue Kaoru as well as of Mutsu. (Oka, *Kindai no seijika*, pp. 99–100.)

Hara's devotion to Mutsu verged on hero worship. Hara followed Mutsu in and out of various ministries, and in 1892, he resigned with Mutsu in protest over government interventions at the polls. Mutsu was then minister of agriculture and Hara a bureau chief. (Maeda, *Hara den*, I, 320, 339–340.)

7. His feelings on this matter can be seen clearly, for example, in his "Seifu to seitō" (The government and the parties), *Hara zenshū*, I, 336–346.

8. See Oka, *Kindai no seijika*, pp. 103–104.

9. *Hara nikki*, III, 313 (June 3, 1909).

10. Hara strengthened this foothold by cementing ties with the Furukawa Mining Company, of which he was elected vice-president in 1904. *Hara nikki*, II sequel, 223 (Apr. 2, 1905); *ibid.*, p. 238 (Apr. 17, 1905). See also Shirayanagi Shūko, *Zoku zaikai taiheiki* (An account of the financial world; Tokyo, 1948), p. 111; and Uzaki Kumakichi, *Chōya no godai batsu* (The five major factions in and out of government; Tokyo, 1912), pp. 11–12.

11. Saionji Kimmochi, *Saionji Kimmochi jiden* (Autobiography), recorded by Koizumi Sakutarō, ed. Kimura Ki (Tokyo, 1949), p. 170.

12. Mitani, 78.5 and 6: 12 and passim. Those closest to Itō were, for example, Saionji Kimmochi, Suematsu Kenchō, Watanabe Kunitake, and Kaneko Kentarō.

13. Itō to Ishikawa Hanzan, quoted in Oka, *Kindai no seijika*, p. 102.

14. Maeda, *Hara den*, II, 32–35. Such prefectures as Gumma, Kōchi, Tokushima, Hiroshima dissolved the party branch offices. An abortive movement was started to re-establish a "Jiyūtō" under Itagaki Taisuke, whom the party had discarded in 1900 in order to join with Itō. Party leaders such as Kataoka Kenkichi, Hayashi Yūzō, and Ozaki Yukio left over this incident. See Maeda, *Hara den*, II, 49–50, and Kobayashi Yūgo, *Rikken Seiyūkai shi* (Official history of the Seiyūkai; Tokyo, 1924), I, 268.

15. Masumi Junnosuke, "Nihon seitō shi ni okeru chihō seiji no shomondai," (Local politics in Japanese party history); *Kokka gakkai zasshi*, 76.1 and 2: 24–25 (September 1962). See also *Seiyū* (Official journal of the Seiyūkai), No. 104: 52–57 (February 1909), in which the numerical strength of the various groups is given, and *Nihon oyobi nihonjin*, No. 512: 1–4 (June 1909), and Uzaki Kumakichi, *Jidai seiryoku no hihan* (A critique on the cliques in power; Tokyo,

1914), pp. 278–279, in which leaders of the various groups are given.

16. Sasakawa Tamon, *Matsuda Masahisa kō* (Biography of Matsuda; Tokyo, 1938), pp. 447–452; Uzaki, *Jidai seiryoku*, p. 284.

17. Uzaki, *Jidai seiryoku*, p. 284.

18. Tokutomi Iichirō, *Sohō jiden* (Autobiography; Tokyo, 1935), pp. 450–451. Ozaki Yukio affirms this view in his *Gakudō kaiko roku* (Memoirs of Ozaki; Tokyo, 1952), II, 32–34. Ozaki, who was not a paragon of an administrator, recalled his impression of Saionji in this way: "When I took his [Saionji's] office in 1898 as minister of education . . . I discovered a 4½ mat Japanese-style room in the back of the official residence. I thought this quite unbecoming for a Western-style official residence of the minister of education. Upon asking why the room was there, I was told it was especially ordered by him [Saionji] during his stay in office. . . . Minister of education and 4½ mats are a strange contrast but it seems that during his tenure as minister of education, the laying of 4½ mats was his one and only accomplishment. I don't think he left behind anything else of workmanlike quality."

19. Saionji, *Jiden*, pp. 81–82; Oka, *Kindai no seijika*, p. 41.

20. Saionji, *Jiden*, p. 24; Oka, *Kindai no seijika*, p. 203. Saionji's role in the affairs of the party was minimal. Many of his speeches were read by others and, for the most part, he stayed at his villa in scenic Ōiso (along the Tōkaidō route). For a brilliant and somewhat sympathetic essay on Saionji, see Oka, *Kindai no seijika*, pp. 199–244.

21. *Hara nikki*, III, 155 (Jan. 25, 1908). In another entry, Hara complained: "It has not been just once that I have rescued Saionji. But he is, as Count Mutsu [Munemitsu] once remarked of him, simple, lacks diligence and moreover, has no will power; he has never exerted himself to the fullest over anything. By the same token, I do not think he recognizes my efforts. It is quite astonishing. . . ." (*Hara nikki*, III, 15–16, Jan. 13, 1907.)

22. Maeda, *Hara den*, II, 52–53. The government group was the Motoda Hajime-Ōoka Ikuzō faction. It was called the *"futsukakai"* and it continued as a group until 1909 when Hara ordered its dissolution on grounds that the Seiyūkai could not tolerate a "party within a party." (*Ibid.*, pp. 128–129.) The Haseba Junkō-Sugita Teiichi group was the remnant of the Jiyūtō faction in the party.

23. In the fall of 1913, rumors were strong that both Hara and Matsuda Masahisa were due for titles. Matsuda accepted, but Hara did not: "I have not wanted a title up to now and I do not want one even after I die. . . ." (*Hara nikki*, V, 333–347, Oct. 30, 1913.)

24. Said to the Seiyūkai following the election of May 1908, quoted in Maeda, *Hara den*, II, 118.

25. A pet phrase of Hara, appearing frequently in his speeches and writings. For example, "Seitai henkō ron" (On changes in political structure) written for the *Yūbin hōchi*, Nov. 4, 1880, quoted in *Hara zenshū*, I, 14–19; "Seifu to seitō" (The government and the parties) written for the *Ōsaka mainichi* of Oct. 28, 1897 (*ibid.*, pp. 336–346); "Seitō naikaku" (Party cabinets) for the *Ōsaka mainichi* of July 4, 1898 (*ibid.*, pp. 390–416).

26. From his speech to the governors in Feb. 1906, *Seiyū*, No. 69: 43–44 (February 1906).

27. Hara's "Seitai henkō ron," *Hara zenshū*, I, 14–19.

28. *Hara zenshū*, I, 17.

29. *Hara nikki*, VII, 251 (Oct. 17, 1917).

30. *Hara nikki*, V, 358 (Nov. 24, 1913).

31. *Hara nikki*, VIII, 377 (Nov. 6, 1919).

32. *Ibid.*, p. 492 (Feb. 20, 1920). Hara knew that as long as a powerful party pushed for manhood suffrage its realization was inevitable. Therefore, he sought to lower the restrictions gradually and ultimately grant the right to vote to all men of draft age.

33. *Hara zenshū*, I, 337. Hara accused parties of abusing their newly acquired status within the government. He saw compromises between government and party as a favorable development, as something being "spurred on by the natural trends." (*Ibid.*, p. 339.) See also his "Sekinin nashi tasū" (Irresponsible majority) written for the *Ōsaka mainichi* of Apr. 7, 1899 (*ibid.*, pp. 443–448), in which he castigates opposition for opposition's sake as irresponsible.

34. Hara's "Seitō naikaku," *Hara zenshū*, I, 392.

35. *Hara nikki*, III, 369 (Oct. 27, 1909). In 1898, Hara's idea on majority had been formed. He argued, for example, that the Ōkuma cabinet of 1898 was not "constitutional government" because it did not control the majority in the Lower House. See his "Seitō naikaku," *Hara zenshū*, I, 390–416.

36. *Hara nikki*, VI, 186 (Nov. 29, 1914).

37. *Hara nikki*, VII, 66 (Nov. 11, 1916). See also *Hara nikki*, VIII, 27 (Sept. 25, 1918).

38. *Hara nikki*, IX, 89 (Oct. 8, 1920).

39. Kobayashi, IV, 11. Also Mitani, 78.5 and 6: 23.

40. Hara to Yamamoto Gonnohyōe, leader of the Satsuma faction. (*Hara nikki*, VI, 13, Mar. 31, 1914.) Hara's view that the majority party should control the cabinet implied, as in his statement that the

prime ministership be granted to "one or the other of the parties that controls the majority," an acceptance in principle of an opposition party. "Although there will be some neutrals in the middle," Itō said to Hara, "in general, the result will be two parties." (*Hara nikki*, III, 99, Sept. 24, 1907.) Hara observed that anti-Seiyūkai activities might very well develop into a second major party and, although the details of this were not yet clear, Itō's assessment was valid. (*Ibid.*) While Hara accepted the right of opposition as a principle, he was a politician interested in power. Hence, his actions were exclusively centered around his party — the Seiyūkai. When he spoke of "party expansion," he did not mean the expansion of political parties but specifically the Seiyūkai; and when he spoke of parties contributing to the state he meant, unequivocally, the Seiyūkai.

41. From Hara's "Seitō naikaku," *Hara zenshū*, I, 396–397. See also Mitani, 78.5 and 6: 16–17. When Hara wrote this, it was still possible for a civilian to be a military minister. In 1899, to prevent civilian and possible party interference in military affairs, Yamagata revised the law so that only generals and admirals on the active list could become military ministers. In 1913 Hara had the law revised so that men on the reserve list could be included as well, opening the way for potential party influence. This subject will be discussed later.

42. *Hara nikki*, IX, 467–468 (Oct. 7, 1921). See also *ibid.*, p. 404 (Sept. 25, 1921). Hara was assassinated on November 4, 1921. An interesting, if futile, question remains as to how Hara would have dealt with the military had he lived on.

43. See Tokutomi Iichirō, *Seijika to shite no Katsura Kō* (Katsura as a politician; Tokyo, 1913), pp. 106–112.

44. For a more favorable interpretation of this term, I suggest Andō, *Zoku O-Koi*, pp. 266–268. (O-Koi was Katsura's mistress.)

45. Saionji, *Jiden*, p. 159.

46. See Tokutomi, *Seijika no Katsura*, pp. 90–93. For greater details, see Tokutomi Iichirō, *Kōshaku Katsura Tarō den* (Biography of Katsura; Tokyo, 1917), I, 847–882, and Masumi, "Chihō seiji," *Kokka gakkai*, 76.5 and 6: 36.

47. *Hara nikki*, II sequel, 235–236 (Apr. 16, 1905). Hara, however, was against stirring the masses, and in this instance even more so because he was certain that "regardless of what the conditions are for ending the war, the majority of the people will not be satisfied" (*ibid.*); and, "even if it means having to bear some disadvantages, the signing of a peace treaty is, for the nation's sake, the best possible plan." (*Ibid.*, pp. 261–262, Mar. 14, 1905.) Under these conditions,

Hara saw that the only realistic alternative was to have Katsura shoulder the responsibility of the treaty and have the Seiyūkai acquire power in the process. (*Ibid.*, pp. 235–236, Apr. 16, 1905.)

48. *Hara nikki*, II sequel, 236 (Apr. 16, 1905); *ibid.*, pp. 263–266 (Aug. 22, 1905).

49. In these talks between Hara and Katsura, Saionji was passive. Hara informed Saionji of the talks after they took place. *Hara nikki*, II sequel, 238 (Apr. 17, 1905).

50. *Ibid.*, pp. 270–271 (Sept. 1, 1905); *ibid.*, p. 283 (Oct. 20, 1905). Public opinion generally still supported the method of unified action by both parties against the cabinet, for the idea was ingrained that a party "existed for the nation and not for selfish ends." The party as a group representing interests was ever-present as a fact, but foreign as an idea. See, for example, *Jiji shimpō* (Nov. 14, 1905), p. 3.

51. *Hara nikki*, II sequel, 271 (Sept. 25, 1902). Saionji delivered a speech to the party on September 2, persuading the members to support the treaty. Sentiment among the rank and file was against the treaty, and such leaders as Haseba Junkō and Sugita Teiichi of the Jiyūtō faction participated actively in the rallies against the treaty. The party as a whole, however, including its regional branches, refrained from active participation. On September 5, when the riots began, Hara was on his way to Morioka. (*Ibid.*, 272, Sept. 5, 1905.) Hence, the demonstrations did not have a decisive impact on the political situation even though they proved to be more violent than expected.

52. *Hara nikki*, II sequel, 293 (Dec. 12, 1905); *ibid.*, pp. 304–305 (Jan. 7, 1906). The minister of communications was Yamagata Isaburō; the minister of agriculture and commerce was Matsuoka Yasutake; the minister of education was Makino Shinken; and the minister of finance was Sakatani Yoshirō.

53. *Hara nikki*, III, 302 (Apr. 18, 1908).

NOTES TO CHAPTER 3

1. James MacGregor Burns, *Roosevelt: The Lion and the Fox* (New York, 1956), pp. 482–487.

2. Tokutomi Iichirō, *Jimu ikkagen* (My views on current affairs; Tokyo, 1913), pp. 19–20, 25. See also Tokutomi Iichirō, *Taishō seikyoku shi ron* (On the political history of Taishō; Tokyo, 1916), pp. 227–228.

3. See Hara's statement to the governors on February 1906, *Seiyū*, No. 69: 43–44 (Feb. 1906); *Hara zenshū*, II, 753–757.

4. Taken from "Senzen no bunkan to seiji" (The civil bureaucracy and politics in pre-war Japan) unpublished paper of Itō Takashi, research assistant, Institute of Social Science, Tokyo University, 1961. As to the growth of the bureaucracy in sheer size, Masumi's analysis shows that with 1890 (the year the first Diet convened) as base of 100 percent, the number of bureaucrats (excluding "employees") had almost doubled by 1907 (198 percent):

1890	29,000	100%
1907	58,000	198%
1908	72,000	244%
1915	80,000	292%
1921	118,000	399%
1922	162,000	547%

Masumi, "Chihō seiji," *Kokka gakkai*, 76.5 and 6: 57.

5. Ijiri Tsunekichi, ed., *Rekidai kenkan roku* (Record of bureaucrats and posts held; Tokyo, 1925), pp. 900–968. As late as the period 1898–1905, Kuribayashi Teiichi mentions 68 prominent governors. Of these, 42 were from the seven Kyūshū prefectures and Yamaguchi prefecture (Chōshū). The remaining 26 governors were divided among 35 prefectures and municipalities. Kuribayashi Teiichi, *Chihō kankai no hensen* (Changes in regional bureaucratic personnel; Tokyo, 1930), pp. 78–80.

6. Makino Shinken (minister of education in Saionji's first cabinet) described the changing nature of Tokyo Imperial University students thus: "Until 1890, or thereabouts, 90 percent of the students were from the ex-samurai class. From 1907 on into the teens and twenties, the overwhelming number were commoners." Makino Shinken's *Kaiko roku* quoted in Masumi, "Chihō seiji," *Kokka gakkai* 76.5 and 6: 53.

7. *Hara nikki*, II sequel, 306 (Jan. 12, 1906).

8. *Ibid.*, p. 333 (Apr. 18, 1906 and Apr. 19, 1906).

9. *Ibid.*, p. 307 (Jan. 16, 1906); Kuribayashi, pp. 22 to Appendix; Masumi, "Chihō seiji," *Kokka gakkai*, 76.5 and 6: 30–81, esp. pp. 50–52.

10. *Hara nikki*, IV, 344 (Sept. 12, 1911).

11. Masumi, "Chihō seiji," *Kokka gakkai*, 76.5 and 6: 51–52.

12. *Ibid.*, p. 59.

13. Kuribayashi, p. 97.

14. From Hara's speech to the governors on May 25, 1906. *Seiyū,* No. 72: 26 (May 1906).

15. Kuribayashi, pp. 96–97. A cabinet minister was empowered under the "law of limiting the bureaucracy" (*bunkan bungen rei*) to suspend at his own discretion. The revision of this law to prevent the power of suspension from above was one of the first objectives of the "new bureaucrats" of the 1930's.

16. Kuribayashi, pp. 98–101.

17. Masumi, "Chihō seiji," *Kokka gakkai,* 76.5 and 6: 59. See also *Hara nikki,* II sequel, 359 (Sept. 28, 1906).

18. *Hara nikki,* III, 117–118 (Nov. 12, 1907).

19. *Ibid.,* p. 186 (Mar. 27, 1908).

20. *Ibid.*

21. *Hara nikki,* IV, 344–345 (Sept. 2, 1911).

22. *Hara nikki,* III, 334 (Aug. 1, 1909).

23. *Ibid.,* pp. 186–187.

24. *Hara nikki,* IV, 345 (Sept. 2, 1911).

25. Masumi, "Chihō seiji," *Kokka gakkai,* 76.5 and 6: 64.

26. Hosoi Hajime, *Seisō to tōhei* (Political struggles and party evils; Tokyo, 1914), pp. 73–74.

27. *Ibid.,* pp. 21–35, 81–87. Hosoi, a newspaper reporter in the post-1905 period, was clearly "anti-Seiyūkai," but he gives a good account (based on newspapers throughout the country) of how the opposition viewed Hara's policies.

28. We can see what the governors meant to the Seiyūkai's party-expansion scheme by taking as an example a prefecture such as Gumma, where the Seiyūkai was chronically weak. After Hara assumed office in 1906, Arita Yoshisuke, an Ōura man, resigned of his own volition after a dispute with Hara; in 1908 Katsura expelled Hara's appointee, Nambu Mitsuomi; in 1911 Hara expelled Katsura's appointee and replaced him with Yoda Keijirō, a strong Seiyū governor; in 1912, Yoda was expelled and an anti-Seiyū governor, Kurogane Taigi, was appointed by Ōura; Hara expelled Kurogane in 1913 and appointed a Seiyū governor, Ōshiba Sōkichi, who was in turn expelled by Ōkuma in 1914. The main economic issue in Gumma involved the development of hydroelectricity. Yoda and Ōshiba manipulated contracts and "gift money" from recipients of contracts to weaken Seiyūkai opposition. Finally, because of pressures of one sort or another by the Seiyū governors, Gumma prefecture went Seiyūkai in the fall of 1913. See Masaki Shigeyuki, *Gumma kensei shi* (Political history of Gumma prefecture; Gumma, 1937), pp. 507–508; and

Hosoi, pp. 29–30. The tactics used by the governors were not entirely new, but earlier they had been used to build up a "pro-governor faction" (*goyōha*) and not a political party. See Kuribayashi, pp. 80–90.

29. A letter from Mori to Mizuno Rentarō, quoted in Mizuno Rentarō, *Ronsaku to zuihitsu* (Writings and jottings), ed. Matsunami Niichirō (Tokyo, 1937), pp. 683–686.

30. Hosoi, pp. 80–81.

31. Kuribayashi, pp. 200–203.

32. From a letter of Takazaki Shinshō to Yamagata on January 28, 1913. Yamagata Aritomo monjo (Papers of Yamagata), kept at National Diet Library, Tokyo, microfilm No. 50-15-6.

33. *Hara nikki*, V, 164 (Dec. 20, 1912).

34. Quoted in Mitani's unpublished version of "Seitō seiji kakuritsu katei," p. 108.

35. Quoted in Masumi, "Chihō seiji," *Kokka gakkai*, 76.5 and 6: 72.

36. For a discussion of this see Mizuno Rentarō, *Gakan dansetsu* (A miscellany of my views; Tokyo, 1930), pp. 160–175.

37. An example of this type was Ōkubo Toshitake, younger brother of the influential Makino Shinken. See Kuribayashi, pp. 107–108.

38. One example is that of Governor Ikematsu Tokikazu, graduate of Tokyo Imperial University in 1898. Kuribayashi, p. 172.

39. In one case Kiyono Chōtarō (graduate of Tokyo Imperial University in 1895), a strong pro-Kenseikai governor, was appointed in 1914 by Ōkuma, suspended by Terauchi in 1916, and not reappointed until 1925 (by Katō Kōmei to Kanagawa prefecture). Kuribayashi, pp. 158–159.

40. I rely heavily in this section on the analysis of Mitani, 78. 7 and 8: 1–66.

41. *Ibid.*, pp. 1–15. Until 1898, the *gun* chief was elected by the *gun* council, but after that he was incorporated into the bureaucracy and given broad police and administrative powers. As regards police powers, the *gun* chief was not a subordinate to the prefectural governor. Yamagata deprived the *gun* council of the right to select its chief because he felt that the elections were becoming too partisan in nature and because the stress on the "election process" per se was not healthy for "self-government."

42. *Seiyū*, No. 69: 43–44 (February 1906).

43. From Hara's defense in the House of Peers of his bill to abolish the *gun*, March 1907. *Hara zenshū*, II, 51–52.

44. Mitani, 78.7 and 8: 54–63.

45. *Hara nikki,* III, 16–17 (Jan. 14, 1907).

46. *Ibid.,* p. 17.

47. *Hara nikki,* II sequel, 324 (Mar. 17, 1906); *ibid.,* p. 324 (Mar. 19, 1906).

48. *Ibid.,* p. 391 (Oct. 25, 1906).

49. *Hara nikki,* III, 13 (Jan. 11, 1907); III, 16 (Jan. 14, 1907). Hara's comment on this opposition in the cabinet was: "I have decided to use the *gun* issue as the opportunity to do battle. If it does not pass, I will resign. The problem of the *gun* is a grave one, which in the end will leave the Yamagata faction completely without power. But the cabinet members, and others as well, cannot grasp this."

50. *Seiyū,* No. 83: 61–62 (March 1907). Also Ōtsu Jun'ichirō, *Dai Nihon kensei shi* (Constitutional history of Japan; Tokyo, 1927), VI, 286–289.

51. Ozaki, *Gakudō kaiko roku,* II, 45. Some of this early group, for example, were the Yarai kurabu, Ban'an kurabu, the Fukuoka-gumi, and the Kairakuen-gumi. Utsumi Nobuyuki, *Kōjin Inukai Bokudō* (Biography of Inukai; Tokyo, 1938), p. 148; Uzaki Kumaki-chi, *Inukai Tsuyoshi den* (Biography of Inukai; Tokyo, 1932), pp. 191–193. Some important leaders of this faction were Kinoshita Ken-jirō, Hatoyama Kazuo, Hiraoka Kotarō, Sasaki Seizō, Katō Masa-nosuke, and, the most important from 1907 on, Ōishi Masami.

52. For the details of the position taken by this reform faction see Kobayashi, II, 353–368; Washio Yoshinao, *Inukai Bokudō den* (Biography of Inukai; Tokyo, 1938), I, 785–798; and Uzaki, *Inukai den,* pp. 193–194.

53. Floor leader (*innai sōmu*) reduced from two to one, Inukai ousted. Secretariat (*kanji*) reduced from seven to five. Directorate (*sōmu*) abolished. Standing committee of 15 established in place of directorate (nine were of the reform faction). Utsumi, pp. 149–150; Washio, *Inukai Bokudō,* I, 786–798.

54. *Hara nikki,* III, 16–17 (Jan. 14, 1907).

55. One member of the Daidō Club switched his vote at the last minute to support the bill. *Jiji shimpō* (Mar. 2, 1907), p. 13; *Jiji shimpō* (Mar. 4, 1907), p. 7; *Seiyū,* No. 83: 61–62 (March 1907); Kobayashi, II, 381–384.

56. *Hara nikki,* V, 50 (Apr. 2, 1912).

57. See, for example, Hara's talks with Hotta Masayasu, an influential figure in the Kenkyūkai. *Hara nikki,* II sequel, 396 (Oct. 13, 1906); III, 18 (Jan. 18, 1907).

58. In early 1908, for example, Hara held a dinner for 13 sympathetic members of the House of Peers. *Hara nikki,* III, 165 (Feb. 14, 1908); III, 166–168 (Feb. 21, 1908); III, 171–176 (Mar. 4, 1908); III, 185 (Mar. 25, 1908).

Also Kobayashi, III, 138–144, 267–272.

59. *Hara nikki,* III, 166 (Feb. 21, 1908); Uzaki, *Jidai seiryoku,* pp. 304–307.

60. *Hara nikki,* III, 295 (Apr. 7, 1909). Katsura asked about Hara's ties with the House of Peers, and Hara denied any "close connections."

61. *Hara nikki,* IV, 74 (July 9, 1910).

62. Hara's intimate connection in the House of Peers, Hotta Masayasu, for example, was expelled from the Kenkyūkai in April 1909 for "bringing the influence of political parties into the House of Peers." *Hara nikki,* III, 302–314 (Apr. 18, 1909).

63. *Hara nikki,* III, 40 (Mar. 21, 1907).

64. See *Hara nikki,* III, 154 (Jan. 23, 1908).

65. *Hara nikki,* III, 204–205 (June 23, 1908). See also Oka, *Yamagata Aritomo,* pp. 104–105. Hara felt that suppression should always be the last recourse in handling the socialists. He continued to be highly critical of the "reckless suppression" of the socialists by the "bureaucratic faction." In 1910, when a plot by anarchists to assassinate the Emperor (the "Great Treason Case," in which Kōtoku Shūsui and twelve others were executed on grounds that remain unconvincing) was uncovered, Hara wrote in his diary: ". . . those who incite the masses will generally emerge victorious. This is not limited to elections, but includes other problems as well. The bureaucratic faction failed to consider this point and suppressed the Socialist party. As a result, a great treason has been attempted." (*Hara nikki,* IV, 75, July 12, 1910.)

Again he wrote: "When I was in office, an Elder Statesman appealed to the throne that my measures of control were too mild. . . . The bureaucratic faction constantly attacked us on this; but what are their thoughts now. Their policy is suppression, but this causes the believers of this ideology to grow secretly thus producing results contrary to what was intended." *Hara nikki,* IV, 78 (July 23, 1910); IV, 113 (Nov. 10, 1910) for further comments.

66. "Is it because Saionji is indifferent to political power," Hara wrote, "that, at the slightest provocation, he wants to resign from his office?" *Hara nikki,* III, 155 (Jan. 25, 1908). Following the May elections Hara would say that Saionji may be "ill" as he pleads, but

that in fact "he has no will power at all." *Hara nikki*, III, 205–206 (June 27, 1908).

<h2 style="text-align:center">NOTES TO CHAPTER 4</h2>

1. Nukada Matsuo, *Tateru Inukai Bokudō* (Biography of Inukai; Tokyo, 1930), p. 81.

2. Tōyama Shigeki and Adachi Kiyoko, eds., *Kindai Nihon seiji shi hikkei* (A handbook on modern Japanese political history; Tokyo, 1961), pp. 188–191.

3. See Vol. 6, *Narikin tenka* (The world of the nouveau riche; Tokyo, 1962), edited by Tsurumi Shunsuke, of the interesting series, *Nihon no hyakunen* (Japan's hundred years), esp. pp. 1–74.

4. Mitani, 79.1 and 2: 94–106. In about a decade after 1905, 295 were arrested for bribery and purchasing of votes in Tsushima. (The electorate in Tsushima numbered only 612.) In the election of May 15, 1912, 660 violations at the polls were prosecuted. About 5,831 persons were involved, of these 4,668 in bribery cases. (Kobayashi, III, 514.) See also *Hara nikki*, IV, 245 (Apr. 26, 1911) and IV, 417 (Dec. 16, 1911) for Hara's argument along these lines to Katsura and Yamagata; and *Hara zenshū*, II, 75–125, for Hara's presentation of these points to support his bill to establish small instead of large electoral districts (January–February 1912).

5. *Seiyū*, No. 142: addendum pp. 1–10 (June 1912). Even men with reputed "iron *jiban*" were barely being elected. Kōno Hironaka, an old hand in the party movement, for example, was elected by a bare 34 votes. Of the new faces we find many Seiyūkai men who would take active part in the Movement for Constitutional Government. Some of these were: Kinoshita Seitarō (Hokkaidō), Koyama Kango and Kosaka Junzō (Nagano), Fukuzawa Momosuke (Chiba), Hayashi Kiroku (Kagawa), and Kikuchi Butoku (Aomori).

6. *Seiyū*, No. 179: addendum pp. 1–13 (April 1915). In the election of 1920, 242 were new faces, and in that of 1924 there were 222 (the membership in the Lower House had grown to 466 by this time). In 1924, according to Katō Seizō, 87 had been elected three times and 14, 10 times or more. See Katō Seizō, *Seitō no hyōri* (A close-up of political parties; Tokyo, 1928), pp. 94–104.

7. *Hara zenshū*, II, 81, and also *Hara nikki*, III, 203 (June 15, 1908). To reach managing-staff status in the party a member usually had to be in the "re-elected three times" class, and in the four- or five-times class to vie for vice-minister and minister positions. See Katō Seizō, pp. 103–104.

8. *Hara zenshū*, II, 75–125, for Hara's presentation and defense of his small district bill. Hara argued to Katsura and Yamagata on the need for establishing small electoral districts to reduce corruption and curb the activities of radicals. The bill was defeated in the House of Peers on Mar. 20, 1912, by a vote of 201 to 28. *Hara nikki*, V, 46 (Mar. 20, 1912).

9. *Hara nikki*, II sequel, 316 (Feb. 19, 1906). When the first Saionji cabinet resigned in August 1908, the massive Kobe harbor project remained to be completed as did telephone expansion, a number of schools (for example, Tōhoku Imperial University), and, of course, railroads. A total of some 220 million yen worth of projects begun between 1906 and 1908 (First Saionji Cabinet), excluding military expenses, remained to be carried out. *Seiyū*, No. 99: 2–6 (August 1908).

10. Maeda, *Rekidai naikaku*, I, 405.

11. Hosoi, p. 6.

12. *Seiyū*, No. 69: 44 (February 1906).

13. Okurashō shuzei kyoku, *Kuni no sainyū ichiran hyō* (Statistical tables on government income; Tokyo, 1956), pp. 1–21.

14. *Ibid.*, p. 76 and addendum. Indirect taxes rose from 96 million yen in 1903 to 152 million in 1905 and, under Hara's spending policy, to 231 million yen in 1908. In 1908, indirect taxes constituted 56.7 percent of the total tax intake.

The total military expense incurred during the war with Russia was 1.7 billion yen or seven times what had been spent 10 years earlier in the Sino-Japanese War (1894–1895). Of this total, 1.4 billion (or about 82 percent) was covered by emergency loans. By 1907, the economy had entered a period of recession and it was felt that domestic loans would not be effective; hence, the Saionji cabinet resorted to raising consumption taxes. The deficit was close to 199 million yen. See Suzuki Takeo, *Zaisei shi* (A financial history; Tokyo, 1962), pp. 84–86, 109.

15. Following the local elections of September 1911, for example, 390 branch and regional rallies were held reaffirming the party's support of a positive policy to stimulate regional industrial development. See *Seiyū*, No. 135: 36–38 (November 1911), and Kobayashi, III, 450–456.

16. *Kokumin hyōron*, No. 2: 79–81 (Dec. 1909).

17. "Where is the focal point of the Seiyūkai — who are the central figures of the Seiyūkai? The focal point is the managing staff; the central figures are in the regions as a whole. And the organizations

that concretely represent these latter are the eight regional groups within the party: Kyūshū, Shikoku, Kantō, Tōhoku, Hokushin, Tōkai, Kinki, and Chūgoku. . . ." *Nihon oyobi nihonjin,* No. 512: 2–4 (June 1909).

In 1909, the relative strength of the regional groups and some of the leaders of each were as follows:

Regional group	Diet members	Major leaders
1. Kantō	38	Hara Kei, Murano Joeimon, Okazaki Kunisuke, Morikubo Sakuzō
2. Kyūshū	33	Matsuda Masahisa, Noda Utarō, Haseba Junkō, Motoda Hajime
3. Hokushin	23	Sugita Teiichi, Takekoshi Yosaburō, Itō Daihachi
4. Tōkai	22	Ebara Soroku, Muramatsu Aizō, Kurihara Ryōichi
5. Kinki	22	Kikuchi Kanji, Oku Shigesaburō
6. Tōhoku	19	Hara Kei, Sugawara Den
7. Chūgoku	19	Yokoi Tokio
8. Shikoku	16	Yamamoto Sachihiko

Seiyū, No. 104: 52–57 (February 1909); Uzaki, *Jidai seiryoku,* pp. 278–279; *Nihon oyobi nihonjin,* No. 512: 1–4 (June 1909).

18. The executive staff (*kambu*) included: directorate (*sōmu*), secretariat (*kanji*), floor leader and assistant (*innai sōmu* and *innai kanji*). All positions were appointed by the president of the party.

19. The board of councillors (*kyōgiin*) acted on decisions made by the executive staff and served as a body to transmit demands from below. Ten members were appointed and 20 were elected by the eight regional groups (Kyūshū and Kantō, the two largest of the regional groups, elected more representatives than the others). For a discussion of the Seiyūkai party structure, see Masumi, "Chihō seiji," *Kokka gakkai,* 76.1 and 2: 1–61.

20. Local power holders (*yūryokusha*) who took part in the welcoming party were made up of people like the following (the case cited here is the welcoming committee at Tokushima prefecture in July 1910):

A. *Rural stop:* Gun chief, police chief, chief of the post office, administrators of government projects, prefectural representatives (11), town and village chiefs (12), "business leaders," *gun* assembly men (7), and about 20 men whose occupations were not known.

B. *Urban stop:* Vice-president of "Business Association" and its secretary, prefectural representatives (3), president of Kyōdō company (and 11 others), president of the Salt Manufacturers' Association, president of the Agricultural and Industrial Bank, town council representatives (about 12), president of the Sanshi Bank, and president of Aha Dyers Association. (Seiyū, No. 120: 38, July, 1910).

21. *Seiyū,* No. 120: 34 (July 1910). Purpose attributed to one Saitō Jirō in touring Fukushima prefecture.

Hara himself took part actively in these tours and rallies. See for example, *Hara nikki,* III, 52–55 (May 4–6, 1907); IV, 103 (Oct. 22, 1910); IV, 157 (Nov. 1, 1910).

Speakers sent from party headquarters included the following — all of executive staff status — Ōoka Ikuzō, Matsuda Genji, Motoda Hajime, Sugita Teiichi, Ozaki Yukio, Itō Daihachi, Oku Shigesaburō, and Sugawara Den. (See Kobayashi, III, 450–456).

22. Hosoi, pp. 7–8.

23. *Hara nikki,* IV, 103 (Oct. 22, 1910).

24. From a Tōhoku regional rally held at Sapporo, September 1906, and attended by Ōoka Ikuzō from the managing staff and 13 others from central headquarters. *Seiyū,* No. 77: 39 (September 1906).

25. From Yamagata prefecture rally, November 1905, in which Haseba Junkō and Sugawara Den were sent from party headquarters. *Seiyū,* No. 67: 39 (December 1905).

26. From a rally at Fukushima, December 1906, in which Sugita Teiichi and Kurihara Ryōichi were sent from party headquarters. *Seiyū,* No. 80: 46–47 (December 1906).

27. From a Tōhoku regional rally held at Sapporo, Hokkaidō, in September 1906. *Seiyū,* No. 77: 39 (September 1906). At the Hokuriku regional rally held at Fukui in November 1906, to which Kurihara Ryōichi and Ueno Yasutarō were sent from party headquarters, the following requests were resolved: reduction of the business tax; building of a technical high school in the area; building of a railroad between Tsuruga and Maizuru; rapid completion of lines connecting with Mikuni Harbor. *Seiyū,* No. 79: 41–42 (November 1906).

At the Hyōgo prefecture rally held in December 1906, in which Sugawara Den took part, the following were resolved: support of the positive policy; completion of the dredging of Kobe Harbor and selection of a "committee of several names" to see that this was agreed upon by the Diet. *Seiyū*, No. 80: 49–50 (December 1906).

28. Mokushū, "Giin to kenkan," (Diet men and prefectural bureaucrats), *Nihon oyobi nihonjin*, No. 513: 74 (July 1909). In December 1906, 260 men from the northwest joined the party. (*Seiyū*, No. 79: 43–44, November 1906.) Between September and December 1907, 678 from Ōita prefecture joined. (*Seiyū*, No. 81: 45–48, January 1907.) In September 1908, 368 more joined from Ōita. (*Seiyū*, No. 100: 52–56, September 1908.) In July 1910 alone, 1,665 men joined from throughout Japan, Yamagata prefecture being the largest with 741. (*Seiyū*, No. 120: 58–65, July 1910.) Between 1910 and 1911, 2,465 joined from Akita prefecture (*Seiyū*, No. 131: 37, June 1911) and in the first few months of 1912, 2,799 joined, the largest groups being Niigata with 872, Gifu with 631, and Aichi with 304. (*Seiyū*, No. 141: addendum, pp. 1–15, May 1912).

29. See Tōyama and Adachi, pp. 162–195; Maeda, *Rekidai naikaku*, I, 317–320. According to the latter, the neutrals and splinter groups often tended to side with the government; in 1904, therefore, about 102 from these splinter groups were actually Katsura supporters and formed the nucleus of the Daidō Club. ,

30. Kobayashi, II, 408–411. *Ibid.*, III, 443–449.

31. Hosoi, pp. 6–8. See also Mokushū, "Tōsei no kakuchō," (The expansion of party power), *Nihon oyobi nihonjin*, No. 516: 73–75 (September 1909). According to the latter article, Diet members wrote letters such as this to party men at local branch offices: "If our party controls all the posts [in the Agricultural and Industrial Bank], it will be useful for you in the matter of borrowing capital. . . . I expect victory at all cost. . . . I will send shareholders to deliver speeches in your area and send the power of attorney to the branch office on behalf of the many who will not be present."

32. Hosoi, pp. 73–74. The letter was written to Hosoi on Nov. 2, 1913, by one Itō Keiichirō. In the same fashion, the Seiyūkai, by using railroad building as bait, cut into the electoral base of old standbys such as Kōno Hironaka of Fukushima. Once dominant in Fukushima, by 1912 Kōno was barely being elected. (*Ibid.*, pp. 170–171.)

33. *Hara nikki*, IV, 103 (Oct. 22, 1910).

34. The best treatment of railroad developments in the context of the Seiyūkai's positive policy is Mitani, 78.11 and 12: 65–118.

35. *Seiyū*, No. 119: 16–19 (June 1910). Hara also delivered a speech with virtually the same content before the Kanazawa branch

rally in October of the same year. *Seiyū*, No. 122: 1–4 (October 1910).

36. *Hara nikki*, II sequel, 314–315 (Feb. 17, 1906). Aside from the fact of Mitsubishi backing, Katō opposed as a matter of principle the purchasing of private investments by the government "by force of law"; he also opposed the "evils of excessive foreign loans." Itō was also undecided on the matter of nationalizing the railroads. *Hara nikki*, II sequel, 314–315 (Feb. 17, 1906). Reflecting the fears of business leaders, the *Jiji shimpō* opposed the nationalization because of the high cost. (See its editorial of Mar. 9, 1906, p. 9.)

37. Hara had this to say on the matter of loans to the governors on February 1906: "This loan [ca. 200 million yen] is extremely crucial. . . . At the same time, it will be rather difficult to appeal directly to popular patriotism as was done during the war. But from the view of financial policy, this loan is as important as any floated during the war. I hope, therefore, that you will exert your entire effort to fulfill this. . . ." *Seiyū*, No. 69: 43–44 (February 1906).

38. Ōkurashō, ed., *Meiji Taishō zaisei shi* (Financial history of Meiji and Taishō; Tokyo, 1940), I, 263–266; also Suzuki, pp. 96–97; and *Seiyū*, No. 99: 2–6 (August 1908).

There had been through 1906 (first line laid in 1872) a total of 3,100 kilometers of railway (7,595 miles). In 1915, a total of 5,500 kilometers (13,475 miles) of railway was laid — an increase of 2,400 kilometers (5,880 miles) in a 10-year period. Tetsudōshō, ed., *Nihon tetsudō shi* (Official history of the railroads; Tokyo, 1919), III, 199–200.

39. Mitani, 78.11 and 12: 75–83 and passim. In 1911–1912 Hara held the post of chief of the railroad bureau jointly with that of home minister. In 1913–1914, he appointed his close supporter Tokonami Takejirō to the post. During his first cabinet (1918–1921) Hara raised this bureau to the status of a ministry.

40. *Ibid.*, pp. 77–85. Gotō is an interesting bureaucrat-politician. A physician by training, he entered the bureaucracy under the auspices of Itagaki Taisuke and rose steadily until he became chief administrator in Manchuria (1898–1905). There he established close ties with Katsura and became his close aide. His part in the broad-gauge plans is documented in Tsurumi Yūsuke, *Gotō Shimpei den*, (Biography of Gotō; Tokyo, 1944), VI, 330–374.

41. Yamagata Meishichi, *Zaisei jūnen* (A financial history of the past ten years; Tokyo, 1914), p. 45; *Hara nikki*, IV, 132–138 (Dec. 4, 1910).

42. *Hara nikki,* III, 289 (Mar. 25, 1909).

43. *Ibid.,* p. 293 (Apr. 7, 1909).

44. *Seiyū,* No. 100: 51 (September 1908). By "vital industries," furthermore, the Kyūshū group meant the completion of railroad lines — Yoshiyama to Ōita, Yashirō to Kagoshima (western coast), Kumamoto to Ōita (to cut Kyūshū laterally), and Yoshizuke to Sasebo.

45. *Seiyū,* No. 104: 52 (February 1909).

46. *Hara nikki,* III, 355 (Oct. 14, 1909).

Here we see the crucial significance of compromise, as Hara could exercise an important influence on political decisions. In the winter of 1909–1910, when the above agreement made its initial influence, for example, projected pay hikes for government employees were reduced from 30 percent to 15 percent. Furthermore, Katsura's plan to lower income taxes was scrapped and land taxes were reduced instead (.008 yen per land unit, roughly 9.4 million yen). Hara argued that "this has drawn considerable support" in the party, and so in the end Katsura had to give in although "he had not expected at all to be confronted with the issue of lowering land taxes." (*Hara nikki,* III, 355, Oct. 14, 1909 and IV, 2–13, Feb. 8, 1910; Suzuki, p. 109.) Finally, in railroad development, 127 million yen in newly committed funds was provided in 1910 as compared with none in 1909 when Seiyūkai influence was at a minimum; in terms of kilometers, this was 217.28 for 1910 and 80.71 for 1909. (Tetsudōshō, III, 91–95; Ōkurashō, I, 264–265.)

47. *Hara nikki,* IV, 21 (Feb. 24, 1910). See also *Hara nikki,* III, 392 (Jan. 4, 1910).

48. *Hara nikki,* IV, 110 (Nov. 9, 1910). Also *Seiyū,* No. 119: 16–19 (June 1910), and No. 122: 1–4 (October 1910).

49. *Hara nikki,* IV, 113 (Nov. 10, 1910); IV, 75–78 (July 12, 1910 and July 23, 1910).

50. *Ibid.,* 178 (Jan. 26, 1911). See also Sasakawa, p. 461. To Hara, the annexation of Korea itself was part of a plan by "Yamagata and his bureaucratic faction to increase their glory." *Hara nikki,* V, 87 (Aug. 29, 1910).

51. See, for example, Sasakawa, p. 461. This controversy, called the *"nambokuchō seijun mondai,"* was over the question of imperial legitimacy in fourteenth-century Japan. An editorial in a leading newspaper (*Yomiuri*) stated that government-approved elementary school textbooks were treating the northern and southern dynasties equally, contradicting the myth of an unbroken imperial line. This issue was taken up in the Diet to embarrass Katsura. The chief of the

textbook division in the Ministry of Education urged that the matter be left to "interpretation" and was duly ousted by Katsura. The northern dynasty was purged from the line of imperial families and only the south was henceforth to be treated in the textbooks; the period of history itself was to be renamed "Yoshino Court Period" instead of the "Period of Northern and Southern Dynasties."

52. From a letter of Terauchi to Yamagata on Feb. 24, 1911. Tokutomi Iichirō, ed., *Kōshaku Yamagata Aritomo den* (Biography of Yamagata; Tokyo, 1933), II, 772.

53. *Hara nikki,* IV, 163 (Dec. 25, 1910).

54. Katsura expressed this in a letter to Yamagata on Dec. 13, 1910, in which he optimistically noted that the views of the leaders of the Seiyūkai "did not differ significantly" from his and that they were interested in coming to terms. Yamagata Aritomo monjo, microfilm No. 50-13-153.

55. *Hara nikki,* IV, 153 (Dec. 14, 1910).

56. *Ibid.,* p. 150 (Dec. 14, 1910).

57. *Ibid.,* pp. 177–178 (Jan. 26, 1911).

Regarding the postponement of the broad gauge plan, Katsura stated to the press that "it is difficult for the government to carry out a plan which the people are unhappy about. . . ." *Jiji shimpō* (Feb. 2, 1911), p. 6.

58. The plan called for 149 new lines or 10,221 kilometers, equal to a 100 percent increase in total. Mitani, 78.11 and 12: 97–103.

59. *Hara nikki,* VII, 300 (Dec. 23, 1917).

60. Kobayashi, III, 384–387. Maeda, *Rekidai naikaku,* I, 379–381. Shortly after the vote of no confidence was defeated, Terauchi wrote to Yamagata revealing an undertone of dissatisfaction with Katsura's leadership: "The Kokumintō submitted a resolution of no confidence on account of the grand treason incident and the textbook incident. Fortunately, it was defeated; but the latter is truly a serious government mismanagement." Tokutomi, *Yamagata den,* II, 772.

NOTES TO CHAPTER 5

1. Shinobu Seizaburō's magnum opus *Taishō seiji shi* (A political history of Taishō; Tokyo, 1954), and his *Taishō demokurashii shi* are undoubtedly the most detailed undertakings to date on the Taishō Political Crisis. The emphasis is on the interaction of the mass movement with the liberal-bourgeoisie and intellectuals. The masses are treated as striking out against "absolutism." Treatment of a similar

nature is in Inoue Kiyoshi, ed. *Kindai* (Modern period; Tokyo, 1960), Vol. 7 of *Nihon jimbutsu shi taikei* (A general history of important Japanese figures), pp. 1–6; 16–22; and Ishii Kin'ichirō, "Kensei shijō ni okeru Kei-On jidai" (Katsura and Saionji in constitutional history), *Shigaku kenkyū* (Researches in history), No. 44: 55–65 (Tokyo, 1951).

Two stimulating discussions that examine, among other questions, the emergence of mass consciousness, are Ishida Takeshi's *Kindai Nihon seiji kōzō no kenkyū* (Researches on the political structure of modern Japan), 3rd ed. (Tokyo, 1959), and from the point of view of intellectual history, especially as regards Yoshino Sakuzō, Matsumoto Sannosuke's "Mimponshugi no rekishiteki keisei," (Formation of the idea of political democracy), *Seijigaku nempō* (The Annals of the Japanese Political Science Association; Tokyo, 1957), pp. 109–131.

One of the more interesting treatments that concentrates on Saionji and the question of imperial rescripts is Satō Isao, "Iwayuru Taishō seihen ni tsuite" (A study on the Taishō Political Crisis) *Seiji keizai ronsō* (Debates on politics and economics), 1.1: 79–97; 1.2: 51–58 (Tokyo, 1949).

For an interesting round table discussion of the subject, see Yamamoto Shingo, et al. *Shinsetsu Nihon rekishi* (A general history of modern Japan; Tokyo, 1959), XI, 297–351.

2. *Hara nikki*, IV, 176 (Jan. 26, 1911).

3. Letter by Katsura to Inoue on Jan. 25, 1911. Inoue Kaoru monjo (Inoue papers), in National Diet Library, Tokyo. There seems to be an explanation for these demands. According to Ōura, in a letter to Yamagata on Jan. 28, 1911 (Yamagata monjo, microfilm No. 50-15-157) there was "great excitement" among the rank and file in response to a promise, designed to "pacify the party," that Seiyūkai men would be asked to join the Katsura cabinet.

4. *Hara nikki*, IV, 175 (Jan. 26, 1911). Even to Yamagata, Katsura wrote: "The transformation of popular feeling is truly frightening — unprecedented since the Meiji Restoration." Katsura to Yamagata on Feb. 26, 1911. Tokutomi, *Yamagata den*, II, 773–774.

5. *Hara nikki*, IV, 180–181 (Jan. 28, 1911).

6. Kobayashi, III, 353–354. See also Tokutomi, *Katsura den*, II, 502–503; *Jiji shimpō* (Jan. 30, 1911), p. 4.

7. *Hara nikki*, IV, 179 (Jan. 26, 1911).

8. *Hara nikki*, IV, 328 (Aug. 26, 1911).

9. *Ibid.*, p. 328.

10. Letter by Katsura to Inoue on Jan. 27, 1911. Inoue monjo, microfilm No. 21-19-5.

11. The Seiyūkai could be manipulated, Katsura would argue, because it had lost Itō, its "inner pillar." (Katsura to Yamagata, Jan. 27, 1911, Yamagata monjo, microfilm No. 50-15-157.) On Mar. 22, 1911, Katsura wrote again to Yamagata to dispel worries the latter might have since there would be no "accidents in the administrative process." Yamagata monjo, microfilm No. 50-15-158.

12. See *Hara nikki*, IV, 227–228 (Apr. 4, 1911), and IV, 237–238 (Apr. 14, 1911). Also, a letter from Terauchi to Yamagata on May 6, 1912 (Yamagata monjo, microfilm No. 50-15-158), reports that Katsura's position was to set up either a cabinet of allies or a Saionji cabinet and not a coalition cabinet as a practical alternative.

13. *Hara nikki*, IV, 287–288 (June 8, 1911). There were some differences of opinion between Hara and Saionji. For example, Hara supported Wakatsuki Reijirō over Yamamoto Tatsuo for finance minister and was not pleased with the choice of Makino Shinken to a cabinet post because of Makino's strong Satsuma orientation. Ozaki Yukio was turned down as a candidate (by Hara) because he had no "common sense" and sought only "personal glory." The point is, the selections were based on the candidates' willingness to cooperate with the Seiyūkai.

14. Tokutomi, *Katsura den*, II, 554. The minister of finance was Yamamoto Tatsuo, former president of the Hypothec Bank of Japan.

15. *Jiji shimpō* (Feb. 1, 1911), p. 4.

16. Kobayashi, III, 408–409; also pp. 528–530 for the final dissolution of the Danwakai.

In April 1912, Hara began once again to build up Seiyūkai strength in the House of Peers by appointing Sugita Teiichi, a Seiyūkai leader of the Hokushin regional group, and Ebara Soroku of the Tōhoku group, to the House of Peers. Commenting on this, Hara wrote with pride: "This is the first time that party men entered the House of Peers. It is not rare in other countries for men with long experience in the Lower House to enter the House of Peers, but in Japan this was the first incidence. . . ." (*Hara nikki*, V, 50, Apr. 2, 1912).

In December 1912, Hara appointed several more Seiyūkai men to the House of Peers. Among them were Mizuno Rentarō, his close supporter, Koga Kenzō (second only to Anraku Kendō as Hara's supporter in the police department), and Minami Hiroshi, a "Seiyū governor." (See *Seiyū*, No. 148: 28, December 1912). These Seiyū-appointees organized themselves into a club but remained weak and almost unheeded by the rest of the house. (Kobayashi, III, 496–498.)

17. *Hara nikki,* IV, 329 (Aug. 26, 1911).

18. Hara had other plans besides an economic policy to expand party influence. Through legal reforms, he first attempted (but failed) to revise the election law which would establish small electoral districts in place of the existing large districts; and second, he planned to revise the civil service appointment act to help expand party influence in the bureaucracy.

(For Hara's plans in the area of legal reform see *Hara nikki,* IV, 288–289, June 8, 1911; IV, 290–304, July 3, 1911.) The election bill was defeated by the House of Peers in the spring of 1912 by a vote of 201 to 28 (compare with the 149–109 vote when Hara's *gun* bill was defeated). "The bureaucratic faction is proud of this," Hara wrote, "but they do not comprehend that they will be despised by the people. . . ." (*Hara nikki,* V, 46, Mar. 20, 1912.) Furthermore, through his appointive powers, Hara relentlessly continued to promote, demote, and expel governors; and through personal influence he managed to have Seiyūkai supporters appointed to the House of Peers.

19. Hara had in mind: Aomori, northern Japan; Yokkaichi in Mie prefecture, central Japan; Shiogama, Kyūshū; and Funakawa, Akita prefecture facing the Japan Sea. Plans for the development of these were being laid by the "Harbor Development Investigation Committee," which Hara had established in the home ministry in 1906.

Hara nikki, IV, 367–368 (Oct. 10, 1911).

20. In the fall of 1913, for example, Yamamoto took part in rallies in northern Japan and Kyūshū announcing his decision to commit himself to the Seiyūkai. Yamamoto Tatsuo Sensei denki hensankai, ed., *Yamamoto Tatsuo* (Yamamoto Tatsuo; Tokyo, 1951), pp. 316, 359–360. See also Hosoi, pp. 33–34.

In the dark years of 1914 and 1915, furthermore, when the Seiyūkai was on the defensive against a powerful coalition, Yamamoto remained faithful to the party; hence, in time, a strong bond of friendship developed between Hara and Yamamoto, and Hara included Yamamoto in his first cabinet in 1918. *Hara nikki,* VIII, 29 (Sept. 25, 1918).

21. *Hara nikki,* IV, 384 (Oct. 30, 1911).

22. Yamamoto Tatsuo hensankai, pp. 301–310; Inoue Kaoru Kō denki hensankai, ed. *Segai Inoue Kō den* (Tokyo, 1934), V, 365–372; 268–274. Also Yamagata Meishichi, *Zaisei jūnen,* pp. 329–330, in which a similar memo of Matsukata's a year later is discussed.

23. *Hara nikki,* IV, 364–365 (Oct. 3, 1911); IV, 383–384 (Oct. 30, 1911); IV, 397 (Nov. 20, 1911); IV, 358 (Sept. 25, 1911).

24. *Ibid.,* pp. 424–425 (Dec. 23, 1911).

25. *Ibid.,* pp. 428–431 (Dec. 24, 1911).

26. *Hara nikki,* V, 9 (Dec. 25, 1911).

There is the possibility that Hara submitted his resignation knowing Saionji could not allow it. Aside from the fact that Hara was, through Katsura, the cabinet's chief contact with Yamagata, Hara's resignation in December 1911 so soon after the cabinet had been formed was an indication of weakness that could not be afforded. At the same time, it does seem that his decision to resign was more than a political gimmick. As a result of his disagreements with Yamamoto, Hara seriously contemplated resigning sometime in February or March of 1912 and using as pretext the failure of his bill to revise the election law, which was actually a foregone conclusion short of an ideological revolution in the House of Peers. His feelings on this matter are clearly reflected in *ibid.,* p. 399 (Nov. 24, 1911); pp. 425–432 (Dec. 23, 1911); also Maeda, *Rekidai naikaku,* I, 403–404.

27. Horikiri Zembei, "Kokumin keizai no hatten to tetsudō no fukyū," (The economic advancement of the people and the expansion of railroads), *Seiyū,* No. 147: 11 (November 1912).

28. Takakura Tetsuichi, *Tanaka Giichi denki* (Biography of Tanaka; Tokyo, 1958), I, 497.

29. Fearing a grand rapprochement among the European powers, Yamagata wrote to Inoue: "A few clashes and disturbances, based on differing interests, between England, France, Russia, and Germany will be unavoidable. But if they devised a grand rapprochement in Europe, inevitably the tip of that sword will be pointed directly at East Asia." (Yamagata to Inoue, Oct. 24, 1907, Inoue monjo, microfilm No. 7-14-3.)

An almost identical letter was sent to Inoue on Oct. 2, 1910 (Inoue monjo, microfilm No. 7-16-3). Again the fear of "becoming isolated" is revealed.

30. Takakura, I, 506–507; 506–517 for entire text. Writing from Korea and criticizing the inept handling of foreign affairs by the cabinet, Terauchi expressed the same fear as Tanaka. Russia, Terauchi claimed, was infiltrating into Mongolia and northern Manchuria and had made these areas virtually dependent on it. (Terauchi to Katsura, Katsura Tarō monjo (Katsura papers), in National Diet Library, Tokyo, Terauchi No. 40.)

31. Yamagata memo, Jan. 14, 1911, Yamagata monjo, microfilm

No. 50-15-164. Outwardly, at least, Katsura was of the same persuasion (for example, Katsura to Yamagata on Dec. 1, 1911, Yamagata monjo, microfilm No. 50-15-163); and so was Terauchi, governor general of Korea (Terauchi to Katsura, Jan. 7, 1912, Katsura monjo, Terauchi No. 28). Terauchi was extremely eager to have troops sent. A round of letters between Terauchi, Yamagata, and Katsura reveal the extraordinary concern of military leaders over the situation in China and their impatience on the matter of sending troops.

32. Yamagata to Katsura, Jan. 15, 1912, Katsura monjo, Yamagata No. 149.

33. Komatsubara Eitarō to Yamagata, Feb. 14, 1912, Yamagata monjo, microfilm No. 50-15-167.

34. Katsura to Yamagata, Feb. 8, 1912, Yamagata monjo, microfilm No. 50-15-166.

35. Yamagata to Katsura, Feb. 9, 1912, Katsura monjo, Yamagata No. 150.

These feelings were expressed by other men in the Yamagata faction. For example, Komatsubara Eitarō, a loyal Yamagata supporter in the House of Peers, wrote to Yamagata: "Since the outbreak of this event, our government has lost opportunity after opportunity in the area of foreign policy. In the matter of sending troops to Manchuria, for example, internally it feared Diet opposition; externally, it feared the powers. Thus, troops were not sent and the opportunity was lost. It is extremely deplorable. . . ." (Komatsubara to Yamagata, Feb. 14, 1912, Yamagata monjo, microfilm No. 50-15-167.)

36. Terauchi to Katsura, Apr. 6, 1912, Katsura monjo, Terauchi No. 34.

37. According to Wakatsuki (in his memoirs and in an interview in 1940) the study of political parties was indeed the main focus of Katsura's trip. See Wakatsuki Reijirō, *Wakatsuki Reijirō jiden: kofūan kaiko roku* (Autobiography: The memoirs of a hermit; Tokyo, 1950), pp. 178–179. See also his unpublished interview of 1940, "Wakatsuki Reijirō Danshaku danwa sokki," in the Diet Library in Tokyo. Wakatsuki, a Tokyo Imperial University graduate (1892), was a bureaucrat in the Finance Ministry. See also Katsura's statement quoted in Ōtsu, VI, 725, in which he denies that going to Europe was part of a plan to form a party.

For Gotō Shimpei's statement on this subject, see Tokutomi, *Katsura den,* II, 563–564. Gotō denies that the trip was in "preparation" for a party but admits that a purpose of the trip was to "investigate" parties. (See also *ibid.,* pp. 561–593.)

38. Yamagata's poem is in Tokutomi, *Katsura den,* II, 571. His

gratitude is expressed in Yamagata to Katsura, July 4, 1912, Katsura monjo, Yamagata No. 155. For a general account of the entire affair see Tokutomi, *Katsura den*, II, 580–605; and Tsurumi Yūsuke, VI, 269–274.

39. Saionji, *Jiden*, pp. 163–164.

40. From a report included in a letter by Gotō to Katsura, "late August" 1912, Katsura monjo, Gotō No. 24.

Editorials in the Asahi newspaper became so vehement that its Aug. 17, 1912, issue was banned. Even Hara, although one step closer to the inside of these affairs than the press in general, wrote: "It is clearly a scheme on the part of the Yamagata faction to gain complete control over the Privy Council and the Imperial Household." *Hara nikki*, V, 96 (Aug. 13, 1912). He also noted, however, that "the bureaucrats cannot continue like this much longer." (*Ibid.*, p. 97.)

41. From a report included in a letter by Gotō to Katsura, "late August" 1912 (marked "secret"), Katsura monjo, Gotō No. 24, in which special note is made of public misunderstanding of the situation surrounding Katsura's retirement. See also Tokutomi, *Seijika no Katsura*, pp. 171–176, and Tokutomi, *Katsura den*, II, 595–600. Also see the corroborating accounts in the various memoirs of Miura Kanju, *Kanju Shōgun kaiko roku* (Memoirs of Miura), ed. Kotani Yasutarō (Tokyo, 1925), pp. 395–396; Kataoka Chokuon, *Kaisō roku* (Memoirs of Kataoka; Tokyo, 1933), pp. 307–308; Adachi Kenzō, *Adachi Kenzō jijoden* (Autobiography of Adachi Kenzō; Tokyo, 1960), pp. 122–124.

42. This same pattern was repeated in the spring of 1912. Writing from Korea, governor general Terauchi urged Yamagata that the army minister selected to replace Ishimoto Shinzō (who died on Apr. 2) should be one thoroughly familiar with conditions in China. The implications were that military action in China would most likely be necessary and, because of this, firm representation was needed by the army for the two divisions. (See, for example, Terauchi to Yamagata, June 2, 1912, Yamagata monjo, microfilm No. 50-15-168.)

Katsura submitted a Chōshū man (General Kigoshi Yasutsuna) to the cabinet; but General Uehara Yūsaku was chosen instead for little reason except that he was a Satsuma man. Public response was favorable to this, taking it as a sign of decreasing Yamagata and Chōshū strength in the army.

43. See Yamagata-Hara talks, *Hara nikki*, VI, 105–106 (Aug. 14, 1914).

44. *Jiji shimpō* (Jan. 29, 1911), p. 5.

45. See Katsura to Yamagata on Nov. 1, 1912, in which he recalls this. Ōtsu, VII, 7–8.

46. Katō Masanosuke, *Katō Masanosuke kaiko roku* (Memoirs of Katō; Tokyo, 1957), p. 136; the activities of the reform faction can be found in the following: Kōnō Hironaka's account in Ōtsu, VII, 13–14; Hongō Naohiko, *Kōbe kensei shi* (Political history of the city of Kōbe; Kōbe, 1913), pp. 202–203; Kataoka, pp. 315–318; Uzaki, *Inukai den*, pp. 225–226; Rōjō, *Batsujin to tōjin*, p. 73; Shirayanagi, pp. 261–264; Adachi, *Jijoden*, pp. 117–118, 122–124.

47. *Hara nikki*, V, 65–66 (May 20, 1912): "A direct conflict with the bureaucratic faction will be unavoidable in the next Diet session because if the present condition continues, the gradual decline of the bureaucratic faction's area of influence will become evident to them — actually, this decline will seem more severe to them than is, in fact, the case. Thus we can count on them to plan a conflict."

48. In 1905, Katsura did his best to keep the demands of the army for six new divisions down to four for the first phase. (*Hara nikki*, II sequel, 294, Dec. 14, 1905). Furthermore, he postponed, between 1908 and 1911, the army's demand for the 2 other divisions in the first phase which remained unfulfilled. (*Hara nikki*, V, 94 (Aug. 9, 1912).

Katsura also kept navy demands down; for example, in 1910 he cut the navy's budget from 450 million yen to 82 million. (Yamagata Meishichi, *Zaisei jūnen*, pp. 296–300.)

49. *Hara nikki*, V, 99 (Aug. 17, 1912).

50. See Egi Yoku's brief account on the annexation of Korea, "Nikkan heigō tōji no kaiko," in Tonedate Masao, ed., *Sono koro o kataru* (Reflections on historical events; Tokyo, 1928), pp. 283–285. For the army's displeasure regarding the cabinet's acceptance of the navy's program, see Takakura, I, 515. The matter of army-navy rivalry is also discussed in Sasakawa, p. 462.

51. Recorded in Takakura, I, 497. In Hara's diary, Yamagata's statement, as relayed by Saionji, was similar — "to carry out the navy's plan and not that of the army is distasteful." *Hara nikki*, V, 132 (Nov. 10, 1912).

52. Takakura, I, 497; Inoue Kaoru hensankai, V, 278–279; and Ōtsu, VI, 749. Yamagata made these points publicly to the *Jiji shimpō* (Dec. 11, 1912), p. 4.

53. Tanaka's activities are discussed in Takakura, I, 483–495; also Rōjŏ, *Batsuijin to tōjin*, p. 92. Tanaka is said to have convinced Inoue of the need for the two divisions by arguing that the army trained

country youth and that therefore, increasing the size of the army would "raise the efficiency of regional industries." See Inoue Kaoru hensankai, V, 281.

54. *Hara nikki*, V, 131 (Nov. 10, 1912): "I have to strive for the security of the cabinet, but at the same time I must also consider the party's opposition."

55. *Ibid.*, p. 134 (Nov. 16, 1912).

56. *Ibid.*, p. 144–145 (Nov. 27, 1912).

57. Although unable to exercise any influence, Uehara personally supported the postponement of the two divisions. (See Maeda, *Rekidai naikaku*, I, 415–417.) Under influence of fellow Satsuma men such as Tokonami, he agreed to the postponement of the two divisions (Nov. 28, 1912); but the next day he reverted to the stand that the two divisions should be carried out in the fiscal year 1913. *Hara nikki*, V, 147–150 (Nov. 29, 1912–Dec. 1, 1912).

58. Matsukata to Hirata, Nov. 24, 1912, Yamagata monjo, microfilm No. 50-15-3.

59. See the exchange of letters between Hirata and Yamagata Nov. 23–26, 1912, in Tokutomi, *Yamagata den*, II, 808–811.

60. Maeda, *Rekidai naikaku*, I, 416–418. See also Takakura, I, 503–504; and Oka, *Yamagata Aritomo*, p. 125.

61. Included in Uehara to Katsura, Nov. 17, 1912, Katsura monjo, Uehara No. 1. In Kiyoura Keigo to Yamagata we find Kiyoura (powerful Yamagata supporter in the House of Peers) lamenting the fact that the crisis had turned into an "army vs. the people" affair. (It might very well be that Kiyoura wrote the circular of Nov. 17, also.) Dec. 7, 1912, Yamagata monjo, microfilm No. 50-15-4.

62. If Saionji had not expected Yamagata to do just that he would have had a better explanation later on (late 1920's) for his resignation than this: "Of course, if I had forced myself, I could still have gone on; but I always felt that it was best to leave some room for maneuver and so I did not persist." (Saionji, *Jiden*, pp. 145–146).

63. *Hara nikki*, V, 153 (Dec. 6, 1912).

64. See Hara's record of talks with Yamagata, *Hara nikki*, VI, 103–104 (Aug. 14, 1914). This was probably the result of the Yamagata-Ōyama talks of Dec. 1, 1912. At that time, Hara simply noted: "It is reported that Ōyama called on Yamagata for a discussion of the present political situation." *Hara nikki*, V, 149 (Dec. 1, 1912).

65. Saionji, *Jiden*, p. 145.

66. Consider, for example, this excerpt from a late August report to Katsura via Gotō Shimpei: "From the point of view of the bu-

reaucrats [that is, Yamagata's faction, not Katsura's] the best plan is of course to have the present cabinet carry it [the two divisions] through. Therefore, the danger of this cabinet collapsing is remote. . . ." The report was included in a letter by Gotō to Katsura, "late August" 1912, Katsura monjo, Gotō No. 24. At this time, Katsura was asked to give especially careful consideration to the prospect of a decline in the popularity of the Saionji cabinet if it compromised with the army.

67. Tanaka to Katsura on behalf of himself and Uehara. Dec. 17, 1912, Katsura monjo, Tanaka No. 1.

68. Hirata to Katsura, Dec. 10, 1912, Katsura monjo, Hirata No. 19.

NOTES TO CHAPTER 6

1. Tsurumi Shunsuke, et al. *Meiji no eikō* (The splendor of Meiji; Tokyo, 1962), Vol. 7 of *Nihon no hyakunen* (Japan's hundred years), pp. 332–349.

2. Natsume Sōseki expressed this feeling of attachment to the Meiji period in the novel *Kokoro:* "I felt then that, somehow or other, the spirit of Meiji began and ended with the Emperor. I was deeply moved by the thought that those of us who had come under the powerful Meiji influence would be out of touch with the times were we to live on. . . ." *Kokoro* (The heart; Tokyo, 1914), p. 345.

3. "Sabakari mo/ medetaki Mikado/ owashikeri/ yo mo kono hi yori/ inishie to naru." *Asahi shimbun* (Aug. 19, 1912), p. 5.

4. Ueda Sotoo, *Taishō no seihen* (The Taishō Political Crisis; Tokyo, 1913), p. 39. Ueda was a reporter with leanings toward the progressive wing of the Seiyūkai. For resolutions from the various branch offices see *Seiyū*, No. 148: 45–54 (December 1912).

5. *Seiyū*, No. 148: 53 (December 1912).

In Hokkaidō on November 23, the bureaucratic faction was denounced as a "serious threat to constitutional government" and at the same time it was resolved "that railroad lines, already agreed to, be rapidly advanced and that the laying of new lines urgently needed in the area be accepted without delay." (*Ibid.*, p. 47.) At Niigata on November 27, the two divisions were denounced and a resolution passed that "our party will complete the administrative retrenchment and furthermore, lay plans for the expansion of industry and transportation facilities." (*Ibid.*, p. 50.) At Fukushima on December 8, a pledge was made to oppose the two divisions and a "bureaucratic cabinet," and "that the party [would] continue to retain the tradi-

tional industrial policies, in particular, the expansion of railroads."
(*Ibid.*, p. 49.)

6. See any one of the resolutions recorded in *Seiyū*, No. 148:
47–54 (December 1912).

7. *Seiyū*, No. 119: 26 (June 1910).

8. *Seiyū*, No. 103: 2–4 (November 1909). The speech was given
in honor of Itō. For a speech with similar content see Hara's address
on the party's tenth anniversary (Sept. 15, 1909) in *Hara zenshū*,
II, 758–760. Hara reaffirmed in private what he had said publicly.
In his diary he entered: "The growth of popular strength everywhere
is amazing. Even Russia, where bureaucratic government has been
rife up to now, has given way to popular will. In Germany, too,
power is about to be taken over by the Imperial Diet. These situations
should be given careful thought in the future management of our
State." *Hara nikki*, III, 278 (Feb. 20, 1909).

9. Thus, preceding and following the mutual understanding of
January 1911, there had been opposition to a compromise with Katsura. For example, the Tokyo branch issued this statement to the
press on Jan. 16, 1911: "The heart of our party's platform is to
establish constitutional government. The present cabinet [Second
Katsura] is a militaristic and despotic one. This branch resolves to act
on party principle and to protect constitutional government." (*Seiyū*,
No. 126: 32, February 1911.)

In the regions, as at a Hokushin regional rally on April 2, 1911,
similar views were voiced: "On the basis of the established principles
of our party, we resolve that unconstitutional activities be erased.
. . ." (*Seiyū*, No. 130: 30, May 1911.)

Matsuda Masahisa, whose task it was to explain the progressive
nature of the mutual understanding to the various regions, expressed
regret over the resolutions; but murmurings of displeasure persisted.
(*Seiyū*, No. 130: 30, May 1911.) See also Sasakawa, pp. 453, 459–
460; and Maeda, *Rekidai naikaku*, I, 379–380.

10. *Taiyō* (Mar. 1913), Special Issue, pp. 193–204. For the activities of one of these men see the short work by Kinoshita Seitarō,
Taishō no seihen to waga kōdō (A personal account of the Taishō
Political Crisis; Tokyo, 1914), esp. p. 36. Kinoshita was a representative from Hokkaidō elected in 1912. His activities point out well the
predicament of those who opposed compromise but who were dependent on party power for the security of their electoral base.

11. See Bokugaku Sanjin, *Taishō ishin seihen no shinsō* (The

actual details of the Taishō Political Crisis; Tokyo, 1913), pp. 39–
41, 65. Also Rōjō, *Batsujin to tōjin*, pp. 61–62.

12. In this group were important and active leaders such as
Okazaki Kunisuke, Yoshiue Shōichirō, and Ōkubo Kishichi of the
Kantō group; Sugita Teiichi of the Hokuriku; Sugawara Den of the
Tōhoku; and Matsuda Genji of the Kyūshū group. See *Taiyō* (March
1913), Special Issue, pp. 200–203. Also Rōjō, *Batsujin to tōjin*, pp.
61–62. Bokugaku, pp. 39–41.

13. From the Seiyūkai rally of Dec. 15, 1912. *Seiyū*, No. 148: 55
(December 1912).

Individually they said: "It is perfectly all right with us if a Yamagata cabinet were established. It was he, after all, who destroyed
the Saionji cabinet. . . . A Katsura cabinet is the same. I would
consider it an enemy of the people, an enemy of constitutional government." (From a speech at the Dec. 17 Seiyūkai rally by Matsuda
Genji. Recorded in *Seiyū*, No. 149: 16, January 1913. Speeches by
Ozaki, Sugita, Yoshiue, Sugawara, Ōkubo, and others are also recorded in this issue.)

Earlier, on Dec. 7, 1912, about 60 Seiyūkai men of differing political shades including Ōoka Ikuzō, Sugawara Den, Okazaki Kunisuke,
Ozaki Yukio, and Takekoshi Yosaburō came together in a rally in
Tokyo; this occurred again on Dec. 10, 15, and 19. On the latter two
occasions between 1,000 and 2,000 persons were said to have been
present. (Bokugaku, p. 65; *Seiyū*, No. 148: 55, December 1912;
Kinoshita Seitarō, p. 36.)

14. Kojima Kazuo, *Kojima Kazuo kaiko roku* (Memoirs of Kojima;
Tokyo, 1951), p. 42. For Kojima's activities during these years see
Washio Yoshinao, *Kojima Kazuo* (Kojima Kazuo; Tokyo, 1950), pp.
860–866. See also Koyama Kango, *Koyama Kango nikki* (Diary of
Koyama; Tokyo, 1955), pp. 166–168. Koyama, a Seiyūkai member
and newspaper reporter, was one of those in the original group. See
also Washio, *Inukai Bokudo*, II, 12.

15. Uzaki Rōjō, "Kōjunsha ron" (On the Kōjunsha), *Chūō kōron*,
pp. 73–84 (May 1913).

16. Known as Kōjunsha an, and also as "shigi kempō," Osatake
Takeki, *Nihon kensei shi no kenkyū* (Researches on Japanese constitutional history; Tokyo, 1943), pp. 275–314.

17. Unlike most social clubs of its day, the Kōjunsha was always
rife with disorganized political gossip. According to Takekoshi Yosaburō, one of the regulars, this was the result of the continuation of

the ideals of Fukuzawa Yukichi. (Takekoshi Yosaburō, "Takekoshi Yosaburō Shi danwa sokki." Recorded, typed interviews with Takekoshi in 1939. In National Diet Library, Tokyo.)

Takahashi Yoshio, a high-ranking member of the Kōjunsha, recorded some of the political gossip that went on in his diary, "Banshō roku" (unpublished and kept at the National Diet Library, Tokyo). To quote from one entry, Sept. 2, 1912, pp. 75–77: "Set out for the Kōjunsha. Kamata Eikichi [leader of Kōjunsha], Fukuzawa Momosuke [business leader and Seiyūkai representative], Aijima Kanjirō [Inukai supporter, Kokumintō], Ishikawa Kammei [editor, *Jiji shimpō*], and others were carrying on a heated political discussion. Saionji's successor will be most likely Terauchi. If so, Hara will reach an agreement with Terauchi and will organize the cabinet. The Seiyūkai is a pro-government party and so it will not resist this and try to form its own cabinet. The Seiyūkai has become a powerful party because it has retained close ties with the government. Naturally, when it ceases to do this, it will split. Thus, the executive staff will not gamble the unity of the party and its ties with the government. Fukuzawa, who had just joined the Seiyūkai, urged party reform. But Aijima said this was absurd because there was no hope for this to be carried out. . . . Aijima had just recently joined the Kokumintō and he said that the leadership of the party was divided between Inukai, Ōishi [Masami], and Kōno [Hironaka] and that unity could not be achieved. . . . Because the Seiyūkai has ties with the government, it draws business support due to interest relationships. But the Kokumintō remains an anti-government party and hence draws only lawyers and those with political grievances. In an emergency, it has no funds and so there is little hope for the future. Under these circumstances, it is a problem to see how long the party lasts. Thus they went on."

18. Some of the regulars at the Kōjunsha:

Itō Kinryō: Keiō, studied in England, *Nihon shimbun*.

Ishikawa Kammei: Keiō, *Jiji shimpō* editor.

Honda Seiichi: Tokyo, traveled in Europe, *Asahi shimbun*.

Koyama Kango: Keiō, ex-*Jiji shimpō* reporter, Seiyūkai representative. (Married to Fukuzawa Yukichi's granddaughter.)

Fukuzawa Momosuke: Keiō, Seiyūkai representative. (Adopted son of Fukuzawa Yukichi.)

Kikuchi Butoku: Keiō, ex-*Jiji shimpō* reporter, Seiyūkai representative.

Shiba Teikichi: Keiō, traveled in Europe, *Yorozu chōhō* reporter.

Takekoshi Yosaburō: Keiō, Seiyūkai representative.
Hayashi Kiroku: Keiō, Seiyūkai representative.
Horikiri Zembei: Keiō, Seiyūkai representative.
Nakano Seigō: Waseda, *Asahi shimbun* reporter.
Yugeta Seiichi: *Asahi shimbun* reporter.
Aijima Kanjirō: Kokumintō representative.
Kojima Kazuo: Kokumintō representative.

Taiyō (March 1913), Special Issue, pp. 193–204; Shinobu Seizaburō, Watanabe Tōru and Koyama Hirotake, eds., *Gendai hantaisei undō shi* (A history of opposition movements in modern Japan; Tokyo, 1960), I, 181–182; Koyama, pp. 162–168; Kojima, p. 42.

19. Ōnishi Rihei, ed., *Fukuzawa Momosuke ō den* (Biography of Fukuzawa; Tokyo, 1939), pp. 298–301; Washio, *Inukai Bokudō*, II, 12.

20. From a speech on Feb. 12, 1913, by Ukita Kazutami, editor of the leading liberal journal, *Taiyō*. Quoted in Bokugaku, p. 219.

21. One example is the critic and editor of the journal *Taiyō*, Ukita Kazutami. For Ukita, the basic elements of constitutional government were: (1) prevention of arbitrary use of power; (2) provision of legal protection for broad areas of personal freedom; (3) establishment of party cabinets controlled by the majority party in the Diet; (4) establishment of a policy based on a broad consensus of the people and not on the views of the few; and (5) assurances that responsibility for all political decisions be made explicit. Any one of Ukita's editorials that appeared regularly in *Taiyō* will bear these points out. One of his clearest statements is his "Rikken seiji no kompongi" (The basic principles of constitutional politics), *Taiyō*, pp. 7–11 (April 1913). The writings of the critic Maruyama Kanji also reflect Ukita's views. For example, his "Minshuteki keikō to seitō" (Democratic tendencies and parties), *Nihon oyobi nihonjin*, No. 597: 72–76 (January 1913).

22. In Japan, the Emperor system was explicitly taught, hence widely understood, as a system in which imperial power was unlimited; university graduates and those in government, however, understood that the power of the Emperor was limited. (See Kunō and Tsurumi, p. 132.) Attempts such as that of Minobe Tatsukichi (his "organ theory") to make explicit and widespread the notion that the Emperor was limited because he was part of the State were meaningful only to the educated elite.

23. Ozaki, *Rikken kinnō ron*, pp. 15–16. The same idea was expressed by Nakano Seigō, who tended toward strident nationalism —

for example, his "Kensei yōgo no kompon ron" (The basic thesis of protecting constitutional government), *Nihon oyobi nihonjin*, No. 604: 61–68 (April 1913); his "Kensei yōgo isshūnen" (One year after the Movement for Constitutional Government), *Nihon oyobi nihonjin*, No. 621: 164–171 (January 1914); and for the same ideas in a historical framework, his *Meiji minken shi ron*. For a brief reference on this subject by a contemporary scholar, see Imai Seiichi, "Seiji shidōsha no shisōteki yakuwari" (The intellectual role of political leaders), in *Kindai Nihon shisō shi kōza* (Lectures on modern Japanese intellectual history; Tokyo, 1960), V, 61–62; and with regard to Yoshino Sakuzō's views, Kunō and Tsurumi, pp. 151–159.

24. Financial support for the movement came from influential business leaders at the Kōjunsha. Some have suggested that the Mitsui men at the Kōjunsha contributed funds to counter a Mitsubishi-Katsura coalition; whatever their reasons, they did contribute funds in the early stages of the movement. Thus Tokutomi Soho (Iichiro), for example, recalled: "The so-called Movement for Constitutional Government was not launched by party men so much as by men who had no ties with the parties at all. They produced the funds from their various pockets and caused party men to start the movement. This is an undeniable fact." (Tokutomi, *Soho jiden*, p. 429.)

The fact of money coming from Asabuki Eiji, a powerful adviser to the Mitsui firm and pro-Seiyūkai, was attested to by Itakura Takuzō at an interview on July 5, 1963. Itakura was a reporter for the *Jiji shimpō* and one of the few eyewitnesses of the events being related who is still alive. A discussion of this aspect of the movement can also be found in Shirayanagi, pp. 259–269, and Uzaki Rōjō, pp. 73–82.

25. Ozaki became minister of education under Ōkuma in 1898. Skillful manipulation by opposition factions of his so-called "Republican Speech" forced Ozaki's resignation, and he was replaced by Inukai. The latter held the post for only four days because the Ōkuma cabinet collapsed.

Ozaki's "Republican Speech" was given before a teachers' association in August 1898. In it he decried the glorification of wealth in Japan, then went on to make this innocuous statement which was seized by his enemies: "It is out of the question that Japan will become a republic. Even if a country has been through thousands of years of history, it does not mean that it will become a republic. But let us assume, for argument's sake, that Japan were a republic and it had a presidential election system, it will probably be a Mitsui or

Mitsubishi man that would be elected president." (Isa Hideo, *Ozaki Yukio den* [Biography of Ozaki; Tokyo, 1951], p. 597.)

The fact that no one came to his defense in this case would cause Ozaki in the 1930's to compare it with the general apathy of the populace regarding the treatment being meted out to Minobe Tatsukichi at that time. For his outspoken comments on this matter see *ibid.*, pp. 597–616.

26. Oka, *Kindai no seijika*, pp. 153–154; Washio, *Kojima Kazuo*, pp. 419, 732–739; Uzaki, *Inukai den*, pp. 20–22.

27. Ozaki was disappointed because neither Ōkuma nor Inukai nor anyone in the party, for that matter, came to his defense in the "Republican Speech" incident; furthermore, as he admitted, he had a high regard for Itō. Ozaki's regard for Ōkuma as party leader had declined considerably in the 1890's; at the same time his respect for Itō's "power of judgement" had grown. Ozaki, *Kensei shi o kataru*, I, 423–426, 454.

28. Ozaki admitted this in his memoirs, *Gakudō kaiko roku*, II, 24.

29. In the 1890's he contended in a bitter factional struggle against Shimada Saburō, although he knew he could serve the cause of Kaishintō unity if he cooperated: "Shimada was already fourth or fifth in the bureaucratic ranking . . . were I to support him I would have become, in most likelihood, a subordinate of his. Finding it distasteful to lower my head to anyone, I naturally struggled against him." (Ozaki, *Kensei shi o kataru*, I, 141.)

30. Rōjō, *Batsujin to tōjin*, p. 63. Uzaki (Rōjō Gakujin, pen name) used this phrase to describe Ozaki's career 1898–1912, but it can be applied to Ozaki's career to its end.

31. For a good discussion of Inukai, see Oka, *Kindai no seijika*, pp. 143–196.

32. Letter to one Inukai Gentarō (not a relative). Washio Yoshinao, *Inukai Bokudō shokan shū* (Collected letters of Inukai; Tokyo, 1940), p. 134.

33. Letter from Inukai to Kobayashi Sozōei, Dec. 12, 1912. Washio, *Inukai shokan shū*, p. 132.

34. Washio, *Inukai shokan shū*, p. 135.

35. Hara preferred to remain flexible for negotiation with Katsura, and for this reason felt that a strong movement was to his advantage. But, to preserve his tactical position, he could not agree with Inukai that he become directly involved in the movement. He therefore offered to Inukai three leaders — Ozaki, Okazaki Kunisuke, and Sugita Teiichi — to represent the Seiyūkai in the movement. Sugita

and Ozaki were leaders from the early party movement, and both had imbibed deeply the activism of that tradition. Both were critical of Hara, and Hara's opinion of them was low; he felt that they, especially Ozaki, were expendable. (*Hara zenshū*, II, 1038–1039, and also *Hara nikki*, IV, 287, June 8, 1911; V, 50, Apr. 2, 1912.) Okazaki was different. He was close to Hara and not expendable as were the other two; in this case, he was willing to act as mediator for Hara in the movement because he disliked Katsura. Okazaki never forgave Katsura for drawing on his support for Yamagata in 1898 and then doing nothing while Yamagata proceeded to carry out a series of anti-party reforms. Okazaki Kunisuke, *Kensei kaiko roku* (Memoirs of Okazaki; Tokyo, 1935), pp. 137–139.

36. Inukai to Kojima Kazuo and Aijima Kanjirō on Dec. 14, 1912, in preparation for meeting at the Kōjunsha on Dec. 14 and 15. Washio, *Inukai shokan shū*, p. 135.

37. Ozaki, *Gakudō kaiko roku*, pp. 61–63. See also Isa, pp. 770–771.

38. Speech at Osaka on Jan. 13, 1913. Bokugaku, pp. 100–101.

39. For example, Ozaki's speech of Dec. 19, 1912, in Tokyo, quoted in Isa, pp. 771–772. See also Ozaki's *Seiji kyōiku ron* (On political education), ed. Sukuri Jūichi (Tokyo, 1913), pp. 46 and 75, in which these points are explicitly made.

40. Speech of Dec. 19, 1912. Uzaki, *Inukai den*, p. 240.

41. Speech of Dec. 27, 1912. Washio, *Inukai Bokudō*, II, 23. Also Bokugaku, pp. 68–70.

42. For a brief description of these meetings, see the account by the tea receptionist for the meetings in Tsurumi Shunsuke, *Narikin tenka*, pp. 40–41.

43. Said by Yamagata to Saionji on Feb. 11, 1913, recorded by Yamagata himself in his own account of the Taishō Political Crisis "Taishō seihen ki" (unpublished), in National Diet Library, Tokyo. See also Irie, p. 156. Any of the biographies of men in this period relate the same details. Tokutomi, *Katsura den*, II, 613–619; Kyōguchi Motokichi, *Kindai Nihon rekishi kōza: Taishō seihen zengo* (Lectures on modern Japanese history: the Taishō Political Crisis; Tokyo, 1940), p. 196.

44. Gotō went on to disapprove of two of Katsura's choices: Ōura Kanetake and Katō Kōmei. In Gotō's view, Ōura was a "schemer" who would draw unnecessary Seiyūkai opposition, while Katō was ignorant of developments in Japan. Gotō to Katsura on Dec. 14, 1912, Katsura monjo, Gotō No. 25.

45. Kiyoura to Yamagata on Dec. 7, 1912. Tokutomi, *Yamagata den*, II, 811.

46. Any account dealing with this period gives the same details. See, for example, Shinobu, *Taishō seiji shi*, p. 149; Tokutomi, *Seijika no Katsura*, pp. 176–181; Tokutomi, *Katsura den*, II, 620; or Kyōguchi, p. 224. From Koyama Kango, a young Seiyūkai member active at the Kōjunsha, who, in retrospect, said that Katsura was loyal: "Society, however, was cynical. Everyone was surprised that the still not old . . . the overly ambitious and unseasoned Katsura should suddenly enter the Imperial Household. Scandalous talk began to mount about the distinction between the Imperial Household and the civil government being thrown into confusion. And then, rumors spread that Katsura, to say nothing of Prince Yamagata in the background, was pulling strings from the Imperial Household to use the two divisions plan to cause the resignation of the Saionji cabinet." (Koyama, p. 292.)

47. See Egi Yoku's account recorded in Ōtsu, VI, 670–671; Tokutomi, *Katsura den*, II, 615–618.

48. Tokutomi, *Sohō jiden*, p. 429.

49. Seki Naohiko, *Shichijūnen no kaiko* (Memoirs of Seki; Osaka, 1933), p. 168. For details of the rally see *Taiyō* (March 1913), Special Issue, p. 198, and Ōtsu, VI, 766. The general resolution read: "The high-handed tactics of clique government has now reached its extreme. Constitutional government has been placed in imminent danger. We resolve firmly to reject compromise and uproot clique government, and on this basis, protect constitutional government."

50. From the resolution at the rally of Dec. 19. See Ōtsu, VI, 766.

51. For resolutions and accounts of the activities of party men: Isa, p. 773; Washio, *Inukai Bokudō*, II, 22–24; Maeda, *Rekidai naikaku*, I, 432.

52. See, for example, Kataoka, pp. 334–335.

NOTES TO CHAPTER 7

1. Tokutomi, *Katsura den*, I, 789–882, 935–944; Okazaki, p. 137.

2. From Gotō's manuscript on the Taishō Political Crisis, "Taishō seihen shimatsu genkō," in Tsurumi Yūsuke, *Gotō Shimpei den*, VI, 309 and passim; also, Nagashima Ryūji, *Seikai hiwa* (A personal account of the political world; Tokyo, 1928), p. 105.

3. *Jiji shimpō* (Jan. 16, 1913), p. 4; Kinoshita Kenjirō, "Kinoshita Kenjirō Shi danwa sokki" (Recorded interview with Kinoshita in 1939), in National Diet Library, Tokyo.

4. Following a visit by Irie Kan'ichi on Jan. 9, 1913. Yamagata Aritomo, "Taishō seihen ki" (An account of the Taishō Political Crisis), in National Diet Library, Tokyo.

5. Takazaki Shinshō to Yamagata on Jan. 28, 1913, Yamagata monjo, microfilm No. 50-15-6.

6. Katsura to Inoue Kaoru on Feb. 8, 1909, Inoue monjo, microfilm No. 21-14-2. Also, Katsura to Yamagata stating the same feelings on Sept. 14, 1910, Yamagata monjo, microfilm No. 50-15-152.

7. Katsura to Yamagata on Jan. 13, 1913, Yamagata Aritomo, "Taishō seihen ki."

8. From Gotō's "Taishō seihen shimatsu genkō," quoted in Tsurumi Yūsuke, VI, 304–305.

9. Hara nikki, VI, 106 (Aug. 14, 1914).

10. Katsura to Yamagata on Nov. 1, 1912 quoted in Ōtsu, VII, 7–8.

11. Ibid., p. 5.

12. Yamagata Aritomo, "Taishō seihen ki."

13. Ibid.

14. Inukai reported this in a letter to Kohashi Sozōei on Dec. 28, 1912, Washio, Inukai shokan shū, pp. 132–133.

15. Den Kenjirō, Den Kenjirō nikki (Unpublished diary of Den), in National Diet Library in Tokyo.

16. Hara nikki, V, 159 (Dec. 18, 1912).

17. Miura, pp. 388–389.

18. Draft enclosed in Watanabe Chiaki to Katsura in late December, Katsura monjo, Watanabe, No. 26.

19. Yamagata Aritomo, "Taishō seihen ki." See also Ōtsu, VII, 16–17. Katsura also warned Yamagata to refrain from making statements to the press injurious to his cabinet. On Dec. 11 Yamagata reiterated the need for the two army divisions in an interview printed in Jiji shimpō (Dec. 11, 1912), p. 4. Katsura's warning to Yamagata on this matter is documented in Irie, pp. 422–424.

20. Katsura to Yamagata on Jan. 12, 1913, Yamagata Aritomo, "Taishō seihen ki." See also Ōtsu, VII, 799–800.

21. Yamagata Aritomo, "Taishō seihen ki."

22. Yamagata to Katsura on Jan. 14, 1913, Yamagata Aritomo, "Taishō seihen ki."

23. Yamagata to Hara, Hara nikki, VI, 102–104 (Aug. 14, 1914).

24. Hara nikki, V, 158 (Dec. 17, 1912).

25. Ibid., 158–159 (Dec. 17, 1912).

26. Ibid., 166–167 (Jan. 16, 1913).

27. See for example Kinoshita Seitarō, pp. 55–56; Ueda, pp. 68–69, 71–72.

28. Den Kenjirō nikki (Jan. 17, 1913).

29. Saionji, *Jiden*, pp. 163–164.

30. See Gotō's notes of his interview with Saionji, "Saionji kaiken oboegaki," Tsurumi Yūsuke, VI, 310–317.

31. *Ibid.*, p. 314.

32. Inukai to Koguri Sadao on Dec. 10, 1908, Washio, *Inukai Bokudō*, I, 795.

33. Katō Masanosuke, pp. 129–133; Kinoshita Kenjirō; Oka, *Kindai no seijika*, pp. 156–158.

34. Kinoshita Kenjirō; Uzaki, *Chōya no godai batsu*, pp. 228–245.

35. Shibutani Sakusuke, *Taketomi Tokitoshi* (Biography of Taketomi; Tokyo, 1934), pp. 145–147.

36. From Ōishi's statement on the need for two parties, "Risōteki nidai seitō no tairitsu" (The ideal of two-party rivalry) in Okumura Akira, ed., *Saikin seikai no shinsō* (The details of recent developments in the political world; Tokyo, 1911), pp. 14–16.

37. For example, Kōno Hironaka's account in Ōtsu, VII, 32–36; Kataoka, pp. 334–335; Bokugaku, pp. 86–91; Ueda, p. 54.

38. Inukai to Kohashi Sozōei on Dec. 28, 1912, Washio, *Inukai shokan shū*, p. 133.

39. Details can be found in Uzaki, *Inukai den*, pp. 228–229; Washio, *Inukai Bokudō*, II, 27–28; Ōtsu, VII, 22–26; and Maeda, *Rekidai naikaku*, I, 437.

40. Kōno's account is in Ōtsu, VII, 36–37.

41. Katsura to Yamagata on January 19, 1913, Yamagata Aritomo, "Taishō seihen ki." Also Ōtsu, VII, 18–19; and Tokutomi, *Katsura den*, II, 682–688.

42. Den Kenjirō denki hensankai, ed., *Den Kenjirō den* (Biography of Den; Tokyo, 1922), pp. 242–245; Hirata Tōsuke to Yamagata, Jan. 16, 1913, quoted in Tokutomi, *Yamagata den*, II, 835.

43. Den Kenjirō hensankai, pp. 242–245.

44. Yamagata Aritomo, "Taishō seihen ki."

45. Tokutomi, *Yamagata den*, II, 840.

46. Takazaki Shinshō to Yamagata on Jan. 28, 1913, in Tokutomi, *Yamagata den*, II, 840–841. In the rest of the letter (Yamagata monjo, microfilm No. 50-15-6), Takazaki attacked Katsura for his arrogance and predicted that he would in the end but compound the evils of the Seiyūkai.

47. From Kōno's account in Ōtsu, VII, 37–38.

48. One who joined with Katsura recalled his move in this way: "Those of us who represented Hyōgo prefecture had then to decide what we were to do. There were nine from our party representing Hyōgo at that time. . . . Six of us decided that under the circumstances, there was little hope for the Kokumintō, so we decided to join Katsura's new party." (Saitō Takao, *Kaiko shichijūnen* [Memoirs of Saitō; Tokyo, 1948], p. 20.)

For similar views, see Hongō, p. 180; Bokugaku, p. 165.

49. Inukai to a friend in his home prefecture of Okayama on Feb. 8, 1913, Washio, *Inukai shokan shū*, p. 137.

50. See *Taiyō* (Mar. 1913), Special Issue, pp. 205–216; Adachi, *Jijoden*, pp. 118–124; Shirayanagi, pp. 182, 223.

51. Gotō to Katsura on Dec. 14, 1912, Katsura monjo, Gotō No. 25.

52. For example, Miura, pp. 394–395; Rōjō, *Batsujin to tōjin*, pp. 50–66. The general comment at the Kōjunsha was along these same lines. See Takahashi, "Banshō roku" (Diary; Sept. 2, 1912), pp. 75–77; (Dec. 16, 1912), pp. 172–174.

53. Katsura was alleged to have given as much as 50,000 yen to one Seiyūkai leader, Itō Daihachi. Maeda, *Rekidai naikaku*, I, 430. See also *Taiyō* (March 1913), Special Issue, pp. 209–210, and Hashimoto Itsuo, *Kinchiku yoei* (Biographical sketches of Ōura Kanetake; Tokyo, 1942), p. 255.

54. Tsurumi Yūsuke, VI, 355.

NOTES TO CHAPTER 8

1. *Hara nikki*, V, 170–171 (Jan. 20, 1913). Because of this optimism, he also saw no need to agree to a union with Inukai, of whom he was rightly suspicious. Thus he rejected another proposal by Inukai in late January for a union: "There is some validity for a union, but the Kokumintō is now in chaos. Since the future of the Kokumintō is quite pessimistic, that party needs a union to brighten its future prospects. . . . Our interests are different from those of Inukai." *Ibid.*, V, 177 (Jan. 28, 1913).

Hara was alleged to have asked Inukai how old he was, implying that if Inukai were younger than Hara, which he was not by one year, he could join the Seiyūkai. Washio, *Inukai Bokudō*, II, 58–59.

2. *Hara nikki*, V, 178 (Jan. 29, 1913); also V, 179 (Jan. 31, 1913).

3. *Ibid.*, p. 171 (Jan. 22, 1913).

4. Seki Naohiko, an Inukai supporter, calculated at least 10,000 at the Osaka rally of Jan. 14. He made his calculation on the basis

of eight persons per mat in the park where the rally was held. Seki, p. 169.

5. Ōno Bamboku, *Ōno Bamboku kaisō roku* (Memoirs of Ōno; Tokyo, 1962), pp. 22–36. Ōno, formerly vice-president of the Jimintō, began his political career as a "non-Diet personnel" (*ingaisha*) in the Seiyūkai during the Taishō Political Crisis. He accompanied Diet men and delivered speeches.

Also, *Jiji shimpō* (Jan. 25 and 26, 1913).

Takahashi Yoshio recorded in his diary (Takahashi, "Banshō roku," Jan. 2, 1913, pp. 44–45): "Den Yoshifumi attended the rally for Constitutional Government today . . . but there was utter confusion and he could not enter the hall."

6. Katsura to Yamagata on Jan. 24, 1913. Yamagata Aritomo, "Taishō seihen ki."

Katsura's trying experience during the Sino-Japanese War was related by his mistress, O-Koi. Katsura was a division commander in Manchuria in 1894. He had been drinking heavily with his staff. When the enemy attacked, he is said to have rushed out into the winter night to shout an order only to fall face downward into the snow, unconscious. The experience gave Katsura insomnia and a variety of bodily aches and pains and caused him to stop drinking. Later he restricted himself to an occasional glass of wine, but he gave that up too. (Andō, *O-Koi monogatari*, pp. 269–271.)

7. Ōtsu, VI, 779–780.

8. Hugh Borton, *Japan's Modern Century* (New York, 1955), Appendix IV, p. 500.

9. Ōtsu, VI, 788–794.

10. Ōnishi, pp. 307–308.

11. Abe Shinnosuke, quoted in Nakano Yasuo, *Chichi, Nakano Seigō den* (A biography of my father, Nakano Seigō; Tokyo, 1958), p. 215.

12. *Hara nikki*, V, 185 (Feb. 5, 1913).

13. *Ibid.*, pp. 185–186 (Feb. 6, 1913).

14. Yamagata Aritomo, "Taishō seihen ki."

15. *Hara zenshū*, II, 1043, and also 1038–1045. For other indirect Katsura-Hara connections see *Hara nikki*, V, 181–182 (Feb. 2, 1912).

16. Katsura to Yamagata on Jan. 24, 1913, Yamagata Aritomo, "Taishō seihen ki."

17. Yamagata Aritomo, "Taishō seihen ki"; Tokutomi, *Yamagata den*, II, 843–846.

18. See Tsurumi Yūsuke, VI, 321–327.

19. See Wakatsuki, *Jiden*, p. 196.

20. For the details of the recorded talks between Katsura and Saionji, Saionji and Katō, see Tsurumi Yūsuke, VI, 330–338; Tokutomi, *Katsura den*, II, 647–652.

21. Yamagata Aritomo, "Taishō seihen ki."

22. Tsurumi Yūsuke, VI, 348–349.

23. The nine men were: Saionji, Hara, Matsuda, Motoda Hajime, Ozaki Yukio, Okazaki Kunisuke, Itō Daihachi, Noda Utarō, and Satake Sakutarō. *Hara nikki*, V, 187–188 (Feb. 9, 1913); Maeda, *Rekidai naikaku*, I, 450. Also Masumi Junnosuke, "Taishō seihen to sono zengo" (A study of the Taishō Political Crisis), *Tokyo toritsu daigaku hōgakkai zasshi* (Journal of the Association of Legal Studies at Tokyo City University), 4.1: 35–36 (November 1963).

24. Inukai was invited to sit in because of the Kokumintō alliance with the Seiyūkai. Some of the details are in: Washio, *Inukai Bokudō*, II, 102–103; Kojima, pp. 49–50; *Hara nikki*, V, 187–188 (Feb. 9, 1913).

25. Isa, p. 788.

26. *Hara nikki*, V, 188 (Feb. 9, 1913).

27. Isa, p. 788.

28. *Hara nikki*, V, 189 (Feb. 9, 1913).

29. See Tokutomi, *Katsura den*, II, 658; Wakatsuki, *Jiden*, pp. 196–197.

30. Tokutomi, *Katsura den*, II, 653–655; *Hara nikki*, V, 189–192 (Feb. 10, 1913).

31. See Washio, *Inukai Bokudō*, II, 111–112.

32. See Ōnishi, p. 301; Tokutomi, *Taishō seikyoku shi ron*, pp. 151–152.

33. *Hara nikki*, V, 190 (Feb. 10, 1913).

34. Washio, *Inukai Bokudō*, II, 106–107.

35. For a discussion of Saionji and the rescript, see Satō, pp. 79–97. For a more scathing interpretation of Saionji, see Masumi, "Taishō seihen," 4.1: 26–47.

36. Bokugaku, p. 191. For an almost identical speech delivered earlier, see Kobayashi, III, 646.

37. *Hara nikki*, V, 191 (Feb. 10, 1913); *Hara zenshū*, II, 1045. A detailed discussion of these events can be found in Masumi, "Taishō seihen," 4.1: 43 and passim.

38. And Katsura was said to have replied: "Thank you, my best regards to Hara also." (*Hara zenshū*, II, 1045.)

39. One of his followers, Wakatsuki Reijirō, recalled his feelings,

as well as those of others, in this way: "We were convinced we could destroy the Seiyūkai and thus wanted to proceed straight on. . . . In those days, once a struggle was underway, force was used at elections so the side of the government could win a majority. Most of us expected to take part in this and were disappointed when Katsura resigned." Wakatsuki, "Wakatsuki Reijirō Danshaku danwa sokki."

40. *Hara nikki*, V, 191 (Feb. 10, 1913).

41. Yamagata memo dated mid-February 1913, Yamagata monjo, microfilm No. 50-15-11.

42. *Hara nikki*, V, 195 (Feb. 13–14, 1913).

43. "Susunde issen subeki ka? Shirizoite kōto o kisubeki ka? Kaisan ya?! Sōjishoku ya?!" (Tsurumi Yūsuke, VI, 310.)

44. According to the account of Itakura Takuzō, reporter for the *Jiji shimpō*, at an interview on July 5, 1963. The ordeal soured Tokutomi on politics in general. He concluded that democracy had become rampant. (Tokutomi, *Sohō jiden*, pp. 434–435; and his *Taishō seikyoku shi ron*, pp. 226–228.)

45. Washio, *Inukai Bokudō*, II, 91–94; Ōno, pp. 15–22; *Taiyō* (March 1913), Special Issue, pp. 233–239.

46. Shinobu, *Taishō demokurashii*, I, pp. 227–238; Hongō, pp. 204–208; Hosoi, p. 182.

47. *Hara nikki*, IV, 75 (July 12, 1910).

48. His views on this are clearest with regard to riots in Sept. 1913. See *Hara nikki*, V, 293–294 (Sept. 14, 1913).

NOTES TO CHAPTER 9

1. *Hara nikki*, V, 189–192 (Dec. 10, 1913); see also Masumi, "Taishō seihen," 4.1: 46.

2. *Hara nikki*, V, 193 (Feb. 11, 1913). Some of the details of this meeting were related by Saionji to Matsumoto Gōkichi: Matsumoto Gōkichi, *Taishō demokurashii ki no seiji: Matsumoto Gōkichi seiji nisshi* (The politics of Taishō democracy: the diary of Matsumoto), ed. Oka Yoshitake and Hayashi Shigeru (Tokyo, 1959), pp. 525–526; see also, Saionji, *Jiden*, pp. 166–167.

3. Seki, p. 173.

4. As Genrō, Saionji thought of himself as successor to Yamagata; he therefore saw little difference between himself and the traditional enemy of the party he headed: "Yamagata is commonly referred to as leaning to the right and I to the left, but I do not believe in re-

publican ideals. I believe in the principle of the Emperor. . . . Yamagata's right and my left are actually one." (Saionji, *Jiden*, p. 153.)

While reconciling his differences in that facile manner, his attitude toward the advocates of party government was naive: "Some say from the standpoint of rational and normal constitutional government that the prime minister should be exchanged between the Seiyūkai, and when its cabinet collapses, the Kenseikai or the Kokumintō. But a Seiyūkai cabinet is not a Seiyūkai cabinet. I consider it the Emperor's cabinet. What books treat the matter of a rational or normal [constitutional order] and what country carries on government according to these ideas?" (Matsumoto Gōkichi, p. 142.)

5. *Hara nikki*, V, 241 (Mar. 25, 1913); see also V, 192–195 (Feb. 11–12, 1913).

6. Saionji to Hara on Mar. 1, 1913, "Saionji Kimmochi shokan, Taishō jidai" (Letters of Saionji to Hara, Taishō period), in National Diet Library, Tokyo, No. 57, and Mar. 31, 1913, No. 58.

7. Saionji, *Jiden*, p. 165.

8. *Hara nikki*, V, 195 (Feb. 13–19, 1913).

9. *Hara nikki*, IV, 288 (June 8, 1911).

10. *Ibid.*, p. 114 (Nov. 11, 1910).

11. *Hara nikki*, V, 301 (Sept. 29, 1913).

12. *Ibid.*, pp. 193–195 (Feb. 12, 1913); and Bokugaku, p. 210.

13. *Hara nikki*, V, 193–194 (Feb. 12, 1913).

14. Kobayashi, III, 678. Okuda became minister of education, Takahashi became finance minister, and Yamamoto became minister of agriculture and commerce.

15. *Hara nikki*, V, 195–197 (Feb. 13–19, 1913); Sasakawa, p. 353.

16. Kinoshita Seitarō, p. 101.

17. Sasakawa, p. 532; Bokugaku, pp. 239–240; Kinoshita Seitarō, pp. 112–113; Ōnishi, pp. 309–310.

18. According to Itakura Takuzō, a reporter at that time, at a personal interview on July 5, 1963.

19. Hongō, p. 212. See also Maruyama Fukumatsu, *Nagano-ken seitō shi* (History of the parties in Nagano prefecture; Nagano, 1928), II, 138–144; *Hara nikki*, V, 217 (Mar. 24, 1913).

20. The hard faction first argued that the talks with Yamamoto should be ceased. Later it asked that: (1) Yamamoto join the Seiyūkai; (2) all the cabinet posts be filled by Seiyūkai men; (3) Inukai be included in the cabinet. This was followed by the following requests: (1) that Yamamoto announce his support of Seiyūkai principles; (2) that non-Seiyūkai cabinet members join the party; (3) that

cooperation with the Kokumintō continue. Sasakawa, pp. 524–525; Kinoshita Seitarō, pp. 104–128; Bokugaku, pp. 212–213.

21. Yokoyama Yūi, *Katō Komei ron sono ta* (Biographical sketches of Katō and others; Toyko, 1917), p. 183.

22. The words of Takekoshi Yosaburō, a member of the hard faction in the Seiyūkai, "Takekoshi Yosaburō Shi danwa sokki." For an interesting discussion, see Masumi, "Taishō seihen," 4.1: 48–61.

23. For example, Asabuki Eiji was alleged to have offered the Seiyūkai 300,000 yen if an election took place. Ōnishi, pp. 302–303.

24. *Hara nikki*, V, 207 (Mar. 1, 1913). Hara was in close touch with Kōjunsha leaders such as Kamata Eikichi and Asabuki Eiji throughout the Taishō Political Crisis. He also held talks with them regarding his plans for regional industrial development. (*Ibid.*, p. 263, July 10, 1913, and pp. 332–333, Oct. 28, 1913.) For Hara-Kōjunsha connections see *Hara nikki*, IV, 360 (Sept. 27, 1911); IV, 401–402 (Nov. 30, 1911); IV, 406 (Dec. 6, 1911); and V, 420 (Feb. 26, 1914).

25. *Hara nikki*, V, 195–201 (Feb. 13–19, 1913).

26. Bokugaku, pp. 232–234; also, Ozaki Yukio, "Taishō seihen no kaiko" (Reflections on the Taishō Political Crisis), *Jiji shimpō* (Jan. 3, 1914), p. 3.

27. Kinoshita Seitarō, pp. 118–121; Maruyama Fukumatsu, II, 138–144, 178–179.

28. Okazaki, p. 137.

Okazaki had not taken active part in the Movement for Constitutional Government for reasons of ideal: this new move of his was, by admission, the result of a desire to strike against Katsura: "Actually, I harbored for many years a desire to strike back at Katsura for a serious breach of faith he committed. This opportunity arose . . . hence, I gave my all to the Movement, which I was neither skilled at [leading] nor of which I was especially fond."

See also *Hara nikki*, V, 203 (Feb. 23, 1913).

29. Nagashima, pp. 102–103; Yokoyama, p. 185; Isa, pp. 792–793. In fact, by early March Hara clearly saw that Ozaki would play into the hands of the Dōshikai (*Hara nikki*, V, 208, Mar. 3, 1913). Later in the month, Saionji also reported from Kyoto that Ozaki was working on behalf of the "bureaucratic faction." (Saionji to Hara on Mar. 31, 1913, "Saionji shokan," No. 58.)

30. Isa, p. 798.

31. Seki, p. 74.

32. Bokugaku, pp. 235–236.

33. Inukai to Kohashi Sozōei on Apr. 7, 1914, Washio, *Inukai shokan shū*, p. 153.

34. Bokugaku, p. 295.

35. Hara to Saionji, *Hara nikki*, V, 241 (Mar. 25, 1913).

36. Hayashi Kiroku, *Kōdō kōwa shū* (Collected speeches of Hayashi Kiroku; Tokyo, 1933), pp. 548–549; Bokugaku, pp. 287–288.

37. There was some complication at the outset. An anti-Seiyū coalition came within one vote in the budget committee of defeating the Seiyūkai budget. The vote was 30–31 on Mar. 14. (*Seiyū*, No. 159: 14–15 [March 1913].) On the floor of the Lower House, furthermore, the situation was touch and go right up through the actual voting. Wrote Hara: "The votes for or against [the budget] remained unclear to the end. I had the party floor whip investigate the votes a number of times . . . it was a truly critical juncture for the government." (*Hara nikki*, V, 214, Mar. 15, 1913.)

The budget passed 186–181 and this set the stage for a concentrated effort toward carrying out administrative retrenchment. As a result of retrenchment, income taxes were reduced by seven million yen. Another four million yen reduction was scheduled for business taxes, but the peers failed to act on that. Ōkurashō, ed., *Meiji Taishō zaisei shi*, III, 727–728; VI, 204; Kobayashi, III, 759–762.

38. *Hara nikki*, IV, 288–304 (June 8, 1911); see also Shinobu, *Taishō seiji shi*, pp. 1038–1040.

39. *Hara nikki*, V, 242–243 (May 28–29, 1913). See also *Seiyū*, No. 166: 12–13 (Apr. 1913).

40. *Hara nikki*, V, 254–275 (June 25, 1913); Oka, *Yamagata Aritomo*, pp. 129–130; Kobayashi, III, 763–764.

41. Hara to Mizuno Rentarō: Mizuno, *Ronsaku to zuihitsu*, p. 642. In this connection, Mizuno expressed readiness to join the Seiyūkai: "I felt it inevitable that bureaucrats from a certain level had to join a political party and take part in politics. Feeling this way, I joined the party [Seiyūkai] in spite of warnings by my predecessors." (Mizuno, *Ronsaku to zuihitsu*, pp. 644–645.)

42. The words of one Kubota Yuzuru, quoted in Mizuno, *Ronsaku to zuihitsu*, p. 643; see also, Kobayashi, III, 772.

43. *Hara nikki*, V, 209 (Mar. 6, 1913). Yamamoto had never been an ardent backer of Yamagata's ruling since its inception, and his attitude inclined definitely toward cooperation with party leaders on this issue. (*Ibid.*) On Mar. 11, for example, Yamamoto admitted in a reply to a question in the Diet that the ruling was detrimental to the function of government. (Kobayashi, III, 722.)

44. *Hara nikki,* V, 210–211 (Mar. 8, 1913); see also Shinobu, *Taishō seiji shi,* p. 190.

45. Kigoshi Yasutsuna to Yamagata on Mar. 11, 1913, Yamagata monjo, microfilm No. 50-15-8.

46. "Teikoku kengun no kompon gi yōgo ni kansuru gi," Mar. 1913, Tanaka Giichi monjo (Papers of Tanaka), in National Diet Library, Tokyo, No. 14.

47. *Hara nikki,* V, 222–234 (Apr. 18–May 8, 1913); and Shinobu, *Taishō demokurashii,* I, 254.

48. Terauchi to Yamagata on June 20, 1913, Yamagata monjo, microfilm No. 50-15-8.

49. *Hara nikki,* V, 207 (Mar. 1, 1913).

50. *Ibid.,* pp. 287–288 (Aug. 20, 1913); *ibid.,* p. 297 (Sept. 22, 1913); *ibid.,* pp. 342–343 (Nov. 8, 1913) and *ibid.,* p. 369 (Dec. 9, 1913).

51. *Ibid.,* p. 285 (Aug. 20, 1913).

NOTES TO CHAPTER 10

1. *Hara nikki,* V, 241 (May 25, 1913).

2. Katsura to Yamagata on May 22, 1913, Yamagata monjo, microfilm No. 50-15-8. Hara saw Katsura at a dinner on March 21. They did not exchange words, but Hara noted that Katsura seemed quite ill. (*Hara nikki,* V, 216, Mar. 21, 1913).

3. Nagashima, pp. 130–131.

4. *Hara nikki,* V, 241 (May 25, 1913).

5. *Hara nikki,* V, 310–311 (Oct. 7, 1913); Nagashima, pp. 130–133.

6. Details of the Siemens Incident are in Ōtsu, VII, 196–211.

7. *Hara nikki,* V, 409–410 (Feb. 10, 1914); Maeda, *Rekidai naikaku,* II, 50–55.

8. Ōtsu, VII, 277; Kobayashi, III, 841–845; *Hara nikki,* V, 423 (Feb. 28, 1914).

9. *Hara nikki,* V, 434–437 (Mar. 13–16, 1914); V, 447–449 (Mar. 22–23, 1914).

10. *Hara nikki,* V, 450–451 (Mar. 24, 1914).

11. Maeda, *Rekidai naikaku,* II, 64.

12. There was no doubt that Kiyoura would be named. He had already begun to pick his cabinet ministers several days beforehand. (*Hara nikki,* VI, 9–11, Mar. 29, 1914).

13. Details are in Ōtsu, VII, 283–285.

14. From Ōkuma's speech of Jan. 20, 1907, Washio, *Inukai Bokudō,* I, 787–788.

15. Ōkuma's views toward the Seiyūkai are clearly expressed in Nobata Kazuo, ed., *Taisei o takkan seyo* (Take a far-sighted view of the times: Some essays of Ōkuma Shigenobu; Tokyo, 1922), pp. 45–46, 68–70; Washio, *Inukai Bokudō*, II, 177.

16. Washio, *Inukai Bokudō*, II, 177.

17. Inoue Kaoru hensankai, V, 344; Oka, *Yamagata Aritomo*, pp. 140–141; Ōtsu, VII, 14.

18. Report from Mochizuki Kotarō to Inoue, Mar. 27, 1914, Inoue monjo, microfilm No. 25-1-2.

19. Inoue Kaoru hensankai, V, 356–358.

20. Inukai to a political supporter and friend in Akita, Otomekawa Yasuhiko, Apr. 20, 1914, Washio, *Inukai shokan shū*, p. 155.

21. For example, see Kobayashi, II, 899–902; *Hara nikki*, VI, 33 (May 4, 1914).

22. *Hara nikki*, VI, 11 (Mar. 30, 1914); VI, 68–69 (June 22, 1914).

23. When Inoue died Hara wrote of his one-time benefactor: "During these past years, Inoue was led astray by slanders of others; . . . hence, he frequently denounced the Seiyūkai. . . . I did not sever ties with him, but . . . our relationship deteriorated." (*Hara nikki*, VI, 315, Sept. 2, 1915).

24. For example, see *Hara nikki*, VI, 69–71 (June 22–28, 1914).

25. *Hara zenshū*, II, 1079–1081, 1090.

26. *Hara nikki*, VI, 83 (July 9, 1914).

27. Report of Mochizuki Kotarō to Inoue, Aug. 10, 1914, Inoue monjo, microfilm No. 25-5-1, and again on Aug. 19, 1914, microfilm No. 25-7-1.

28. *Hara nikki*, VI, 98–101 (Aug. 12, 1914).

29. *Ibid.*, p. 106 (Aug. 14, 1914).

30. *Ibid.*, p. 107 (Aug. 14, 1914).

31. *Ibid.*, pp. 138–210 (Sept. 22, 1914–Dec. 19, 1914).

32. *Ibid.*, pp. 235–236 (Mar. 25, 1915).

33. *Ibid.*, pp. 235–238 (Mar. 28, 1915); Kobayashi, IV, 132–145; Maruyama Fukumatsu, II, 205.

34. *Hara nikki*, VI, 238 (Mar. 28, 1915).

35. Sakai Chūshichi, *Kanazawa seisen shi* (An account of political struggles in Kanazawa; Tokyo, 1915), esp. pp. 1–3, 32–35; Maeda, *Rekidai naikaku*, II, 110–116; *Hara nikki*, VI, 235–236 (Mar. 28, 1915).

36. Maeda, *Rekidai naikaku*, II, 122–123.

37. *Hara nikki*, VI, 235–236 (Mar. 28, 1915).

38. Kanazawa was in Ishikawa prefecture. Ōkuma supporters from

Waseda University led the campaign on behalf of the Dōshikai candidate, Yokoyama Akira, a business leader in Kanazawa. They hailed Ōkuma and the Dōshikai as the progressive new party and denounced the "party evils" of the Seiyūkai, especially as regards the Seiyūkai's complicity with corrupt naval officers. From Dōshikai headquarters Finance Minister Wakatsuki Reijirō was sent to take part. Wakatsuki waged a spirited campaign attacking the Seiyūkai's positive economic policy, arguing for cutbacks in loans and the restoration of the balance of trade. On the Seiyūkai side the candidate was Nakahashi Tokugorō, a supporter of Hara, a powerful Osaka financier, and a rising figure in the Seiyūkai. Nakahashi was a prestige candidate and his victory was a must for the party. He campaigned on the traditional Seiyūkai platform — the positive economic policy; he countered Wakatsuki's economic policy as passive and urged the floating of more loans to stimulate the economy through spending. From Tokyo, Takahashi Korekiyo (former finance minister) was sent. Takahashi, known for his support of Hara's economic policy, toured the city on behalf of Nakahashi refuting the arguments of Wakatsuki. The first official returns indicated a landslide victory for the Dōshikai candidate. A month after the election was held, however, the validity of the Kanazawa election was appealed in court. (Sakai, throughout; Maeda, *Rekidai naikaku,* II, 118–121.)

39. *Hara nikki,* VI, 172 (Nov. 4, 1914).

40. *Ibid.,* p. 221 (Jan. 10, 1915); *ibid.,* pp. 226–227 (Jan. 25, 1915).

41. Saionji to Hara, Apr. 14, 1915, "Saionji shokan," No. 73.

42. *Hara nikki,* VI, 306–307 (Aug. 18, 1915).

43. *Hara nikki,* VIII, 27 (Sept. 25, 1918). An almost identical statement can be found in VII, 66–67 (Nov. 11, 1916).

44. *Hara nikki,* VII, 455 (July 10, 1918).

NOTES TO CONCLUSION

1. Yoshino, *Gendai no seiji,* pp. 15–16.

2. A concise discussion on party developments in Germany is Sigmund Neumann, "Germany: Changing Patterns and Lasting Problems," in Sigmund Neumann, ed., *Modern Political Parties* (Chicago, 1956), pp. 354–390.

3. See, for example, J. P. Mayer, *Max Weber and German Politics* (London, 1956), p. 82 and passim.

4. Maurice Duverger, *Political Parties,* tr. Barbara and Robert North (New York, 1955), p. 246 and passim.

Adachi Kenzō 安達謙蔵 . "Adachi Kenzō Shi danwa sokki"
安達謙蔵氏談話速記 . Recorded, typed interviews
with Adachi, Tokyo, 1939. In National Diet Library, Tokyo.

------Adachi Kenzō jijoden 安達謙蔵自叙伝 (Autobiography
of Adachi Kenzō). Tokyo, 1960.

Akita, George. The Meiji Constitution in Practice: The First
Diet," Journal of Asian Studies, 22.1:31-46 (November 1962).

------Foundations of Constitutional Government in Modern Japan,
1868-1900. Cambridge, Mass., 1967.

Andō Teru 安藤照 . O-Koi monogatari お鯉物語 (Memoirs
of O-Koi), and Zoku O-Koi monogatari 続お鯉物語
(Sequel to the memoirs of O-Koi). 2 vols.; Tokyo, 1927.

Asahi shimbun 朝日新聞 .

Bokugaku Sanjin 木学山人 . Taishō ishin seihen no shinsō
大正維新政変の真相 (The actual details of the Taishō
Political Crisis). Tokyo, 1913.

Borton, Hugh. Japan's Modern Century. New York, 1955.

Burns, James MacGregor. Roosevelt: The Lion and the Fox.
New York, 1956.

Chūō kōron 中央公論

Den Kenjirō denki hensankai 田健治郎伝記編纂会 , ed.
Den Kenjirō den 田健治郎伝 (Biography of Den).
Tokyo, 1922.

Den Kenjirō nikki 田健治郎日記 (Diary of Den). In National
Diet Library, Tokyo.

Duus, Peter. "The Kenseikai and the Politics of Taishō Japan."
Ph. D. thesis; Harvard University, 1965.

Duverger, Maurice. Political Parties, tr. Barbara and Robert
North. New York, 1955.

Gerth, H. H. and C. Wright Mills, tr. and ed. From Max Weber:
Essays in Sociology. New York, 1958.

Gotō Takeo 後藤武夫. Ozaki Yukio Shi cho rikken kinnō ron
尾崎行雄氏著立憲勤王論 (A rebuttal to Ozaki's
thesis on constitutional government). Tokyo, 1918.

Hackett, Roger F. "Yamagata Aritomo: A Political Biography,"
Ph. D. thesis; Harvard University, 1955.

Hanzawa Gyokujō 半沢玉城. Taishō seisen shi 大正政戦史
(A history of power struggles in Taishō). Tokyo, 1914.

Hara Kei nikki 原敬日記 (Diary of Hara). 9 vols.; Tokyo, 1951.

Hara Kei zenshū 原敬全集 (Collected works of Hara), ed. Tanaka
Asakichi 田中朝吉. 2 vols.; Tokyo, 1929.

Hashimoto Itsuo 橋本五雄. Kinchiku yoei 金竹余影
(Biographical sketches of Ōura Kanetake). Tokyo, 1942.

Hayashi Kiroku 林毅陸. Kōdō kōwa shū 弘堂講話集
(Collected speeches of Hayashi Kiroku). Tokyo, 1933.

Hayashi Shigeru 林茂, ed. Gendai shi 現代史 (A history of
modern Japan). 2 vols.; Tokyo, 1957.

Hobsbawm, E. J. Primitive Rebels. New York, 1959.

Hongō Naohiko 本郷直彦. Kōbe kensei shi 神戸権勢史
(Political history of the city of Kōbe). Kōbe, 1913.

Horikiri Zembei 堀切善兵衛. "Kokumin keizai no hatten to
tetsudō no fukyū" 国民経済の発展と鉄道の普及
(The economic advancement of the people and the expansion of
railroads); Seiyū, No. 147:11 (November 1912).

Hosoi Hajime 細井肇. Seisō to tōhei 政争と党弊 (Political struggles and party evils). Tokyo, 1914.

Ienaga Saburō 家永三郎. Kindai Nihon no shisōka 近代日本の思想家 (Some thinkers of modern Japan). Tokyo, 1962.

Ijiri Tsunekichi 井尻常吉, ed. Rekidai kenkan roku 歴代顕官録 (Record of bureaucrats and posts held). Tokyo, 1925.

Ike, Nobutaka. The Beginnings of Political Democracy in Japan. Baltimore, 1950.

Imai Seiichi 今井清一. "Seiji shidōsha no shisōteki yakuwari," 政治指導者の思想的役割 (The intellectual role of political leaders); in Kindai Nihon shisō shi kōza 近代日本思想史講座 (Lectures on modern Japanese intellectual history). 8 vols.; Tokyo, 1960, V, 61–103.

Inoue Kaoru Kō denki hensankai 井上馨侯伝記編纂会, ed. Segai Inoue Kō den 世外井上公伝 (Biography of Inoue). 5 vols.; Tokyo, 1934, Vol. 5.

Inoue Kaoru monjo 井上馨文書 (Inoue papers). In National Diet Library, Tokyo.

Inoue Kiyoshi 井上清, ed. Kindai 近代 (Modern period). Tokyo, 1960, Vol. 7 of Nihon jimbutsu shi taikei 日本人物史大系 (A general history of important Japanese figures), 7 vols.

Inukai Bokudō Shi dai enzetsushū 犬養木堂氏大演説集 (Collection of Inukai's speeches). Tokyo, 1927.

Inukai Tsuyoshi 犬養毅. Bokudō dansō 木堂談叢 (Collection of Inukai's speeches). Tokyo, 1922.

Irie Kan'ichi 入江貫一. Yamagata Kō no omokage 山県公のおもかげ (Biographical sketches of Yamagata). Tokyo, 1922.

Isa Hideo 伊佐秀雄. Ozaki Yukio den 尾崎行雄伝
(Biography of Ozaki). Tokyo, 1951.

Ishida Takeshi 石田雄. Kindai Nihon seiji kōzō no kenkyū
近代日本政治構造の研究 (Researches on the political
structure of modern Japan). 3rd ed.; Tokyo, 1959.

------Meiji shisō shi kenkyū 明治思想史研究 (Researches on
Meiji intellectual history). 4th ed.; Tokyo, 1961.

Ishii Kin'ichirō 石井金一郎. "Kensei shijō ni okeru Kei-On jidai"
憲政史上における桂園時代 (Katsura and Saionji in
constitutional history); Shigaku kenkyū 史学研究 (Researches
in history), No. 44:55-65 (Tokyo, 1951).

------"Taishō no seihen" 大正の政変 (A study of the Taishō
Political Crisis); Shigaku kenkyū, No. 30:71-82 (Tokyo, 1953).

Ishiyama Kenkichi 石山賢吉, ed. Itō Kinryō ronshū 伊藤欽
亮論集 (Collected works of Itō). 2 vols.; Tokyo, 1930.

Itakura Takuzō 板倉卓造. Notes of an interview I had with
Itakura Takuzo on July 5, 1963.

Itō Takashi 伊藤隆. "Senzen no bunkan to seiji" 戦前の文官
と政治 (The civil bureaucracy and politics in pre-war
Japan). Unpublished paper, 1961.

------"Taishō shoki Yamagata Aritomo danwa hikki" 大正初期
山県有朋談話筆記 (Record of Yamagata Aritomo's con-
versations in early Taishō); Shigaku zasshi 史学雑誌
(Journal of historical studies), 75.10:63-78 (October 1966).

Jansen, Marius B., ed. Changing Japanese Attitudes Toward
Modernization. Princeton, 1965.

Jiji shimpō 時事新報.

Kamata Eikichi Sensei denki oyobi zenshū kankōkai 鎌田栄吉
先生伝記及び全集刊行会, ed. Kamata Eikichi zenshū

鎌田栄吉全集 (Collected works of Kamata). 3 vols.; Tokyo, 1934.

Kataoka Chokuon 片岡直温 . Kaisō roku 回想録 (Memoirs of Kataoka). Tokyo, 1933.

Katō Fusazō 加藤房蔵 . Nihon kensei honron 日本憲政本論 (The essence of Japanese constitutional government). Tokyo, 1913.

------Hirata Tōsuke den 平田東助伝 (Biography of Hirata). Tokyo, 1927.

Katō Masanosuke 加藤政之助 . Katō Masanosuke kaiko roku 加藤政之助回顧録 (Memoirs of Katō). Tokyo, 1957.

Katō Seizō 加藤正造 . Seitō no hyōri 政党の表裏 (A close-up of political parties). Tokyo, 1928.

Katsura Tarō monjo 桂太郎文書 (Katsura papers). In National Diet Library, Tokyo.

Kawasaki Katsu 川崎克 , ed. Bokudō seiron shū 木堂政論集 (Collection of Inukai's political speeches). Tokyo, 1913.

Kikuchi Butoku 菊池武徳 . Seitō isshin ron 政党一新論 (On the renovation of parties). Tokyo, 1915.

Kinoshita Kenjirō 木下謙次郎 . "Kinoshita Kenjirō Shi danwa sokki" 木下謙次郎氏談話速記 . Recorded interview with Kinoshita in 1939. In National Diet Library, Tokyo.

Kinoshita Seitarō 木下成太郎 . Taishō no seihen to waga kōdō 大正の政変と我が行動 (A personal account of the Taishō Political Crisis). Tokyo, 1914.

Ko Hakushaku Yamamoto Kaigun Taishō denki hensankai 故伯爵山本海軍大将伝記編纂会 , ed. Yamamoto Gonnohyōe 山本権兵衛伝 (Biography of Yamamoto). 2 vols.; Tokyo, 1938.

Kobayashi Yūgo 小林雄吾. Rikken Seiyūkai shi 立憲政友 会史 (Official history of the Seiyūkai). 4 vols.; Tokyo, 1924.

Koizumi Sakutarō 小泉策太郎. Zuihitsu Saionji Kō 随筆 西園寺公 (Notes on Saionji). Tokyo, 1939.

Kojima Kazuo 古島一雄. Kojima Kazuo kaiko roku 古島一 雄回顧録(Memoirs of Kojima). Tokyo, 1951.

Kokumin daigakkai 国民大学会, ed. Kensei oyobi kensei kokumin 憲政及び憲政国民 (Constitutional government and a constitutional people). Tokyo, 1914.

Kokumin hyōron 国民評論.

Kokuritsu kokkai toshokan 国立国会図書館, ed. Gikai seiji bunken mokuroku 議会政治文献目録 (Bibliography of political and Diet materials). Tokyo, 1961.

Kornhauser, William. The Politics of Mass Society. Glencoe, Ill., 1959.

Koyama Kango 小山完吾. Koyama Kango nikki 小山完吾日記 (Diary of Koyama). Tokyo, 1955.

Kudō Takeshige 工藤武重. Taishō kensei shi 大正憲政史 (Constitutional history of the Taishō period). 2 vols.; Tokyo, 1927.

Kunō Osamu 久野収 and Tsurumi Shunsuke 鶴見俊輔. Gendai Nihon no shisō 現代日本の思想 (Thought in modern Japan). Tokyo, 1956.

------, Sumiya Mikio, et al. 隅谷三喜男. Kindai Nihon shisō shi kōza 近代日本思想史講座 (Lectures on modern Japanese intellectual history). 8 vols.; Tokyo, 1960, Vol. 5.

Kuribayashi Teiichi 栗林貞一. Chihō kankai no hensen 地方 官界の変遷 (Changes in regional bureaucratic personnel). Tokyo, 1930.

Kyoguchi Motokichi 京口元吉 . Kindai Nihon rekishi kōza: Taishō seihen zengo 近代日本歴史講座：大正政変 前後 (Lectures on modern Japanese history: The Taishō Political Crisis). Tokyo, 1940.

La Polombara, Joseph, and Myron Weiner, eds. Political Parties and Political Development. Princeton, 1966.

Laswell, Harold D., and Abraham Kaplan. Power and Society. New Haven, 1950.

Lipsett, Seymour M. Political Man. New York, 1963.

MacIver, R. M. The Web of Government. Rev. ed.; New York, 1965.

Maeda Renzan 前田蓮山 . Hara Kei den 原敬伝 (Biography of Hara). 2 vols.; Tokyo, 1943.

------Rekidai naikaku monogatari 歴代内閣物語 (A chronological account of cabinets). 2 vols.; Tokyo, 1961.

Maruyama Fukumatsu 丸山福松 . Nagano-ken seitō shi 長野県政党史 (History of the parties in Nagano prefecture). 2 vols.; Nagano, 1928.

Maruyama Kanji 丸山幹治 . "Minshuteki keikō to seitō" 民主的傾向と政党 (Democratic tendencies and parties); Nihon oyobi nihonjin, No. 597:72-76 (January 1913).

Maruyama, Masao. Thought and Behavior in Modern Japanese Politics. New York, 1963.

Masaki Shigeyuki 正木重之 . Gumma kensei shi 群馬県政 史 (Political history of Gumma prefecture). Gumma, 1937.

Masumi Junnosuke 升味準之輔 . "Nihon seitō shi ni okeru chihō seiji no shomondai" 日本政党史に於ける地方 政治の諸問題 (Local politics in Japanese party history); Kokka gakkai zasshi 国家学会雑誌 (The journal of the Association of Political and Social Sciences), 75.9 and 10:1–32 (August 1962); 76.1 and 2:1–61 (September 1962); 76.5 and 6:30–81 (December 1962).

------"Taishō seihen to sono zengo" 大正政変のその前後 (A study of the Taishō Political Crisis); Tōkyō toritsu daigaku hōgakkai zasshi 東京都立大学法学会雑誌 (Journal of the Association of Legal Studies at Tokyo City University), 4.1:26–61 (November 1963).

------Nihon seitō shi ron 日本政党史論 (A study on Japanese party history). 2 vols.; Tokyo, 1966.

Matsumoto Gōkichi 松本剛吉 . Taishō demokurashii ki no seiji: Matsumoto Gōkichi seiji nisshi 大正デモクラシー期の政治： 松本剛吉政治日誌 (The politics of Taishō democracy: The Diary of Matsumoto), ed. Oka Yoshitake and Hayashi Shigeru. Tokyo, 1959.

Matsumoto Sannosuke 松本三之介 . "Mimponshugi no rekishiteki keisei" 民本主義の歴史的形成 (Formation of the idea of political democracy); Seijigaku nempō 政治学年報 (The Annals of the Japanese Political Science Association). Tokyo, 1957, pp. 109–131.

Mayer, J. P. Max Weber and German Politics. London, 1956.

Michels, Robert. Political Parties, tr. Eden and Cedar Paul. New York, 1962.

------First Lectures in Political Sociology, tr. Alfred de Grazia. New York, 1965.

Mitani Taichirō 三谷太一郎 . "Seitō seiji kakuritsu katei ni okeru seiji shidō to sono jōkyō, Hara Kei o chūshin to shite" 政党政治確立過程における政治指導とその 状況 — 原敬を中心として (Political leadership and conditions in the emergence of party government, with special

emphasis on Hara Kei); Kokka gakkai zasshi, 78. 5 and 6:1-34
(November 1964); 78. 7 and 8:1-66 (February 1965); 78.11 and
12:64-118 (July 1965); 79.1 and 2:93-125 (September 1965).

------Nihon seitō seiji no keisei: Hara Kei no seiji shidō no tenkai
日本政党政治の形成：原敬の政治指導の展
開 (The formation of party politics in Japan: The development
of the political leadership of Hara Kei). Tokyo, 1967. A
collection of the articles in entry above.

Miura Kanju 三浦観樹. Kanju Shōgun kaiko roku 観樹将軍
回顧録 (Memoirs of Miura), ed. Kotani Yasutarō.
Tokyo, 1925.

Miyake Setsurei 三宅雪嶺. Meiji shisō shōshi 明治思想
小史 (A short intellectual history of Meiji). Tokyo, 1913.

Mizuno Rentarō 水野錬太郎. Seikan 静感 (Quiet thoughts).
Tokyo, 1915.

------Gakan dansetsu 我観談屑 (A miscellany of my views).
Tokyo, 1930.

------Ronsaku to zuihitsu 論策と随筆 (Writings and jottings),
ed. Matsunami Niichirō 松波仁一郎. Tokyo, 1937.

Mokushū 黙洲. "Tōsei no kakuchō" 党政の拡張 (The expansion
of party power); Nihon oyobi nihonjin, No. 516:73-75
(September 1909).

------"Giin to kenkan" 議員と県官 (Diet men and prefectural
bureaucrats); Nihon oyobi nihonjin, No. 513:74 (July 1909).

Moore, Barrington, Jr. Political Power and Social Theory.
New York, 1965.

Nadel, George H., ed. Studies in the Philosophy of History.
New York, 1965.

Nagashima Ryūji 長島隆二 . Seikai hiwa 政界秘話 (A personal account of the political world). Tokyo, 1928.

Nakamura Kikuo 中村菊男 . "Taishō seihen to Hayashi Kiroku" 大正政変と林毅陸 (Hayashi Kiroku in the Taishō Political Crisis); Hōgaku kenkyū 法学研究 (Researches on legal studies), 24.9 and 10:105-128 (September 1951).

Nakano Seigō 中野正剛 . Meiji minken shi ron 明治民権 史論 (A history of the popular rights movement in Meiji). Tokyo, 1913.

------"Kensei yōgo no kompon ron" 憲政擁護の根本論 (The basic thesis of protecting constitutional government); Nihon oyobi nihonjin, No. 604:61-68 (April 1913).

------"Kensei yōgo isshūnen" 憲政擁護一周年 (One year after the Movement for Constitutional Government); Nihon oyobi nihonjin, No. 621:164-171 (January 1914).

Nakano Yasuo 中野泰雄 . Chichi, Nakano Seigō den 父, 中野 正剛伝 (A biography of my father, Nakano Seigō). Tokyo, 1958.

Nakase Toshikazu 中瀬寿一 . "Kensei yōgo shisō no shinshutsu to tenkai - dai ichiji goken undō no shidō riron" 憲政擁護 思想の進出と展開 ─ 第一次護憲運動の指導 理論 (The emergence and development of the idea to protect constitutional government); Shigaku zasshi, 72.2:48-79 (February 1963).

Natsume Sōseki 夏目漱石 . Kokoro (The heart). Tokyo, 1914. A novel.

Neumann, Sigmund, ed. Modern Political Parties. Chicago, 1956.

Nezu Masashi 禰津正志 . Hihan Nihon gendai shi 批判日本 現代史 (A critique of modern Japanese history). Tokyo, 1958.

Nihon oyobi nihonjin 日本及び日本人 .

Nobata Kazuo 野畑一男 , ed.   Taisei o takkan seyo 大勢を
達観せよ (Take a far-sighted view of the times: Some
essays of Ōkuma Shigenobu). Tokyo, 1922.

Nukada Matsuo 額田松男. Tateru Inukai Bokudō 起てる犬
養木堂 (Biography of Inukai). Tokyo, 1930.

Oka Yoshitake 岡義武.   Kindai Nihon no seijika 近代日本の
政治家 (Politicians of modern Japan). Tokyo, 1960.

------Yamagata Aritomo 山県有朋 (Biography of Yamagata).
Tokyo, 1961.

Okazaki Kunisuke 岡崎邦輔.   Kensei kaiko roku 憲政回顧
録 (Memoirs of Okazaki). Tokyo, 1935.

Okumura Akira 奥村亮 , ed.   Saikin seikai no shinsō 最近政
界の真相 (The details of recent developments in the political
world). Tokyo, 1911.

Ōkurashō 大蔵省 , ed.   Meiji Taishō zaisei shi 明治大正
財政史 (Financial history of Meiji and Taishō). 20 vols.;
Tokyo, 1940, Vols. 1, 3, and 6.

Ōkurashō shuzei kyoku 大蔵省主税局 , ed.   Kuni no sainyū
ichiran hyō 国の歳入一覧表 (Statistical tables on government income). Tokyo, 1956.

Olson, Lawrence A., Jr.   "Hara Kei, a Political Biography." Ph.D.
thesis; Harvard University, 1954.

Ōnishi Rihei 大西理平 , ed.   Fukuzawa Momosuke ō den 福沢
桃介翁伝 (Biography of Fukuzawa). Tokyo, 1939.

Ōno Bamboku 大野伴睦.   Ōno Bamboku kaisō roku 大野伴
睦回想録 (Memoirs of Ōno). Tokyo, 1962.

Osatake Takeki 尾佐竹猛.   Nihon kensei shi no kenkyū 日本
憲政史の研究 (Researches on Japanese constitutional
history). Tokyo, 1943.

Ostragorski, M.   Democracy and the Organization of Political Parties. 2 vols.; New York, 1964.

Ōtsu Jun'ichirō 大津淳一郎. Dai Nihon kensei shi 大日本憲政史 (Constitutional history of Japan). 10 vols.; Tokyo, 1927.

Ōura Shi kinen jigyō kai 大浦氏記念事業会, ed. Ōura Kanetake den 大浦兼武伝 (Biography of Ōura). Tokyo, 1921.

Ozaki Yukio 尾崎行雄. Seiji kyōiku ron 政治教育論 (On political education), ed. Sukuri Jūichi 宿利重一. Tokyo, 1913.

_____"Taishō seihen no kaiko" 大正政変の回顧 (Reflections on the Taishō Political Crisis); Jiji shimpō (Jan. 3, 1914).

_____Rikken kinnō ron 立憲勤王論 (On constitutional loyalism). Tokyo, 1918.

_____Nihon kensei shi o kataru 日本憲政史を語る (Reflections on Japanese constitutional history). 2 vols.; Tokyo, 1938.

_____Gakudō kaiko roku 咢堂回顧錄 (Memoirs of Ozaki). 2 vols.; Tokyo, 1952.

Parsons, Talcott, ed.   Max Weber: The Theory of Social and Economic Organization. New York, 1965.

Rōjō Gakujin, see Uzaki Kumakichi.

Rudé, George.   The Crowd in History. New York, 1964.

Saionji Kimmochi 西園寺公望. Saionji Kimmochi jiden 西園寺公望自伝 (Autobiography). Recorded by Koizumi Sakutarō 小泉策太郎, ed. Kimura Ki 木村毅. Tokyo, 1949.

"Saionji Kimmochi shokan, Taishō jidai" 西園寺公望書翰, 大正時代 (Letters of Saionji to Hara, Taishō period). In

National Diet Library, Tokyo.

Saitō Takao 斎藤隆夫 . Kaiko shichijūnen 回顧七十年
(Memoirs of Saitō). Tokyo, 1948.

Sakai Chūshichi 堺忠七 . Kanazawa seisen shi 金沢政戦史
(An account of political struggles in Kanazawa). Tokyo, 1915.

Sasakawa Tamon 笹川多門 . Matsuda Masahisa kō 松田正
久稿 (Biography of Matsuda). Tokyo, 1938.

Satō Isao 佐藤功 . "Iwayuru Taishō seihen ni tsuite" いわゆる
大正政変について (A study on the Taishō Political Crisis);
Seiji keizai ronsō 政治経済論争 (Debates on politics and
economics), 1.1:79-97; 1.2:51-58 (Tokyo, 1949).

Scalapino, Robert. Democracy and the Party Movement in Pre-war
Japan. Berkeley, 1953.

------and Masumi Junnosuke. Parties and Politics in Contemporary
Japan. Berkeley, 1962.

Seiji jittai kenkyūkai 政治実態研究会 , ed. Seitō kenkyū
bunken mokuroku 政党研究文献目録 (Bibliography on
researches on the parties), No. 3. Tokyo, 1956.

Seiyū 政友 .

Seiyūkai sanjūgonen shi hensambu 政友会三十五年史編
纂部 , ed. Seiyūkai sanjūgonen shi 政友会三十五
年史 (A thirty-five-year history of the Seiyūkai). Tokyo,
1936.

Seki Naohiko 関直彦 . Shichijūnen no kaiko 七十年の回顧
(Memoirs of Seki). Osaka, 1933.

Shibutani Sakusuke 渋谷作助 . Taketomi Tokitoshi 武富時
敏 (Biography of Taketomi). Tokyo, 1934.

Shinobu Seizaburō 信夫清三郎 . Meiji seiji shi 明治政
治史 (A political history of Meiji). Tokyo, 1950.

------Taishō demokurashii shi 大正デモクラシー史 (A history of

Taishō democracy). 3 vols.; Tokyo, 1954.

------Taishō seiji shi 大正政治史 (A political history of
Taishō). Tokyo, 1954.

------, Watanabe Tōru 渡部徹 and Koyama Hirotake 小山弘
健, eds. Gendai hantaisei undō shi 現代反体制運
動史 (A history of opposition movements in modern Japan).
2 vols.; Tokyo, 1960.

Shirayanagi Shūko 白柳秀湖. Zoku zaikai taiheiki 続財界
太平記 (An account of the financial world). Tokyo, 1948.

Susukida Teikei 薄田貞敬. Nakano Buei no shichijūnen
中野武営の七十年 (Biography of Nakano). Tokyo, 1934

Suzuki Takeo 鈴木武雄. Zaisei shi 財政史 (A financial
history). Tokyo, 1962.

Tagawa Daikichirō 田川大吉郎. Seitō oyobi seitō shi
政党及び政党史 (On parties and party history).
Tokyo, 1929.

Taiyō 太陽.

Takahashi Yoshio 高橋義雄. "Banshō roku" 万象録
(Diary). In National Diet Library, Tokyo.

Takakura Tetsuichi 高倉徹一. Tanaka Giichi denki 田中
義一伝記 (Biography of Tanaka). 2 vols.; Tokyo, 1958.

Takekoshi Yosaburō 竹越与三郎. "Takekoshi Yosaburō Shi
danwa sokki" 竹越与三郎氏談話速記. Recorded,
typed interviews with Takekoshi in 1939. In National Diet
Library, Tokyo.

Tamura Naoomi 田村直臣. Waga mitaru Hara Shushō no
omokage 我が見たる原首相の面影 (A personal view
of Hara Kei). Tokyo, 1922.

Tanaka Giichi monjo 田中義一文書 (Papers of Tanaka). In
National Diet Library, Tokyo.

Tanaka Kōtarō 田中貢太郎 . Saionji Kimmochi 西園寺 公望 (Biography of Saionji). Tokyo, 1940.

Tetsudōshō 鉄道省 , ed. Nihon tetsudō shi 日本鉄道史 (Official history of the railroads). 3 vols.; Tokyo, 1919.

Tokutomi Iichirō 徳富猪一郎 (Tokutomi Sohō 徳富蘇峰). Jimu ikkagen 時務一家言 (My views on current affairs). Tokyo, 1913.

------Seijika to shite no Katsura Kō 政治家としての桂公 (Katsura as a politician). Tokyo, 1913.

------Taishō seikyoku shi ron 大正政局史論 (On the political history of Taishō). Tokyo, 1916.

------Kōshaku Katsura Tarō den 公爵桂太郎伝 (Biography of Katsura). 2 vols.; Tokyo, 1917.

------, ed. Kōshaku Yamagata Aritomo den 公爵山県有朋伝 (Biography of Yamagata). 3 vols.; Tokyo, 1933.

------Sohō jiden 蘇峰自伝 (Autobiography). Tokyo, 1935.

Tokutomi Sohō, see Tokutomi Iichirō.

Tonedate Masao 刀禰館正雄, ed. Sono koro o kataru その頃を語る (Reflections on historical events). Tokyo, 1928.

Toyabe Shuntei 鳥谷部春汀 . Shuntei zenshū 春汀全集 (Collected works of Toyabe). 2 vols.; Tokyo, 1909.

Tōyama Shigeki 遠山茂樹 and Adachi Kiyoko 安達淑子 , eds. Kindai Nihon seiji shi hikkei 近代日本政治史必携 (A handbook on modern Japanese political history). Tokyo, 1961.

Tsukada Masao 塚田昌夫 , ed. Rikken Minseitō shi 立憲民政党史 (History of the Minseitō). 2 vols.; Tokyo, 1935.

Tsurumi Shunsuke 鶴見俊輔 , et al. Narikin tenka 成金天下 (The world of the nouveau riche), Tokyo, 1962; and Meiji no eikō 明治の栄光 (The splendor of Meiji). Tokyo, 1962;

Vols. 6 and 7 of Nihon no hyakunen 日本の百年 (Japan's hundred years). 10 vols.

Tsurumi Yūsuke 鶴見祐輔. Gotō Shimpei den 後藤新平伝 (Biography of Gotō). 10 vols.; Tokyo, 1944.

Ueda Sotoo 上田外男. Taishō no seihen 大正の政変 (The Taishō Political Crisis). Tokyo, 1913.

Ukita Kazutami 浮田和民. "Rikken seiji no kompongi" 立憲政治の根本義(The basic principles of constitutional politics); Taiyō, pp. 7-11 (April 1913).

Utsumi Nobuyuki 内海信之. Kōjin Inukai Bokudō 高人犬養木堂 (Biography of Inukai). Tokyo, 1938.

Uzaki Kumakichi 鵜崎熊吉. Chōya no godaibatsu 朝野の五大閥 (The five major factions in and out of government). Tokyo, 1912.

------(Uzaki Rōjō 鵜崎鷺城). "Kōjunsha ron" 交詢社論 (On the Kōjunsha); Chūo kōron, pp. 73-84 (May 1913).

------(Rōjō Gakujin 鷺城学人). Batsujin to tōjin 閥人と党人 (Oligarchs and party men). Tokyo, 1913.

------Jidai seiryoku no hihan 時代勢力の批判 (A critique on the cliques in power). Tokyo, 1914.

------Inukai Tsuyoshi den 犬養毅伝 (Biography of Inukai). Tokyo, 1932.

Uzaki Rōjō, see Uzaki Kumakichi.

Wakatsuki Reijirō 若槻礼次郎. "Wakatsuki Reijirō Danshaku danwa sokki" 若槻礼次郎男爵談話速記. Recorded, typed interviews with Wakatsuki in 1940. In National Diet Library, Tokyo.

------Wakatsuki Reijirō jiden: kofuan kaiko roku 若槻礼次郎自伝：古風庵回顧録 (Autobiography: The memoirs of a hermit). Tokyo, 1950.

Ward, Robert E. and Dankwart A. Rustow, eds. Political
　　Modernization in Japan and Turkey. Princeton, 1964.

Washio Yoshinao 鷲尾義直 . Inukai Bokudō den 犬養木堂
　　伝 (Biography of Inukai). 3 vols.; Tokyo, 1938.

------Inukai Bokudō shokan shū 犬養木堂書簡集 (Collected
　　letters of Inukai). Tokyo, 1940.

------Kojima Kazuo 古島一雄 (Kojima Kazuo). Tokyo, 1950.

Yamagata Aritomo 山県有朋 . "Taishō seihen ki" 大正政変
　　記 (An account of the Taishō Political Crisis). In National Diet
　　Library, Tokyo.

Yamagata Aritomo monjo 山県有朋文書 　(Papers of Yamagata).
　　In National Diet Library, Tokyo.

Yamagata Meishichi 山県明七 . Zaisei jūnen 財政十年
　　(A financial history of the past ten years). Tokyo, 1914.

Yamamoto Shingo 山本新吾 , et al. Shinsetsu Nihon rekishi
　　新説日本歴史 (A general history of modern Japan).
　　12 vols.; Tokyo, 1959.

Yamamoto Shirō 山本四郎 . "Orimono shōhi zei haishi undō ni
　　tsuite" 織物消費税廃止運動について (On the
　　movement to abolish textile consumption taxes); in Kokushi
　　ronshū 国史論集 (Essays on national history), ed.
　　Kyōto daigaku bungakubu 京都大学文学部 (Kyoto
　　University Department of Letters), pp. 1602-1622. Kyoto, 1959.

------"Taishō seihen" 大正政変　(The Taishō Political Crisis);
　　Gendai 現代 (Modern period). Tokyo, 1963; in Iwanami kōza
　　Nihon rekishi 岩波講座日本歴史 (Iwanami lectures on
　　the history of Japan), 23 vols.; XVIII, 245-285.

Yamamoto Tatsuo Sensei denki hensankai 山本達雄先生伝記

編纂会 , ed. Yamamoto Tatsuo 山本達雄 (Yamamoto Tatsuo). Tokyo, 1951.

Yokoyama Yūi 横山雄偉. Katō Kōmei ron sono ta 加藤高明論その他 (Biographical sketches of Katō and others). Tokyo, 1917.

Yoshino Sakuzō 吉野作造. Gendai no seiji 現代の政治 (Modern politics). Tokyo, 1915.

------Kōjin no jōshiki 公人の常識 (Common sense of a public person). Tokyo, 1929.

------Sūfu to naikaku hoka 枢府と内閣他 (The Privy Council and the cabinet, and other essays). Tokyo, 1950.

Abe Hiroshi 阿部浩

Abe Shinnosuke 阿部真之助

Aijima Kanjirō 相島勘次郎

Akita 秋田

Akiyama Teisuke 秋山定輔

Andō Kensuke 安藤謙介

Anraku Kendō 安楽兼道

Aoki Shūzō 青木周蔵

Aomori 青森

Arita Yoshisuke 有田義資

Asabuki Eiji 朝吹英二

Ban'an kurabu 万安倶楽部

banki kōron 万機公論

batsuzoku daha 閥族打破

bunkan bungen rei 文官分限令

bunkan nin'yō rei 文官任用令

Chiba 千葉

chihō dantai 地方団体

chihō kyoku chō 地方局長

chihō yūryoku sha 地方有力者

Chōshū 長州

Chūgoku 中国

daha 打破

Daidō 大同

danshaku 男爵

Danwakai 談話会

doboku kyoku chō 土木局長

Dōshikai 同志会

Ebara Soroku 江原素六

Egi Yoku 江木翼

Ehime 愛媛

fukoku kyōhei 富国強兵

Fukui 福井

Fukui Saburō 福井三郎

Fukuoka 福岡

Fukuoka-gumi 福岡組

Fukushima 福島

Fukuzawa Momosuke 福沢桃介

Fukuzawa Yukichi 福沢諭吉

Futsukakai 二日会

gen'eki shōkan 現役将官

genkun yūgu no i 元勲優遇の意

Genrō 元老

goyōha 御用派

Gumma 群馬

gun 郡

guzu guzu グズグズ

haikin no fū 拝金の風

Hamaguchi Yūko 浜口雄幸
Hamamatsu 浜松
hambatsu 藩閥
han 藩
Hanai Takuzō 花井卓蔵
Haseba Junkō 長谷場純孝
Hata Toyosuke 秦豊助
Hatoyama Kazuo 鳩山和夫
Hayashi Yūzō 林有造
hinkoku kyōhei 貧国強兵
Hiraoka Kōtarō 平岡浩太郎
Hirata Tōsuke 平田東助
Hiroshima 広島
hiyorimishugi 日和見主義
Hōchi shimbun 報知新聞
Hokkaidō 北海道
Hokuriku 北陸
Hokushin 北信
hombu 本部
Honda Seiichi 本田精一
Hoshi Tōru 星亨
Hotta Masayasu 堀田正養
hyōgiin 評議員
Hyōgo 兵庫

Ibaraki 茨城
Ikematsu Tokikazu 池松時和
ikkun bammin 一君万民
ingaidan 院外団
ingaisha 院外者

innai kanji 院内幹事
innai sōmu 院内総務
Inoue Kakugorō 井上角五郎
Inoue Tokutarō 井上篤太郎
Inoue Tomoichi 井上友一
Inuzuka Katsutarō 犬塚勝太郎

Ishihara Kenzō 石原健三
Ishikawa 石川
Ishikawa Hanzan 石川半山
Ishikawa Kammei 石川幹明
Ishikawa Takuboku 石川啄木
Itagaki Taisuke 板垣退助
Itakura Nakaba 板倉中
Itō Daihachi 伊藤大八
Itō Hirobumi 伊藤博文
Itō Kinryō 伊藤欽亮
Itō Miyoji 伊藤己代治
Ito Yōzō 伊藤要蔵
Iwakoshi 岩越
Iwate 岩手
Izawa Takio 伊沢多喜男

jiban 地盤
jimukan 事務官
jisei 時勢
Jiyūtō 自由党
jōi tōgō 情意投合

Kabukiza 歌舞伎座

Kagawa 香川

Kagawa Teru 香川輝

Kagoshima 鹿児島

Kaikakuha 改革派

Kairakuen-gumi 偕楽園組

Kaishintō 改進党

kambu 幹部

Kamiyama Mitsunoshin
上山満之進

kan 官

Kanazawa 金沢

Kaneko Kentarō 金子堅太郎

kangeikai 歓迎会

kanji 幹事

kanjichō 幹事長

Kantō 関東

Kasai Shin'ichi 笠井信一

Kataoka Chokuon 片岡直温

Kataoka Kenkichi 片岡健吉

Katayama Sen 片山潜

Katō Tomosaburō 加藤友三郎

Kawaguchi Hikoji 川口彦治

Kawakami Chikaharu 川上親晴

Kawashima Junkan 川島純幹

Kazama Reisuke 風間礼助

Keiō 慶応

kemmin taikai 県民大会

Kenkyūkai 研究会

kensei no kami 憲政の神

kensei yōgo batsuzoku daha
憲政擁護閥族打破

Kenseihontō 憲政本党

Kenseikai 憲政会

Kenseitō 憲政党

Kigoshi Yasutsuna 木越安綱

Kinki 近畿

kinnō 勤王

Kinoshita Kenkichi 木下健吉

Kita Ikki 北一輝

Kiyono Chōtarō 清野長太郎

Kiyoura Keigo 清浦奎吾

Kobashi Ichita 小橋一太

Kōbe 神戸

Kōchi 高知

Kodama Gentarō 児玉源太郎

Koga Renzo 古賀廉造

Kōjunsha 交詢社

Kōjunsha an 交詢社案

Kokumin shimbun 国民新聞

Kokumintō 国民党

Komatsubara Eitarō 小松原英太郎

Kōno Hironaka 河野広中

konshinkai 懇親会

Kosaka Junzō 小坂順造

Kōtoku Shūsui 幸徳秋水

Koyama Tanizō 小山谷蔵

Kubota Kiyochika 久保田政周

Kuga Katsunan 陸羯南
Kumagai Kiichirō 熊谷喜一郎
Kumamoto 熊本
kummin kyōji 君民共治
Kuroda Kiyotaka 黒田清隆
Kurogane Taigi 黒金泰義
kyōgiin 協議員
Kyūshū 九州

Makino Shinken 牧野伸顕
Matsuda Genji 松田源治
Matsuda Masahisa 松田正久
Matsukata Masayoshi
　　松方正義
Matsumoto Gōkichi 松本剛吉
Matsuoka Yasutake 松岡康毅
Meiji 明治
Meiji to Shōwa no tanima
　　明治と昭和の谷間
min 民
Minami Hiroshi 南弘
Minobe Tatsukichi
　　美濃部達吉
Minoura Katsundo 箕浦勝人
mintō gōdō 民党合同
Mishima Yatarō 三島弥太郎
Mito Chūzō 三土忠造
Mitsubishi 三菱
Mitsui 三井
Miyagi 宮城

Miyako shimbun 都新聞
Mochizuki Keisuke 望月圭介
Mochizuki Kotarō 望月小太郎

Mokuyōkai 木曜会
Mori Masataka 森正隆
Morioka 盛岡
mosaren 猛者連
Motoda Hajime 元田肇
Mutsu Munemitsu 陸奥宗光

Nagashima Ryūji 永島隆二
Nakae Chōmin 中江兆民
Nakahashi Tokugorō
　　中橋徳五郎
Nakai Hiroshi 中井弘
Nakamura Junkurō 中村純九郎
Nakamura Keiji 中村敬二
Nakano Buei 中野武営
nambokuchō seijun mondai
　　南北朝正閏問題
Nambu Mitsuomi 南部光臣
narikin tenka 成金天下
Nichinichi shimbun 日日新聞
Nihon shimbun 日本新聞
Niigata 新潟
niko-pon-shugi にこぽん主義
Noda Utarō 野田卯太郎
nōkai 農会
nōkō ginkō 農工銀行

Nomura Yasushi　野村靖

O-Koi　お鯉
Ogawa Heikichi　小川平吉
ōi ni ogori tamae
　多いに奢りたまえ
Ōishi Masami　大石正己
Ōita　大分
Oka Kishichirō　岡喜七郎
Okabe Jirō　岡部次郎
Okada Taizō　岡田泰蔵
Okayama　岡山
Okazaki Kunisuke　岡崎邦輔
Oku Shigesaburō　奥繁三郎
Ōkubo Kishichi　大久保喜七
Ōkubo Toshimichi　大久保利通
Ōkubo Toshitake　大久保利武
Okuda Yoshindo　奥田義人
Ōkuma Shigenobu　大隈重信
Ōoka Ikuzō　大岡育造
Ōsaka mainichi　大阪毎日
Ōshiba Sōkichi　大芝惣吉
Ōsugi Sakae　大杉栄
Ōura Kanetake　大浦兼武
oyabun　親分
Ōyama Iwao　大山巌

Rikken dōshikai　立憲同志会
Rikken tōitsutō　立憲統一党
rōnin　浪人

Sabakari mo　さばかりも
/medetaki Mikado　めでたき帝
/owashikeri　おわしけり
/yo mo kono hi yori　世もこの日より
/inishie to naru
　いにしえとなる

Saigō Takamori　西郷隆盛
Saitama　埼玉
Saitō Hanji　斎藤班次
Saitō Makoto　斎藤実
Sakamoto Kin'ya　坂本金弥
Sakatani Yoshirō　阪谷芳郎
sangyō kumiai　産業組合
Sapporo　札幌
Sasaki Seizō　佐佐木正蔵
Satake Sakutarō　佐竹作太郎
Satsuma　薩摩
seii　誠意
Seiyū kurabu　政友倶楽部
Seiyūkai　政友会
Seiyūkai seiken yōgo
　政友会政権擁護
Sendai　仙台
Senge Takatomi　千家尊福
Sengoku Mitsugu　仙石貢
Shiba Teikichi　斯波貞吉
Shibata Kamon　柴田家門
Shida Yoshio　指田義雄
Shiga　滋賀
Shigi kempō　私擬憲法

Shikoku 四国

Shimada Saburō 島田三郎

Shimane 島根

Shimonoseki 下関

Shimooka Chūji 下岡忠治

Shimpotō 進歩党

Shinagawa Yajirō 品川弥二郎

Shirane Sen'ichi 白根専一

Shizuoka 静岡

Soeda Keiichirō 添田敬一郎

sōmu 総務

sōmuin 総務員

sōshi 壮士

Suematsu Kenchō 末松謙澄

Sugawara Den 菅原伝

Sugita Teiichi 杉田定一

Sugiyama Shigemaru 杉山茂丸

Surugadai 駿河台

Susunde issen subeki ka?
進んで一戦すべきか/Shirizoite
koto o kisubeki ka? 退いて
後図を期すべきか /Kaisan
ya? 解散乎 /Sōjishoku ya?
総辞職乎

Taigyaku jiken 大逆事件

Taishō 大正

Taishō seihen 大正政変

Takahashi Korekiyo 高橋是清

Takashima Tomonosuke
高島鞆之助

Takazaki Shinshō 高崎親章

Taketomi Tokitoshi 武富時敏

Tanaka Yoshitake 田中義武

Terauchi Masatake 寺内正毅

tōbatsu 党閥

tōhei 党弊

Tōhoku 東北

Tōkai 東海

tokkan 突貫

Tokonami Takejirō
床次竹二郎

Tokushima 徳島

Tomizu Kanjin 戸水寛人

Tottori 鳥取

Tōyō jiyū 東洋自由

Toyokawa Ryōhei 豊川良平

Tsukamoto Seiji 塚本清治

Tsuruga 敦賀

Tsuruhara Teikichi 鶴原定吉

Tsushima 対馬

Uehara Yūsaku 上原勇作

Ushio Shigenosuke 潮恵之輔

Uzawa Sōmei 鵜沢總明

Waseda 早稲田

Watanabe Kunitake 渡辺国武

Watanabe Shōzaburō
渡辺勝三郎

Yamagata Isaburō
山県伊三郎

Yamaguchi 山口

Yamamoto Gonnohyōe
山本権兵衛

Yamamoto Teijirō
山本悌次郎

Yamato shimbun 大和新聞

Yamazaki Jun'ichirō
山崎淳一郎

Yano Fumio 矢野文雄

Yarai kurabu 矢来倶楽部

Yatsushiro 八代

Yoda Keijirō 依田銈次郎

Yokoyama Akira 横山章

Yomiuri shimbun 読売新聞

Yorozu chōhō 万朝報

Yosano Akiko 与謝野晶子

Yoshikawa Akimasa 芳川顕正

Yoshiue Shōichirō 吉原三郎

Yoshiwara Saburō 吉植庄一郎

Yoshiyama 吉山

Yoshizuke 吉漬

Yuasa Kurahei 湯浅倉平

Yūbin hōchi 郵便報知

Yugeta Seiichi 弓削田精一

Yūkō kurabu 猶興倶楽部

yūryokusha 有力者

zaibatsu 財閥

zettaishugi 絶対主義

307

Index

HARVARD EAST ASIAN SERIES